PRACTICAL MANAGEMENT SERIES

Successful
Negotiating
in Local Government

Successful Negotiating
in Local Government

Edited by
Nancy A. Huelsberg
William F. Lincoln

PRACTICAL MANAGEMENT SERIES
Barbara H. Moore, Editor

Successful Negotiating in Local Government
Capital Financing Strategies for Local Governments
Creative Personnel Practices
The Entrepreneur in Local Government
Human Services on a Limited Budget
Microcomputers in Local Government
Police Management Today
Practical Financial Management
Shaping the Local Economy
Telecommunications for Local Government

The Practical Management Series is devoted to the
presentation of information and ideas from diverse
sources. The views expressed in this book are those of
the contributors and are not necessarily those of the
International City Management Association.

Library of Congress Cataloging in Publication Data

Main entry under title:
Successful negotiating in local government.
  (Practical management series)
  Bibliography: p.
  1. Local government—Addresses, essays, lectures. 2.
Negotiation—Addresses, essays, lectures. I. Huelsberg,
Nancy A.   II. Lincoln, William F.
III. Title.
JS91.S83   1985   352'.00047'25   85-8275
ISBN 0-87326-045-7

Printed in the United States of America.
91908988878685
54321

Foreword

Today's managers are, by the very nature of their jobs, negotiators. They negotiate in working with their staffs and governing bodies, in reconciling competing interests in the community, in creating public-private arrangements for service delivery, development, and land use, and in working out intergovernmental agreements and grants.

This reality was predicted in 1980, when ICMA's Committee on Future Horizons of the Profession reported its vision of local government in the year 2000. The committee made this observation about training for managers: "In the past the focus has been on the technology of service delivery, the analytical skills of administration, and the strategies of direction from the top down. In the future, the prime skill of management will be brokering and negotiation."

Successful Negotiating in Local Government provides an overview of the basics of negotiation—the procedures, the processes, the psychology, and the skills. Through case examples it provides models of successful negotiation in local government settings, showing how experienced mediators and negotiators have worked with conflicting parties to forge successful agreements.

This book is part of ICMA's continuing Practical Management Series, which is devoted to serving local officials' needs for timely information on current issues and problems.

We appreciate the cooperation of the organizations and individuals who granted ICMA permission to reprint their material and to Nancy A. Huelsberg and William F. Lincoln of the National Center for Collaborative Planning and Community Services, Inc., Montpelier, Vermont, who organized and compiled the volume. Thanks also go to the following persons, who were of great help to the editors and the ICMA staff when this book was in the formative stages: Roger Richman, Associate Professor of Public Administration, Old Dominion University, Norfolk, Virginia; James Kunde, Program Director, the Kettering Foundation, at Texas Christian University, Fort Worth, Texas; Christine M. Carlson, Program Officer, the Kettering Foundation, Dayton, Ohio; William Drake, Deputy Director, National Institute for Dispute Resolution, Washington, D.C.; Bill Potapchuk, Associate Director, the Conflict Clinic, University of Missouri, St. Louis, Missouri; Susan Carpenter, Associate Director,

ACCORD Associates, Boulder, Colorado; Chester A. Newland, Professor, University of Southern California, Sacramento, California; and to David S. Arnold, ICMA staff, who was of great help in planning the entire Practical Management Series.

William H. Hansell, Jr.
Executive Director
International City
    Management Association

Successful Negotiating
in Local Government

The International City Management Association is the professional
and educational organization for chief appointed management executives in local government. The purposes of ICMA are to strengthen
the quality of local government through professional management
and to develop and disseminate new approaches to management
through training programs, information services, and publications.

Managers, carrying a wide range of titles, serve cities, towns,
counties, and councils of governments in all parts of the United
States and Canada. These managers serve at the direction of elected
councils and governing boards. ICMA serves these managers and
local governments through many programs that aim at improving
the manager's professional competence and strengthening the quality of all local governments.

The International City Management Association was founded
in 1914; adopted its City Management Code of Ethics in 1924; and
established its Institute for Training in Municipal Administration
in 1934. The Institute, in turn, provided the basis for the Municipal
Management Series, generally termed the "ICMA Green Books."

ICMA's interests and activities include public management
education; standards of ethics for members; the *Municipal Year
Book* and other data services; urban research; and newsletters, a
monthly magazine, *Public Management*, and other publications.
ICMA's efforts for the improvement of local government management—as represented by this book—are offered for all local governments and educational institutions.

About the Editors and Authors

Nancy A. Huelsberg is deputy director of the National Center for Collaborative Planning and Community Services, Inc. A professionally trained mediator, her particular expertise lies in the areas of public policy, municipalities, and environmental mediation. She is the primary developer of training materials and curriculum for the National Center in addition to being one of its primary trainers. Huelsberg is also the Vermont associate of the New England Environmental Mediation Center.

William F. Lincoln is director of the National Center for Collaborative Planning and Community Services, Inc. He is a nationally recognized trainer and practitioner of negotiations and mediated negotiation. Lincoln's experience in dispute resolution includes prison uprisings, racial disputes, Native American affairs, environmental disputes, and court diversion and restitution projects. He is a former federal commissioner on the U.S. Commission to Hear and Examine Proposals for a National Academy of Peace and Conflict Resolution.

Following are the affiliations of the other contributors to *Successful Negotiating in Local Government* at the time of writing:

Lawrence S. Bacow, Associate Professor of Law and Environmental Policy, Massachusetts Institute of Technology, Cambridge, Massachusetts

Christine Carlson, Program Associate, Charles F. Kettering Foundation, Dayton, Ohio

Susan Carpenter, Associate Director, ACCORD Associates, Boulder, Colorado

A. Bruce Dotson, Associate Professor, Division of Urban and Environmental Planning, School of Architecture, University of Virginia

Wendy Emrich, Project Planner and Coordinator, Environmental Management Center, Brandywine Conservancy, Chadds Ford, Pennsylvania

Roger Fisher, Harvard University, Cambridge, Massachusetts

Randolph J. Forrester, City Manager, Wyoming, Ohio

Matalyn Harp, Assistant to the Director, Dallas Water Utilities, Dallas, Texas

W. J. D. Kennedy, Executive Director, ACCORD Associates, Boulder, Colorado

Jeff S. Luke, Assistant to the Dean, College of Public Affairs and Community Service, University of Nebraska at Omaha

Leah K. Patton, Vice President, The Mediation Institute, Seattle, Washington

Roger Richman, Associate Professor of Public Administration, Old Dominion University, Norfolk, Virginia

Jeffrey Z. Rubin, Tufts University, Medford, Massachusetts

Thomas E. Taylor, Director, Dallas Water Utilities, Dallas, Texas

Michael Wheeler, Director of Education and Research, Lincoln Institute for Land Policy, Cambridge, Massachusetts

Orion White, Jr., Professor, Center for Public Administration and Policy, Virginia Tech University, Blacksburg, Virginia

Mark Woodhams, Northeastern University, Boston, Massachusetts

Contents

PART 1

Introduction

Introduction

Nancy A. Huelsberg

This book of readings has been compiled to address the specific negotiating needs of local government officials. A few years ago, such
a project would have been more cut and dried. Then, the concept of
negotiating was typified by late-night bargaining sessions in
smoke-filled rooms as management and union reps hammered out
the fine points of a new contract. Failure to finalize a contract by
midnight would have meant a morning of heavy press coverage,
work stoppages, and picket lines around City Hall. In those days, a
collection of essays on collective bargaining and contract negotiations would have sufficed.

More recently, however, negotiating and the literature surrounding it have taken on a varied and colorful life of their own. Two
things have happened in the last few decades to contribute to that
change: first, the increased complexity of governing, both within the
local context and also where local government interests intersect
with other interests, has greatly complicated the role of local government officials. And second, a spiraling interest in conflict resolution—its strategies, forms, techniques, and styles—has caused the
forums and applications of negotiation to be greatly expanded.

Another factor that has helped make negotiating a growth industry relates to the escalating costs of unresolved conflict. Such
increases may involve the direct costs of litigation and other more
expensive forms of dispute resolution, or they may be the indirect
social and political costs that result from delays in planning and
implementing projects. The unavailability of expedient and equitable dispute resolution processes also contributes to the need for local
government officials to be skilled negotiators. To the extent that a
public administrator is proficient in negotiating, he or she will be
able to avoid the added costs of intervention.

Currently there exists a substantial (and growing) literature on negotiations by theoreticians, academics, and practitioners. Curiously, however, little has been offered that specifically takes into account the role, functions, needs, and negotiating environments of local government managers. Yet it is indisputable that negotiating is an integral part of their professional lives and functions.

The fact is that local government officials, like everyone else, negotiate continually. As Jeff Luke notes in the article that begins this collection: "Administrators negotiate daily—in dealing with department heads, elected officials, supervisors or staff members. Managers negotiate in allocating resources, in getting increased intergovernmental transfers, in meeting with business entrepreneurs and developers, and in dealing with special interest groups."

Local government managers' negotiating activities are not confined to their own jurisdictions. They must be prepared to negotiate at many points of contact with the surrounding environment as well. These points of contact or interface may involve, for example, racial or minority tensions or disputes, zoning and land use issues, or resource allocation and distribution—both natural and fiscal. Such points of contact also occur where one locality's interests intersect with an adjoining one, or with county, regional, state, and even federal jurisdictions. These points of intersection are myriad; the potential for conflict—and for negotiating—is correspondingly diverse.

Just as the range of environments and contexts that require negotiating is expanding, so too are the forms, techniques, and styles of negotiating. Interest, research, and experimentation in the field of conflict management and resolution have given birth to numerous offspring. Among them are facilitation, joint problem solving, mediation, negotiated investment strategy, and "med-arb"; all of those forms depend on negotiating skills. As this list suggests, the vocabulary associated with negotiating is growing rapidly, and the underlying concepts can be usefully incorporated into the negotiating repertoire of local government managers.

The articles in this collection have been selected from a diverse, current literature. The selections are predicated on two assumptions: one, they assume that local government managers, like everyone else, have a basic, if not instinctual, grasp of negotiating. After all, we were all children once and subject to the rigors of sibling rivalry or mere survival. And we made it this far. Second, they assume that most people have had little or no formal training in the art of negotiating. This collection, then, provides an opportunity for local government managers to benefit from the interest, research, social-psychological study, experience, and dedication of experts in the field. It is our belief that these writings will be useful to local government officials who wish to become more effective negotiators. Effective negotiating skills will also contribute to their overall effectiveness in serving their local constituencies.

Content

After considerable deliberation as to the most effective way to organize the articles in this collection, we have grouped them under three general headings: basic principles and processes, psychological factors, and applications. The reader is not expected to sit down and read this collection from beginning to end as she or he would a good spy thriller. Instead, it is our hope that the local government administrator will dip randomly into the collection, his or her interest piqued by a title or subject that is relevant to particular circumstances. Accordingly, each article stands on its own.

Jeff Luke's article, "Arenas of Local Government Negotiating and Bargaining," serves as an introduction to this collection. In it, Luke discusses in some depth the need for local government administrators to increase their bargaining skills, particularly as they relate to public-private and intergovernmental negotiations.

Part 2, "The Basics," covers a range of topics from definitions and terminology to a survey of current processes and strategies involved in successful negotiations. This section also provides matter-of-fact responses to some of the "what," "how," "when," and "what ifs" of negotiating. While it is acknowledged that most managers already have an intuitive grasp of many of the concepts discussed here, the articles provide insight, clarity, and specific information that will be helpful and instructive in their own negotiations.

"The Basics of Negotiation and Mediation," from the Kettering Foundation, opens the section with a description of some basic tools for negotiators. It discusses the meaning of conflict, the nature of negotiation, and mediated negotiation. The article concludes with practical checklists of factors leading to the success or failure of negotiations.

The second article, "Managing Conflict by Applying Common Sense," offers principles that are important in the negotiation process. Using a format contrasting "the right way" with "the wrong way," the authors provide seven common-sense negotiating principles, first an ineffective approach (the wrong way), then the alternative procedure (the right way) to approach negotiating. Although the examples focus on situations involving natural resources, the principles have wide applicability to managers in diverse negotiating situations.

Leah Patton's article, "Settling Disputes through Mediation," is a brief introduction to environmental mediation—a negotiating form that has gained currency among negotiators in the past decade. In addition to describing the negotiating form and its uses, Patton discusses possible impediments that may hinder negotiations and conditions to settlement.

The next two articles focus on what has come to be known as N.I.S. or negotiated investment strategy. Developed at the Kettering Foundation, N.I.S. has found wide application in approaching complex intergovernmental issues. Unlike more traditional approaches to conflict resolution, which resort to negotiation only after impasse has occurred, N.I.S. takes a holistic approach to problem solving; it encompasses all stages of public decision making, from the planning stages, through negotiations, to implementation, review, and monitoring. Christine Carlson provides an overview of this process, followed by an excerpt from the Kettering Foundation publication that presents, in a question and answer format, specific information relating to the uses of negotiated investment strategy.

Next are two selections concerned with labor-management negotiations. In "Negotiations in Public Sector Labor Relations," Randolph Forrester presents down-to-earth guidelines for local government managers as they prepare to negotiate with employees. In the informal, anecdotal manner of "one who's been there," Forrester talks through the strategies and processes he has found to be useful in his own experience in local government. This article is followed by questions and answers giving specific information on labor-management negotiations. The excerpted information focuses on organizing for bargaining, procedures for bargaining, and tips on effective communication at the bargaining table. These preliminary preparations can ultimately contribute to the successful outcome of negotiations.

Part 3 focuses not so much on the "how tos" of negotiating as on the psychological factors that contribute to the "whys" of negotiating—why parties may or may not decide to negotiate, why power is an important force to acknowledge and reckon with in negotiating, and what emotional and interpersonal dynamics must be taken into account for negotiations to proceed or succeed. These dynamics, while not obvious during the negotiating process, are an important component in any negotiation. For that reason managers must be aware of the psychological, behavioral side of negotiation.

Jeffrey Rubin begins this section with an overview of some interpersonal, psychological aspects of negotiating. His essay is followed by Roger Fisher's treatment of power relationships—how power is gained and used.

Next, Michael Wheeler and Lawrence Bacow introduce the idea of decision analysis and its relationship to successful negotiations. Decision analysis is a way of looking at negotiating strategies based on anticipation of others' responses to any action and consideration of the various options open to each party. The approach to negotiating offered by Bacow and Wheeler uses four illustrations or "problems" to clarify the kinds of decisions that take place.

Finally, Orion White looks at conflict resolution in the context of underlying psychological and behavioral factors. Using as an example a city-county boundary dispute in Virginia, White looks beneath the superficial processes of negotiating to examine the emotional and interpersonal needs, perceptions, and interchanges that can impede and possibly halt negotiations.

Part 4 shows how negotiating skills and techniques have been put to work in actual situations. It links Parts 2 and 3 by presenting cases in which negotiation has been effectively or, in some cases, not so effectively carried out. The cases illustrate both the processes and the impact of psychological factors on negotiation. In addition to providing cases that illustrate the principles and processes of negotiation, this section covers a variety of contexts in which today's public administrators are likely to find themselves using their negotiating skills.

Part 4 begins with a case study illustrating the application of the Kettering N.I.S. (negotiated investment strategy) in Walden, Massachusetts. In that instance, the N.I.S. was used effectively to engage the entire community, including local developers and government officials, in a process of determining and establishing long-range planning goals.

A second article discusses a potentially volatile city-county annexation dispute in Virginia. In the course of developing and analyzing the case, Roger Richman elaborates on negotiating techniques and processes, including competitive bargaining, joint problem solving, the use of mediation, and the settlement process. The article provides a relevant example of intergovernmental negotiations, which are becoming increasingly common as city, county, and state administrators find their spheres of influence intersecting and overlapping.

In a third case, a largely constricted negotiation process involving water allocation is reopened through the use of "shuttle diplomacy." This one-on-one approach to the impasse that had developed served to reestablish channels of communication among the numerous parties and allowed for a successful resolution of the impasse. Again, this case illustrates the dynamics of intergovernmental negotiations.

Wendy Emrich's essay, "Let Us Reason Together" presents a brief scenario of a case involving an increasingly common problem—siting a local landfill. Using the case as a frame of reference, Emrich describes the use of environmental mediation to handle the dispute. In addition, she offers alternative dispute resolution approaches that can be useful in avoiding impasses. These approaches include negotiated development (paralleling N.I.S.), joint problem solving, and facilitation. Emrich offers a general compendium of approaches to negotiating complex issues. Again, while couched in an environmental framework, these strategies are broadly applicable to the many arenas in which local government officials serve.

The final selection, Bruce Dotson's "Who and How? Participation in Environmental Negotiation," presents three case studies, all involving land use issues. Through these cases, he illustrates the importance of structure in determining the outcome of a dispute resolution process—who will be involved, what their role will be, and in what context. Dotson's illustrations describe several modes of interaction—e.g., face-to-face, shuttle diplomacy, and indirect bargaining—as well as describing the roles of individuals, their motives, and means of empowerment in negotiating.

Conclusion

These articles represent the experience and expertise of many individuals who are prominent in the field of negotiation and conflict resolution, particularly at the local level. As we have indicated, the potential for conflict and the need for negotiating skills is growing rapidly—among local government officials and for the public in general. For local administrators, the need to be skilled in negotiating is directly proportional to the increasing complexity of governing, both at the local level and in intergovernmental arenas. The ability of a government administrator to negotiate will greatly enhance his or her success in gaining, allocating, and using the municipality's human, environmental, and fiscal resources. To that end, this book is an important contribution.

Arenas of Local Government Negotiating and Bargaining

Jeff S. Luke

The art of negotiation is too often overlooked as a necessary skill for local government managers. When the term "negotiation" is used, it generally conjures up images of labor negotiations and union contracts—the annual confrontation over the bargaining table. However, this particular bargaining process represents only a fraction of the negotiating behavior a local government manager actually engages in. *Administrators negotiate daily*—in dealing with department heads, elected officials, supervisors, or staff members. Managers negotiate in allocating resources in getting increased intergovernmental transfers, in meeting with business entrepreneurs and developers, and in dealing with special interest groups.

Administrators are now required to negotiate more and more, particularly with actors outside the organization. The art of negotiation is increasingly important for effective local government management. Much management now occurs at the boundaries of the organization due to the interconnected web of networks—both intergovernmental and intersectoral—that is, between the public and private sectors. Collaborative strategies, including negotiation, are increasingly required for administrators to effectively formulate and implement public policy in such an environmental context.

The emerging environmental context

In the last decade, the boundaries of public organizations have become more permeable than ever before. City governments are less autonomous and more interdependent with governmental and nongovernmental actors in their environments. The emerging interdependence sets new requirements for administrative performance and self-governance, seriously challenging the viability of traditional jurisdictions and the historical mechanisms of public management and public action. Increasing interdependence limits local governments' capacity to perform in conventional ways.

First, local governments generally have a *reduced capacity to act unilaterally.* No one person or agency controls the essential elements of a policy-making system that is now both intergovernmental and intersectoral. The existence, intentions, and jurisdictions of other actors substantially reduce functional autonomy and often create a strong sense of powerlessness. Any systematic solution to a public problem requires public managers to enter the intergovernmental and public-private network. Policy formulation and program implementation require multilateral cooperation across traditional boundaries and jurisdictions. There is considerable evidence, much of it in doctoral dissertations by younger public administration professionals, that the successful implementation of local government policies in transportation, housing, and economic development necessitate negotiation with increasing numbers of relevant actors, both governmental and nongovernmental.[1]

Second, local government organizations *share their environment* with a multitude of other service providers and beneficiaries. This leads to expanding and crowded policy environments in which everything depends increasingly on everything else and the danger of unanticipated consequences becomes greater. Local government managers find it necessary to involve in decisions those individuals who share in the interorganizational policy-making network.[2] This suggests an increase in "collective strategies"[3] by public organizations, nonprofit agencies, and local business enterprises that collaborate and negotiate in order to pursue specific policy outcomes.

Third, problem solving in a shared and crowded policy environment will necessarily *move forward more slowly.* Effective multijurisdictional problem solving takes time; it requires

that the real political and administrative decision makers must be involved, but the details must be left to the operatives; that the focus must be on the specifics of the issues at hand; that the constant testing and negotiating of solutions are essential; and that eventually the decision makers must reach an agreement, put it on paper, and carry it out through the relevant jurisdictions.[4]

In addition, interconnectedness inevitably *increases the openness and vulnerability to outside influences* that are outside local government control and difficult to buffer. The impact of corporate disinvestment by multinational enterprises on the economic deterioration of a local economy provides a poignant example. Effective administrators react to this vulnerability by entering into the crowded policy environment and *negotiating* policy outcomes. Yet to do this, new skills are required.

As interdependence increases, *there is an increase both in requisite levels of coordination and in potential for conflict.*[5] As new forms of cooperation emerge, so do new forms of conflict. Actors find it necessary to make increased use of cooperative, collective approaches, including:

1. Collaborative problem solving
2. Cooptation and consolidation
3. Coalition formation
4. Negotiation and bargaining.

The recent heralding of public-private partnerships is merely the tip of the collaborative iceberg. It is now generally recognized that public-private partnerships, although not new, offer significant potential for improved policy making and problem solving in local communities. To facilitate such partnerships, local government managers need the negotiation skills to bring disparate parties together to develop cooperative approaches to local issues.

Emerging arenas for negotiating

Negotiating and bargaining are not new to city and county managers. Formal and informal bargaining have been commonplace in local government agencies for decades. What is new, however, is the increasing requirement to negotiate in the manager's external environment—to bargain with external actors in order to achieve local policy objectives. Three general arenas have now emerged requiring the development and effective use of negotiating skills:

1. The *intersectoral* arena, which includes public-sector, private-sector, and third-sector (non-profit) relations such as contracting out, equity partnerships with private developers, and negotiating regulations
2. The *intergovernmental* arena, which encompasses contracting with governmental agencies, grant formulas, intergovernmental regulations, and other grant negotiations
3. The *neighborhood* arena, which is the setting for triangular partnerships and land use decisions.

These arenas are discussed in the following sections.

The intersectoral arena

Contracting Local governments are choosing to contract with private enterprises for the provision of a variety of public goods and services. A survey conducted by the California Tax Foundation found that local governments gained specific advantages by contracting for services and support operations, and that increasing numbers of cities, counties, school districts, and special districts were utilizing the private sector.[6]

Government contracts to the private sector range from the mundane to the politically sensitive. They include provision and maintenance of facilities and equipment, problem analysis and definition, program design, service delivery, executive search, and program monitoring and evaluation.[7]

Whether contracting with a private for-profit or a private non-profit agency, a complex mix of political, economic, and technical factors needs to be taken into account in negotiating a fair, equitable, and politically acceptable contract agreement. At least six factors must be agreed on: *costs; time schedules; quantity; quality of performance; liability;* and *administration.* Each of these must be considered in terms of legal limitations, political sensitivities, and fiscal feasibility. It appears that contracting is on the rise and the local government managers will increasingly negotiate with private enterprises for the provision of specific goods and services. Yet public-private contracting requires managers to do more than refine their negotiation skills; several observers have warned that, in addition, a nonadversarial climate must be developed and nurtured.[8]

Negotiating government regulations   A second area of increased negotiation in the public-private arena is regulations. In the last two decades, local governments have enlarged their spheres of regulation from basic health and safety (typically state mandated) to more geographically specific regulations such as land use control (e.g., rent control) and local franchising (e.g., cable television and public transportation). In negotiating regulations, both sides generally engage in a face-to-face dialogue of problem-solving (rather than winning battles) and early public negotiation (rather than waiting for formal public hearings). Susskind and Persico suggest that regulatory negotiation holds the most promise when:

1. Issues are relatively well defined
2. A limited number of parties are involved and each has sufficient power and resources to tie up the rulemaking process in court
3. A rule or ordinance will inevitably be promulgated in the near future.[9]

Regulatory negotiation is presently occurring at the local level, primarily as a result of increasing government interest in the formation and expansion of small businesses and the attraction of larger industries. The recognition of the interdependence between the local government and the private sector has increased the public manager's attention to economic development through public-pri-

vate partnerships. Cities in the Northeast and Midwest are negotiating a variety of local ordinances, particularly land use regulations, in order to keep or attract business enterprises. Zoning
variances, for example, are increasingly negotiated in order to allow
an existing company to expand, or to entice an industry to relocate
in a particular area. Some company executives have demanded certain variances on the threat of moving to the Sunbelt.

In addition, effective negotiation has become crucial in arriving
at appropriate local government regulations that can stimulate
housing and community development. In housing, for example, bargaining between developers and local jurisdictions occurs in several
other arenas of local regulation:

1. Development agreements (a city and developer agree to subdivision plans that are at variance with the comprehensive
   plan)
2. Density bonus incentives for affordable housing
3. Transfer of development rights, and
4. Assessment districts.[10]

Kirlin and Kirlin conclude that "both the public and private sectors
have begun to recognize the benefits to both parties in a more open,
creative approach to land development and provision of public improvements and services."[11]

Joint ventures and equity partnerships   Perhaps the most recent
and challenging use of bargaining skills by local government managers occurs in the negotiation of equity partnerships and joint ventures between the traditionally separate public and private sectors.
Increasing attempts at public-private collaboration and joint ventures produce a hybrid between the two sectors. Joint business, community, and government committees—other than the more sedate
"blue ribbon committees"—often are established to focus on one
task. The Los Angeles Olympic Committee provides an excellent example of this task force approach, while local community development corporations (CDCs) provide an example of a more institutionalized partnership.

More "radical" partnerships are developed when local governments join in equity partnerships with private enterprises; city governments, for example, have created equity positions with community cable television companies. Economic development programs
seek to generate a healthier economy through new forms of public-
private partnerships, particularly in two areas: equity positions
with private developers, and triangular partnerships between the
government agency, private enterprise, and neighborhood organizations.

Redevelopment projects often involve complex bargains hammered out through public-private negotiations. It has not been un-usual for city mangers, for example, to act as brokers in private land development negotiations.[12] Recent extensions of this broker role involve city governments in equity partnerships with private devel-opers, with the city capturing a percentage of the developer's profit in return for providing the public infrastructure or other public im-provements. In Fairfield, California, for example, the city manager negotiated an equity partnership position with Ernest Hahn, Inc., in the development and management of a regional shopping center on a 26-acre site. The city purchased the site as part of a redevelopment project, assembled the land parcels, improved access to the site, im-proved drainage, and moved an elementary school that was adja-cent to the site to a better location.[13] In addition to the increased tax revenues generated by the shopping mall through the property tax increment, sales taxes, and business license fees, the city negotiated substantial non-tax revenues from the developer; it will receive 10% of any net annual cash flow between $250,000 and $500,000 and 15% after that.

Other types of equity positions and negotiated agreements in-clude:

1. Private developer construction of public improvements in a project area
2. Lump sum payments from the developer to the jurisdiction, sometimes plausibly related to the project
3. Joint public and private use of shared facilities constructed by the developer
4. Private developer provision of services, reducing both capital and operating budgets of a jurisdiction
5. Private developer maintenance and operation of public facili-ties or places
6. Conditions on the developer which facilitate accomplishment of a jurisdiction's policies
7. Modification of project to meet public policy purposes
8. Acquisition of real property (unimproved or improved) by a developer, who transfers title to the jurisdiction or otherwise uses or disposes of it according to the directions of the juris-diction
9. Private development of public property as a source of public sector revenue.[14]

The three most important contextual variables in entering into such negotiations are:

1. Applicable legal restrictions on the extent of public equity provisions
2. Philosophical attitudes by the jurisdiction's governing body that may hesitate at such government intervention

3. Mutual understanding by both parties of the goals, objectives, and peculiar constraints on both the local public and private sector.

The intergovernmental arena   Much public policy making and implementation occurs in the intergovernmental policy network, which consists of a large number of public organizations at the federal, state, and local levels. Successful local government managers know the importance of working the intergovernmental web of relationships, either to ensure effective delivery of services or to affect public policy. Negotiations in the intergovernmental sphere typically take three forms: intergovernmental contracting for services, legislative grant formulas, and specific intergovernmental grant allocations.

Intergovernmental contracting   It has not been unusual for small municipalities to contract with surrounding cities or counties for police and fire protection. More recently, cities have begun contracting for such services as water supply, libraries, sewage treatment, and health care.[15] The efficiency of contracting with a larger jurisdiction, and the expected economies of scale, provide the primary motivation to purchase such services from other governments.

Many cities successfully collaborate in joint agreements to provide a regional service, such as industrial development and environmental control. This is a variation of unilateral contracting that requires interjurisdictional negotiations among multiple parties. Contiguous cities, for example, negotiate "joint powers agreements" for such things as liability and workers' compensation self-insurance and the provision of regional training and development programs.

Intergovernmental formulas   Wright notes that a considerable amount of negotiating and bargaining occurs in establishing intergovernmental transfer formulas for such programs as revenue sharing, block grants, and categorical grants.[16] The bargaining occurs horizontally between the legislative and executive branches of government, as well as vertically, in the intergovernmental realm of federal-state-local relations. Wright describes this "formula game" as a strategic process of attempting to modify the formulas by which federal and state funds are allocated. It usually involves the "big seven" public interest lobbies (among them the National League of Cities, the National Association of Counties, and the U.S. Conference of Mayors). This is a very significant arena for bargaining; in 1981, for example, formula grant programs were 80 percent of the $96 billion in federal and state intergovernment funds distributed that year.[17]

Intergovernmental regulations   Regulations are another arena for such intergovernmental "games," with the ultimate impact being the delimitation of local government authority and autonomy. There are 1,200 national mandates and 3,500 state regulations that constrain, guide, or direct the activities of local jurisdictions.[18] These mandates provide a second, and more recently recognized, arena requiring intergovernmental negotiation.

Grant negotiations   The utilization of Urban Development Action Grants (UDAGs) also has forced jurisdictions into intergovernmental and public-private negotiations. Aimed at leveraging private-sector investment in economic development, UDAGs to local governments are, more often than not, negotiated grants. It is not uncommon for a city manager, mayor, and local private-sector representatives to travel to Washington, to negotiate a UDAG. This move, of course, occurs after the local public and private sectors have already completed their negotiations for the specific economic development project.

This process of multilateral negotiations for specific grant funds is being institutionalized by the *negotiated investment strategy* (NIS), a process developed by the Kettering Foundation. The NIS is an experimental process of mediated intergovernmental negotiations for a specific geographical area that seeks an agreement to target public intergovernmental grants and private investments in an attempt to collectively pursue specific policy goals. An NIS agreement commits the actors to leveraging private commitments and maximizing the use of public (local, state, and federal) resources. The NIS process assumes that intergovernmental financial relations are competitive, not necessarily cooperative, and it employs a negotiation and conflict resolution model to facilitate an agreement on policy goals and specific resource allocation issues in a particular geographical area. This process is described in detail later in the book.

The neighborhood arena   City managers and local officials negotiate not only with intergovernmental and private-sector actors, but with local neighborhood groups and agencies as well. Two key areas where negotiating skills are increasingly required are in triangular partnerships and in negotiating various planning and local land use issues.

Triangular partnerships   A variation of the public-private partnership is the triangular partnership which includes "third-sector" neighborhood organizations in equity positions in local economic development and revitalization projects.[19] The process builds cooperation among three key sectors of a community vital to local economic development: city government, private sector and foundations, and neighborhood organizations.

Triangular partnership projects exist in Oakland, Los Angeles, Tucson, Dayton, and Denver, and are typically characterized by:

1. Relatively equal standing and weight of each of the partners
2. An ongoing organizational structure, which provides the basis for systematic communications and meetings by the partners
3. Joint investment in economic development projects in which the neighborhood partner has an equity stake. The equity share of the neighborhood group may come from federal funds, such as an Urban Development Action Grant (as in the San Antonio Hyatt Regency deal), funds voted by the city council (as Tucson's City Council did in 1981 for a triangular project in its developmental stages), from a foundation (as a project in its developmental stages), from a foundation (as a portion of the neighborhood organization's funds did in the Flint Hyatt deal), from the resources of the neighborhood group itself, or from other sources.[20]

Triangular partnerships are generally negotiated for two types of projects:

1. *Real estate or business development projects* which require some public support or leveraging to be feasible in the market context. This type of project focuses primarily on generating opportunities for profit-making ventures by leveraging public and private funds . . .

2. *Neighborhood or small business wealth-producing activities*, which require some front-end support to attain levels of self-sufficiency.[21]

The U.S. Conference of Mayors, a prime mover in triangular partnerships, notes that there are five steps in a typical project:

Step One: Building support for the triangular concept and building linkages as equals in the partnership

Step Two: Organizing for action from informal arrangements to more formal nonprofit corporation status

Step Three: Agreeing on specific projects to be pursued

Step Four: Identifying and sharing the risks inherent in the project

Step Five: Identifying and securing funds for the partnership. Each of these steps requires negotiation skills on the part of the public managers and other local public officials that are participating.

Planning and land use   Although not all professional planners yet agree, many now argue that political negotiation is necessary and inescapable for getting agreement on community plans.[22] These planners believe "that as planners they contribute to consensus building using various skills of interpretation, communication, group work, and bargaining.[23]

In the planning sphere, negotiation and bargaining occur between local governments and private developers for the purposes of managing growth, developing parkland, maintaining open space, and reducing industrial pollutants. The problem of locating or siting such public facilities as airports, landfills, drug rehab centers, and now hazardous waste treatment facilities generates considerable local conflict and requires mediation and negotiation strategies.

More recently, negotiation strategies have been developed and utilized in annexation disputes. Annexation attempts create significant interjurisdictional conflict due to potentially large shifts in tax bases—for example, when a city annexes from a county such developed land as shopping malls or industrial parks. In many states, Virginia for example, annexation conflicts are increasingly resolved out of court through negotiated settlements.[24]

Developing negotiation skills

This aggregation of recent policy-making and service provision strategies into three general arenas is by no means exhaustive. There is an infinite variety of policy-making processes and service provision alternatives, many of which require negotiation at one stage or another. However, these three arenas have increased in importance in the last decade and suggest the necessary expansion of negotiation techniques for effective public management in the future. Several approaches require the use of a mediator who acts as a nonpartisan facilitator of mutually acceptable settlements. Many, however, can be facilitated by a skillful manager who bargains with intergovernmental, private-sector, and neighborhood actors, within the local legal and political contexts, to obtain a particular public policy objective.

Building competencies How are negotiating skills developed? Review of recent literature in public administration, organization theory, and the applied behavioral sciences indicates that four steps are crucial.

First and foremost, local government managers must change their fundamental assumptions about the separateness of the public and private sectors and the myth of autonomous local self-government. No jurisdiction is independent today; each exists in a web of subtle and direct interdependencies and interconnections that inhibit unilateral policy making. In creating the future they desire for their jurisdictions, managers must now enter into the intergovernmental and intersectoral web, especially in the areas of infrastructure development, affordable housing, economic development, and employment and training. The primary barrier to moving in these

directions is attitudinal.[25] Fundamental attitude changes by both
public- and private-sector leadership are a prerequisite to effective
bargaining and negotiation. The mistrust resulting from assumed
adversarial roles and the negative stereotypes of "the other guy"
need to be overcome.

The second step in developing effective negotiation skills is understanding the basics of the negotiation process. Much has been
published in the last several years. Yet, it is important to emphasize
that *there is no one theory of negotiating* that is applicable to different levels of analysis (the individual, the group, or the organization)
and different types of bargaining arenas (unilateral, bilateral, or
multilateral).[26] However, we know significantly more now than we
did ten years ago, most of it emerging from economic/game theory
literature, social psychological research, and anecdotal accounts offered in popular books.

Research from economics typically provides high-level abstrac-
tions based on economic assumptions of rational behavior, and such
economic principles as maximization of gain and availability of
complete information regarding alternatives and utilities.[27] Unfortunately, such academic assumptions seldom prove accurate and
provide limited guidance to administrators in real conflicts.

The anecdotal literature[28] argues that "everything is negotiable" and provides an encyclopedic array of proverbs for negotiation.
However, due to the situational nature of effective bargaining,
many of the proverbs are contradictory, providing little but "helpful
hints."

The applied behavioral sciences may provide the most useful
guides. Rubin has reviewed the growing body of behavioral research
on negotiation and has identified six major themes in negotiating
effectively (these are fully developed in his article, which is reprinted in this volume):

1. Be aware of the "negotiation tightrope" each party is
    walking.
2. Beware of the need to impress others.
3. Be sensitive, but not overly sensitive, to the other's moves
    and gestures.
4. Allow the other to feel, even induce, a sense of bargaining
    competence.
5. Avoid commitments to tough, irrevocable, take-it-or-leave-it
    positions.
6. Take account of the intensity of the negotiations.[29]

The third step in developing bargaining competencies is understanding the various strategies of negotiation available. Pruitt suggests a "dual concern model" indicating four choices available to a
public manager (Figure 1).

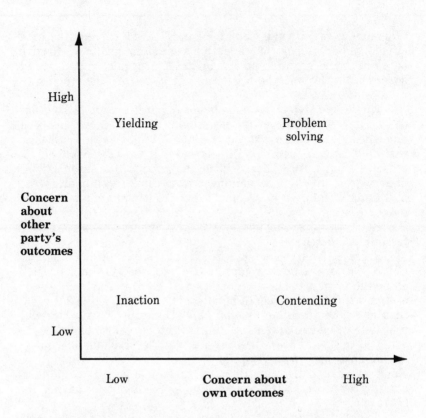

Figure 1.

Source: D. G. Pruitt, "Strategic Choice in Negotiation," *American Behavioral Scientist*, November/December 1983, pp. 167-194.

This model, drawing on Blake and Mouton and Thomas[30] assumes that a negotiator has concerns in two distinct dimensions:

1.   Concern about one's own outcomes
2.   Concern about the other party's outcomes.

Pruitt suggests four strategies and provides the following predictive statements:

Concern about both own and other party's outcomes encourages a problem-solving strategy; concern about only one's own outcomes encourages contending; concern about only the other party's outcomes encourages yielding; concern about neither party's outcomes encourages inaction.[31]

The strategy of "compromise," typically shown in the middle of the model, is excluded because compromises are seen as arising from lazy problem solving involving a half-hearted attempt to satisfy both parties' interests. In other words, it seems unnecessary to postulate a separate strategy to explain the development of compromises.[32]

Which strategy is initially chosen appears to depend on three variables. However, initial strategies will need to change as the negotiation unfolds, as perceptions are clarified, and as these variables shift.

1. *Your perceived power position.* Milward suggests several areas for consideration, including: amount of resource dependencies in the situation; position in the interorganizational network; your mandated authority; and interpersonal skills (temperament and character, as well as skills).[33]
2. *The parameters for the agreement.* Public administrators have considerably more constraints than their private-sector counterparts, the most important being legal parameters, political considerations, and budgetary constraints.
3. *Perceived existence of a "fixed-pie" pool of resources.* If the actors share a relationship of "commensalism," which means "eating from the same table,"[34] win-lose strategies will likely emerge. Although such "fixed-pies" do exist occasionally, it is too often hastily assumed, precluding any "win-win" solution from being generated. Bazerman argues that this fixed-pie assumption is fundamentally false and hinders finding creative and integrative solutions.[35]

The fourth step in acquiring and refining negotiation skills is practicing them in real life conflicts. This is an obvious point and is based on the principle that people *learn by doing.* One cannot learn how to be an effective negotiator by reading abstract principles or anecdotal techniques. The real learning comes from experience, as both an observer and a participant. However, the experience needs to be framed by a conceptual understanding of negotiation processes.

End note

Cooperation, collaboration, and negotiation are not easy behaviors to foster in the intergovernmental and intersectoral networks. These behaviors force a rearrangement of perceptions; a change in attitudes; a redefinition of traditional, comfortable roles; and the development of managerial competencies in negotiation, bargaining, and collaborative problem solving. However, the development of negotiating skills may be the biggest challenge for local government managers in the 1980s and beyond.

1. Transportation policy is discussed in: Myrna Mandel, "The Century Freeway: Interorganizational Network Analyses," Ph.D. diss., University of Southern California School of Public Administration, 1981; housing is examined in: Christine Reed, "Political Dynamics in the Evolution of Federal Housing Policy: The Gautreaux Case, 1966-1982," Ph.D. diss., Brown University, 1983; and economic development is discussed in: Jeff Luke, "Interdependence: Key Element in Public Administration in Its Second Century as a Discipline," Ph.D. diss., University of Southern California, 1982.

2. Robert Agranoff and Valerie Lindsay, "Intergovernmental Management: Perspectives from Human Services Problem Solving at the Local Level," *Public Administration Review* 43 (1983):227-37.

3. Graham Astley and Charles Fombrun, "Collective Strategy: Social Ecology of Organizational Environments," *Academy of Management Review* 8, 4 (1983):576-587.

4. Agranoff and Lindsay, p. 236.

5. James Thompson, "Society's Frontiers for Organizing Activities," *Public Administration Review* 33, 4 (1973):327-335; and Eric Trist, "Collaboration in Work Settings: A Personal Perspective," *Journal of Applied Behavioral Science* 13, 3 (1977):268-278.

6. California Tax Foundation, "Contracting for Service," (Sacramento, 1981), mimeographed.

7. Ira Sharkansky, "Policy Making and Service Delivery on the Margins of Government," *PAR*, March-April 1980, pp. 116-123.

8. James Mercer, "Growing Opportunities in Public Service Contracting," *Harvard Business Review*, March-April 1983, p. 178ff; and John Kirlin and Anne Kirlin, *Public Choices—Private Resources* (Sacramento, Calif.: Tax Foundation, 1982).

9. Lawrence Susskind and Sebastian Persico, *Guide to Consensus Development and Dispute Resolution Techniques* (Cambridge: Harvard Negotiation Project, 1983).

10. Kirlin and Kirlin, *Public Choices*.

11. Ibid.

12. International City Management Association, *Negotiating Business Development*, Innovations Report No. 34 (Washington, D.C.: ICMA, 1981).

13. Kirlin and Kirlin, *Public Choices*.

14. Ibid.

15. Lloyd Nigro, "Developing Human Resources for the Public Sector," in Eddy (ed.), *Handbook of Organization Management* (New York: Marcel Dekker, 1983), pp. 279-296.

16. Deil Wright, "Managing the Intergovernmental Scene," in Eddy (ed.), *Handbook of Organization Management* (New York: Marcel Dekker, 1983).

17. Ibid.

18. Katherine Lovell and Charles Tobin, "The Mandate Issue," *Public Administration Review* 41, 3 (1980):318-330.

19. U.S. Conference of Mayors, *A Guide to Triangular Partnerships* (Washington, D.C.: USCM, 1983).

20. Ibid., p. 6.

21. Ibid., p. 8.

22. Howell Baum, "Politics, Power and Profession." *Planning*, December 1983, pp. 18-21.

23. Ibid., p. 18.

24. Roger Richman, "Structuring Interjurisdictional Negotiations: Virginia's Use of Mediation in Annexation Disputes," *Resolve*, summer 1983.

25. Kirlin and Kirlin, *Public Choices*.

26. J. Z. Rubin, "Negotiation: An Introduction to Some Issues and Themes," *American Behavioral Scientist*, November-December 1983, pp. 135-149.

27. S. B. Bacharach and E. J. Lawler, *Bargaining: Power, Tactics and Outcomes* (New York: John Wiley, 1981).

28. Herb Cohen, "How to Negotiate Anything," *Public Management*, January 1983, pp. 2-5; J. Ilich and B. Jones, *Successful Negotiation Skills for Women* (Reading, Mass.: Addi-

son-Wesley, 1981); M. Schatzki, *Negotiation: The Art of Getting What You Want* (New York: Signet, 1981).

29. Rubin, "Negotiation."
30. Fred Blake and Jane Mouton, *The Managerial Grid* (Houston: Gulf, 1964); K. W. Thomas, "Conflict and Conflict Management," in D. M. Dunnette (ed.), *Handbook of Industrial and Organizational Psychology* (Chicago: Rand McNally, 1976).
31. D. G. Pruitt, "Strategic Choice in Negotiation," *American Behavioral Scientist*, November-December 1983, p. 172.

32. Ibid., p. 173.
33. H. Brinton Milward, "Interorganizational Policy Systems and Research on Public Organizations," *Administration and Society* 13, 4 (1982):457-478.
34. A. Hawley, *Human Ecology* (New York: Ronald Press Company, 1950), p. 39.
35. Max H. Bazerman, "Negotiator Judgement: A Critical Look at the Rationality Assumption," *American Behavioral Scientist* 27, 2 (1983):211-228.

PART 2

The
Basics

The Basics of Negotiation and Mediation

The Kettering Foundation

Negotiation

Disagreements are pervasive in our culture. They frequently occur between individuals, within groups, and between groups. Most disagreements are resolved at an interpersonal level, but occasionally, when two or more parties are unable to resolve a disagreement—that is, when they are not willing to accept the *status quo* or to accede to the demands of the other party—the disagreement becomes a dispute.

Individuals and groups have developed a variety of ways of settling disputes. These include:

1. **Fighting**—using physical violence which may range from fist fights to full scale war
2. **Avoiding**—settling a dispute by moving away or refusing to take action
3. **Substituting**—using symbolic acts such as witchcraft, voodoo, or sporting contests to take the place of direct confrontation
4. **Adjudicating**—allowing outside intervenors such as judges and juries to resolve the matter for conflicting parties
5. **Negotiating**—settling the dispute directly and peacefully between the parties.

While all these methods have at one time or another succeeded in settling differences, negotiation is the most promising means by which disputes are likely to *stay* settled. Negotiation is a means of addressing conflict productively; unlike other adversarial approaches, it need not result in winners and losers.

Negotiation and Mediation, © 1982 and reprinted with the permission of the Kettering Foundation.

Conflict   In order to deal with conflict usefully, parties must understand its nature. Following are some commonly held views of human conflict which are, in fact, serious misconceptions. It is often thought, for example, that:

1. Harmony is the normal state of affairs, while conflict is abnormal.
2. Conflicts and disagreements are the same phenomenon.
3. People who exhibit conflict behavior are "frustrated," "anxious," "blocked," or "neurotic."

In fact:

1. In a relationship that endures over time, neither continuous harmony nor continuous conflict is the norm. Conflict is a normal element of any ongoing relationship, emerging, subsiding, and reemerging at intervals.
2. Conflicts, which involve incompatible goals, are more serious than disagreements, which may often be solved by defining terms and understanding the other party's point of view.
3. Expressions of anger and frustration are legitimate and normal when persons are unable to progress toward their desired goals.

Parties are often unable to remedy a dispute—or, at least, unable to make mutual progress in addressing common problems—because they suppress conflict, never allowing it to come to the surface so it can be resolved. Some traditional approaches to dealing with conflict suggest ways to manage, reduce, or avoid it, but they seldom provide ways to use conflict creatively. In fact, in seeking mutually satisfactory resolutions to serious disputes, it is often appropriate to foment conflict when it does not emerge naturally.

The nature of negotiation   Negotiations are used to address interpersonal disputes between members of the same family or between disagreeing citizens. Negotiations are a means of resolving conflicts between tenants and landlords, and between workers and employers. States and countries settle differences by means of negotiations.

Elements in a true negotiation include: (1) *multiple parties,* who are (2) *interdependent* and who (3) *seek to influence* each other by means of (4) *exchanging information* in various forms, including arguments, appeals, threats, and promises, (5) over *time,* suggesting that the parties are likely to learn about each other and about themselves and as a result positions may change.

Negotiation encourages cooperation in order to reach a mutually agreeable outcome. Ideally, the interests of all the parties—as well as others who have a stake in the issue—will be met completely.

The minimum criterion for an appropriate negotiated outcome is its genuine acceptance by the parties. Another mark of an agreement's success is that it is consistent with the broader community's view of fairness; an objective observer would judge that the interests of the parties (and stakeholders) had been adequately taken into account.

Negotiation is often confused with arbitration or adjudication. Arbitration and adjudication are processes by which parties submit their differences to settlement by an outside intervenor. An arbitrator may be chosen by mutual agreement of the parties or according to statutory provisions, as in a labor dispute. In the case of adjudication, a judge makes the decision by applying predetermined rules of law.

Negotiation differs from bargaining in that negotiation is a broader process involving all of the interaction between the parties. Bargaining, on the other hand, is limited to discussion of specific proposals, and it usually involves the allocation of scarce resources. Bargaining is often a part of the negotiation process. Our most vivid image of bargaining is the interaction which occurs between labor and management over specific terms of a contract.

The benefits of negotiation   While the principal means of resolving disputes in our society is the court system, it is often more beneficial to negotiate than to adjudicate a dispute. The courts will not accept some kinds of cases, and others simply are not appropriate for the courts. Moreover, it is both costly and time-consuming to resolve disputes in the courts.

In addition to bringing genuine conflict to the surface, there are other advantages associated with the negotiations process. If the parties know that they are about to participate in negotiations, they will have to prepare their positions. Often such preparation will require each party to define its concerns and set priorities within them.

Once at the table and participating in the give-and-take of negotiations, a clear differentiation of the parties' positions is likely to emerge. Then the participating groups can realize the ultimate benefit of participating in negotiations—producing "win-win" solutions that satisfy all parties. If all the parties participate in the development of a negotiated outcome, they are more likely to honor and abide by the solution.

Stages of negotiation   Negotiations usually pass through four distinct stages, each involving a range of tasks.

Stage 1: Organizing for negotiations   During this stage, persons responsible for the negotiations undertake some or all of the following tasks. They:

1. Recognize the conflict and define the boundaries of the dispute
2. Determine and accept the parties involved in the dispute
3. Select a mediator (optional)
4. Conduct team-building activities
5. Decide on the place (the "arena") where the negotiations will be conducted
6. Set the time frame.

Stage 2: Informal exchange of information   During this stage, parties to the negotiations perform some or all of the following tasks. They:

1. Define the rules which govern the negotiation
2. Develop their respective issues
3. Request information from the other party or parties
4. Exchange information with the other party or parties
5. Prepare preliminary positions
6. Present their own preliminary positions and react to those of the other party or parties.

Stage 3: Bargaining process   During this stage, parties to the negotiations perform some or all of the following tasks. They:

1. Draft formal positions
2. Resolve differences over formal positions
3. Select a mediator (optional)
4. Draft agreements.

Stage 4: Review and monitoring of agreement   During this stage, parties to the negotiation perform one or both of the following tasks. They:

1. Review and adopt the agreement
2. Monitor performance/compliance.

A typical negotiation usually involves some of the tasks in all four stages. The tasks are often undertaken in the order listed here. It should be remembered, however, that the preceding is descriptive and not prescriptive; not all the tasks are performed in any one negotiations process; the tasks are not always performed in the same sequence; and, occasionally, certain of the tasks are repeated.

Mediation
Central to the success of many complex negotiations are the services of a mediator. When disputing parties are willing but unable to resolve their differences through negotiations, they may turn to an impartial agent—preferably one trained in the art of mediation—to

help them reach an agreement. President Carter served in this capacity in the forging of the Camp David accords, as did a little-known Algerian statesman in bringing about the settlement of the Iranian hostage crisis.

Mediation is a process in which a mediator works with negotiating parties in an attempt to find a mutually satisfactory solution to the dispute and to obtain a set of commitments with which the participants can reasonably live.

The mediator's role   The disputing parties should select a mediator who is acceptable to all and who is perceived as impartial to the outcome of the dispute. The trust the mediator builds with the parties is essential to his or her effectiveness in directing the groups toward settlement. For example, a bond of trust would enable the mediator to receive confidential information which, in turn, could provide clues to the direction the negotiations would have to take in order to achieve settlement.

The mediator can play an important part in the resolution of a dispute in each of the four stages that most negotiations follow. In the preliminary stages, she or he can assure the representation of important parties during the negotiations, can encourage exchanges of information, and can help define disputed issues more precisely. In the latter stages of the negotiation, the mediator assists the parties in reaching a mutually acceptable solution. The mediator moves the process along, functioning as a catalyst as she or he reasons, persuades, clarifies, or seeks data, identifies issues, and manages the process so agreement becomes possible.

Mediation can create a setting in which each party to the dispute can explain its position, understand the views of the other party or parties, and negotiate an agreement acceptable to all. Direction of the negotiations by an experienced mediator reduces the likelihood that permanent obstacles to agreement will develop.

The parties involved in negotiations should remember that the mediator has no authority to impose a settlement; a mediator does not function as an arbitrator or a judge. Similarly, the participants should not look to the mediator for substantive information; she or he is not there to do their homework for them. The mediator's primary role is as the facilitator of the negotiations process, not as a member of one of the negotiating teams.

When to use a mediator   Mediation is most often thought of as an "intervention." That is, usually only after the negotiating parties have reached an impasse is the mediator brought in. However, in the case of complex disputes, it is often preferable to have the mediator present from the beginning. The earlier the mediator is able to perform the central functions of clarification and management of ideas, the more likely it is that negotiations will conclude success-fully.

The principal advantage of early involvement by the mediator is that a broader range of alternatives for settling the dispute is likely to be available. The parties will be more open to change be-cause they have not yet made substantial commitment to a particu-lar plan.

It is appropriate to turn to mediation during the course of a dispute if:

1. The issues become too complex for the parties to disentangle
2. Negative feelings among the parties are so great that they cannot engage in fruitful, rational discussion
3. The parties have reached an impasse in their discussions, that is, no progress is being made toward resolution of the dispute and it is unlikely further progress will be made
4. The parties want to resolve their differences
5. The parties are willing to consider reasonable compromise.

The use of mediation is appropriate at the outset of a negotia-tion if the negotiation involves a combination of the following ele-ments:

1. A complex problem
2. Numerous parties from different sectors
3. The need for extensive coordination in order to achieve re-sults
4. A problem of high priority for all or most of the parties
5. Parties who realize a decision is necessary
6. An urgent need for resolution.

Negotiations checklists

When negotiations may fail   Parties can negotiate about any disagreement. However, a negotiation is likely to be substantially more difficult if the discrepancy in power between the parties is too great, and if there is no time constraint on the outcome of the nego-tiation.

Thus, in certain situations the costs of conducting an effective negotiation will outweigh the benefits of proceeding. Negotiation is probably not time- and cost-effective when:

1. The right people will not (or cannot) be at the table negotiat-ing
2. Viable alternative solutions to the dispute are outside the domain of the conflicting parties
3. One or more of the parties does not accord another minimal legitimacy

4. One or more of the parties is not willing to bargain in good faith
5. The discrepancy in power between the parties is too great for them to engage equally in the development of a mutually satisfying outcome
6. One or more of the parties is not sufficiently clear about their positions and a considerable amount of time will be required to develop them
7. There is no deadline or time constraint on the outcome of the negotiation
8. The parties have already engaged in negotiations and failed.

All of these situations can be dealt with by negotiation, but doing so contributes substantially to the time and cost of a negotiation.

Conditions for successful negotiations   It is appropriate to use negotiations to resolve a dispute if:

1. Two or more parties are involved
2. The parties are unwilling to accept the *status quo* or accede to the demands of the other party
3. The parties desire to produce win-win solutions that satisfy all the parties
4. Negotiation is viewed by all parties as a more attractive alternative for resolving the dispute than fighting, avoidance, substitution, or adjudication
5. It is desirable to bring conflict to the surface and resolve it between the parties
6. It is desirable for each of the parties to define and rank its concerns
7. It is important that all the parties honor and abide by the solution.

Managing Conflict by Applying Common Sense

——————————— Susan Carpenter and W. J. D. Kennedy

Our society has become conscious of the risks and costs of not dealing effectively with complex public disputes, but we have not
adopted new methods for reaching solutions. Some of these disputes
are so convoluted—the storage of hazardous waste, for example—
that many officials avoid dealing with them. In some cases parties
go to court or argue adversarial positions before regulatory bodies.
They turn their interests over to lawyers or government administrators, who, whatever their professional competence may be, have
no direct stake in the outcome. The courts are overwhelmed with an
ever-increasing load of cases, many of which are so complex and
technical that judgments based on points of law only exacerbate the
problems.

Frustrations over the consequences of delay, the failure to involve the public effectively, and the uncertainty and cost of litigation have led individuals and organizations around the country to
explore better ways of dealing with conflict. For over a decade, AC-
CORD[1] has been in the business of designing and applying alternative procedures to resolve large-scale public disputes and environmental controversies. We have adapted to our work lessons learned
in international peacemaking, community dispute settlement, and
interpersonal conflict resolution. Problems we have dealt with
range from municipal water supply to air quality standards, land
acquisition, forest access, coal leasing, and urban development. All
of these controversies are as much social and economic as they are
"environmental." Our intervention activities may take anywhere
from a few days to several years depending on the nature of the

"Managing Environmental Conflict by Applying Common Sense," by Susan Carpenter and W. J. D. Kennedy," *Negotiation Journal*, April 1985. Reprinted with permission.

conflict and the number of parties. We have worked with all levels of government, private industry, and public-interest groups.

Individuals who get caught up in conflict fall prey to an apparently universal phenomenon: as the conflict progresses, they become less capable of using common sense. This article will examine seven principles which, in our experience, are commonly violated by well-intentioned managers of complex issues. While our illustrations are drawn from our experiences with natural resources, the principles are applicable to other fields of dispute resolution activities. We provide an example of what happens when a principle is ignored and describe at least one alternative procedure.

Principle 1: To find a good solution, you have to understand the problem

Conflicts are rarely what they seem. Personalities, motives and relationships are as important as the substance of the issue. What appears to be a straightforward collision of purposes can be more complicated because human beings are less predictable than technical facts. Adversarial positions, especially publicly stated ones, may result from a great variety of pressures and purposes that do not accurately reflect the actual needs of the contending parties. Instead of leaping to conclusions, one should begin by untangling the muddle of emotions, perceptions, needs, and cross-purposes that surround any given conflict.

A government agency wanted to resolve a controversy over ground water in western Colorado. Agency personnel started with the assumption that three groups were involved in the issue: federal land managers, the state Department of Natural Resources, and a state-wide environmental organization. All three groups were based in an urban eastern part of the state. Representatives of the groups met in a series of discussions and, after heavy negotiation, reached agreement. Immediately thereafter, livestock organizations from the western half of the state, who were familiar with the issue and would be directly affected by the agreements, declared that the discussions had been based on invalid information and, therefore, were irreparably flawed. As a consequence, months of negotiations were dismissed, because a party critical to the discussion was overlooked.

Alternative: analyzing the conflict   A person who wants to deal constructively with a conflict should begin by identifying the groups and individuals involved, their relationships to each other, and the substance of the dispute, through visits with individuals directly affected by the dispute and with others who are less involved but well informed about the situation. By a combination of listening, cautious probing, and cross-checking with other sources, the conflict manager attempts to understand what the parties are trying to accomplish and why. He or she looks for differences in perceptions and assesses the consequences for each party if a solution is not found.

Careful analysis of a conflict establishes a base for building a resolution strategy. Analysis should continue throughout the conflict resolution effort and should be adjusted constantly to accommodate new information. Especially in the later stages of a hot dispute, when feelings run high, it is almost impossible for the parties to assess the interests of their adversaries accurately. It is even surprisingly difficult for them to look objectively at what they themselves really need.

Efforts to avoid unnecessary confrontation, to manage an escalating conflict, or to mediate a dispute can be substantially improved by a simple analysis plan that defines specific steps for assessing the situation. A typical analysis plan would:

1.   Identify the parties and the persons who can best represent them
2.   List the apparent central issues
3.   Develop a tentative list of interests and concerns
4.   Analyze relationships between individuals and groups
5.   Assess the consequences for each party if no solution is found
6.   Describe the power each party has to advance its position
7.   List the positions taken.

Analysis of this kind helps the manager in a dispute to assess it in an orderly way. It is important for the manager to avoid relying on assumptions and to fill out the list only after talking with people who have differing views of the situation. If personal visits are impossible, telephone inquiries will serve if the manager listens carefully for perspectives that disagree with his or her own, because they are the checks against reality.

A private land trust purchased land that it wanted to preserve in its natural state. Representatives of the trust declared their intention to allow the nearby community to manage the land, but, without considering the consequences, also announced their support of the National Park Service proposal to clear the title of the land through legal action so it could be added to the national park. The two positions seemed contradictory to the community and it felt betrayed. Communication became thoroughly confused, and suspicion increased dramatically. Accusations flew in all directions, frustrating the citizens and embarrassing the Park Service and the private land trust.

When we were asked to help the parties find a solution to the controversy, we began by reading all the available articles about it and talking with people who were familiar with the history of the dispute. We concluded that the situation was a great deal more complicated than the single issue of land ownership. Behind the arguments were long-standing fears and resentment over other issues. We had to analyze this apparently simple situation carefully before we could design a plan to make the most of the knowledge and experience of the people at the meetings.

Many controversies over natural resources are a great deal more complicated than the land trust situation. At the other end of the scale, the Metropolitan Water Roundtable, an eighteen-month negotiation program to decide how best to meet Denver's water needs, dealt with a highly complex system of separate disputes. The thirty-one participants in the Roundtable represented interests that involved the entire state of Colorado, many of which had been quarreling for decades. Before any formal meetings were held, we took three months to analyze the web of interrelated struggles and, as much as possible, the potential obstacles to resolution.

Whether a dispute is limited to a few parties in a single location or has regional or national scope and brings in many individuals and groups, the conflict manager must understand what issues are important, who is involved, and what the relationships are among the parties. Above all, he or she must avoid leaping to unsubstantiated conclusions.

Principle 2: Planning a strategy can help you reach a better solution

A building contractor does not construct a house by installing the plumbing first, then shingling the roof, and then pouring the foundation, but that is often the way people try to manage conflict. They focus on defining solutions before developing an efficient and logical plan for understanding the nature of the problem and the options available for solution.

Investors and planners in a large western city convened a group of leading citizens interested in developing the last large tract of available land in the downtown area. They intended to reach agreements on the type of development that should occur, but they found themselves talking about narrow issues such as the types of roads that would be needed before they had any idea of how the land would be used. The discussions foundered because no one proposed a process for moving the participants logically from one topic to another toward general agreement on an overall approach.

Alternative: developing a plan for resolution   Moving to resolution without a logical sequence of steps can delay progress and jeopardize success. Under the pressure of conflict, people naturally focus on finding solutions, but taking time to plan and follow a strategy can produce better results and do it faster.

After reviewing the initial conflict analysis, a conflict manager must define the problem. In one situation, the parties defined the problem in three different ways. Each definition suggested a different strategy for resolving the problem. At issue was a federal ban on the use of Compound 1080, a poison used to kill coyotes. Compound 1080 was banned in 1973 because it also killed eagles and other wildlife. After the ban was imposed, wool growers, who already had many serious economic problems, complained that they were losing more lambs. The contending parties had to decide whether the issue was: *(a)* to use 1080 or not, *(b)* how to kill coyotes, or *(c)* how to save lambs. Each alternative required a particular mix of parties at the negotiating table and a different set of technical resources. It was necessary to select one of the three issues as the explicit focus of the discussions to prevent the entire effort from breaking down into irrelevant quarrels over divergent goals.

The next step in developing a strategy is to determine an appropriate conflict-management goal based on the specific problem. The goal may be a formal written set of agreements between the parties, a series of jointly determined recommendations to a decision-making body, or it may be simply to create an effective system of communication. Defining the problem and establishing a goal determines the direction of subsequent activities.

Once the goal is determined, the manager needs to identify the parties and individuals who should participate in the program. Suggestions for participants should be sought in the analysis interviews. If the analysis is thorough, most of the parties will have been identified. The conflict manager works with the parties to determine how many representatives from each group should participate and who they should be. The representatives should be knowledgeable about the issues and able to get along reasonably well with representatives from the other groups.

Then the manager needs to determine what activities should be included in the conflict-management plan and their sequence. Is it desirable to establish ground rules? Are issues and concerns well defined, or should they be clarified? Is technical research required? Have reasonable options been identified, or do they need to be developed? The conflict manager outlines a logical sequence of activities that will move the discussions toward resolution of the problem.

The next step is to decide the most appropriate type of meeting and method for organizing each activity. Data discrepancies might best be handled by an advisory group of technical experts representing each of the disputing sides or by outside specialists who are acceptable to all parties. In disputes involving many parties, a public workshop may be the most effective way to identify the community's interests and concerns. On the other hand, decisions between a city and a single developer may best be handled by having a small negotiating team review what each party needs to satisfy its constituency and then brainstorm possible solutions.

Other steps in developing a strategy include determining who should initiate the conflict-management activity, who should invite the participants, who should chair or facilitate the sessions, the appropriate length of time for the process, the location of the meetings, and the preparation necessary before the meetings.

Several management approaches will appear to be feasible in any complex conflict situation, and the conflict manager must be careful not to lock in on an exact design too early. Timing, the cast of characters, and many other elements may change as the separate components of the problem are more clearly defined. During the first few months of one project, several participants vociferously insisted that the entire effort should take no more than six months. Others, looking at a history of four decades of conflict, thought it would require at least two years. The consensus was that we should wait and see. As the dimensions of the problem emerged, it became clear to everyone that more than six months would be required to collect and analyze data, negotiate agreements, and carry them out.

Flexibility does not imply haphazard planning. A strategy is a preliminary blueprint that gives initial direction but is continuously modified as the situation evolves and appropriate methods are identified.

Principle 3: Human relationships are as important as technical data

Efforts to solve complicated problems by technical criteria alone often cause more conflicts than they resolve. Most complex controversies involve technical questions, and it is easy to assume that the problem will be solved if technical solutions can be found. Although accurate and consistent data are essential to understanding natural resource issues, data alone will not resolve them. Equal attention must be given to human relationships.

Experts on technical problems usually are most comfortable working in their field of competence, and they are often uneasy when faced with "people problems." Nobody likes to be confronted with distrust and even hatred (if the conflict has gone on long enough), especially when defending a position that is based on solid facts. Yet feelings people have about each other are just as real as scientific data, and emotions condition the way people handle information. Decisions are made and battles are fought not by numbers and computers, but by complicated and unpredictable human beings.

Adversaries cannot break off from fighting while they are exchanging verbal blows. People in conflicts readily agree that verbal attacks prevent progress and increase hostilities, but once they start trading insults it is hard to stop. No one wants to appear

weaker than the other side. Yet the rhetoric must cease before negotiations can begin. Sooner or later the parties must start to trust
each other so commitments can be made and solutions found.

Alternative: applying ground rules for behavior   Professional
conflict managers emphasize the importance of building and maintaining trust between adversaries. But colliding interest groups
have a difficult time reorganizing their relationships. It is hard for
them to reestablish the kind of trust that is needed for negotiation,
especially if they have been attacking each other personally.

One straightforward and logical way for people to change the
way they deal with each other is to adopt ground rules for behavior
that all participants in a negotiation are expected to follow. Ground
rules specify how participants will treat each other inside and outside formal negotiation sessions. They may also describe how the
participants will deal with people who are not part of the negotiating effort, such as representatives of other constituencies or the
press. The conflict manager may propose the ground rules, or they
may be developed by the negotiating parties.

Despite long-standing adversarial relationships and intense
feelings about the many issues under discussion, the thirty-one
members of the Metropolitan Water Roundtable were able to exchange information effectively by employing a set of ground rules.
The three pages of rules stipulated such caveats as:

1. Personal attacks will not be tolerated.
2. The motivations and intentions of participants will not be im-
    pugned lightly.
3. All statements, documents, or other communications used in
    the course of Roundtable meetings will not be offered or uti-
    lized as evidence in any administrative or judicial proceeding.
4. When discussing the Roundtable with reporters, participants
    should be careful to present only their views and not those of
    other participants or of the Roundtable. The temptation to
    discuss someone else's statement or position should be
    avoided.

The Roundtable members accepted these explicit standards for behavior with some skepticism in the beginning, but the rules soon
produced a more relaxed and open atmosphere than anyone had
thought possible.

Participants in the Water Roundtable approved and maintained standards of behavior because they recognized them as the
most efficient method for getting on with their work. They had experienced less effective ways of negotiating differences, and they
endorsed the discipline of behavior standards as a more sensible
way of getting things done.

Alternative: encouraging social interaction   Except for a few individuals who gain financially or emotionally from keeping a controversy alive, most people dislike being part of a conflict and find quarreling a disagreeable waste of time. Therefore they may resent those responsible for subjecting them to such an unpleasant experience. Even in a relatively small local dispute, the parties are likely to stop regarding their adversaries as neighbors and fellow human beings and start seeing them as two-dimensional embodiments of greed, immorality, and irresponsibility.

Individuals who represent contending interests must come to realize that their adversaries may have redeeming human qualities and that, if they are not necessarily admirable or lovable, they are at least acceptable and worthy of consideration. *People* negotiate, not the groups they represent.

Exchanges that take place before or after some more formal affair or over a meal are an essential element in managing conflict. Coffee and doughnuts before a meeting, mid-morning breaks, and extended lunch and dinner periods give people the opportunity to find out that their adversaries are people too, and to adjust their personal relationships.

We conducted a series of meetings for the Colorado Air Quality Control Commission about highly controversial visibility regulations. Thirty-five representatives of electric utilities, environmental groups, the forest products industry, oil shale companies, and local governments attended the sessions. At the end of each day, everyone was invited to stay for drinks and snacks. The participants soon were using the time as a chance to continue discussions in an informal setting without the pressure of speaking for or against any position. Social interaction opens the lines of communication that are needed to solve problems.

Principle 4: Lack of necessary information encourages conflict

As people become caught up in the dynamics of conflict and animosities grow, they stop talking with each other. This happens both because it becomes distasteful to talk with adversaries and because communication with the enemy may be viewed with suspicion by one's own associates. Of course, when the flow of information between the parties ceases, it becomes difficult for them to clarify perceptions and transmit or receive new data needed to solve the problem. The parties cannot discuss alternatives or make adjustments. Instead, they generate information that promotes their own positions and convey it, often with irritating inaccuracies, through third parties or the news media. When the conflict has thus become seriously polarized, even useful and accurate information is received with distrust and falls on deaf ears.

If communication ceases, misconceptions cannot be corrected, and people leap to the worst possible interpretations of their adversaries' statements and actions. Distrust builds on itself and is fed by each new hostile move and angry statement. As a result, people may miscalculate the motives of the other side and make destructive decisions.

Almost every major construction project begins amid countless uncertainties about government requirements, financial commitments, market conditions, and access to an adequate work force. Management may decide that it does not need "people problems" at this early stage and thus defer making detailed statements about its plans to local officials until it can forecast them with more certainty. The community, operating in an information vacuum, will probably make up its own "facts."

The company is first seen as uncooperative and then as malevolent. Many people automatically mistrust large organizations anyway, and it is easy for them to suspect the motives of a company that is reluctant to share information with people who will be affected by its actions. The company can find itself deep in "people problems" long before it turns the first shovel of dirt if it decides not to communicate with the community to avoid "stirring up the natives."

Alternative: establishing regular and predictable communication   Communication between people who have stopped talking with each other must be reestablished sooner or later, because they have final responsibility for solving their problems. Individuals may be able to solve a problem completely through informal conversation, and all that is needed is to get them together. Talking informally face-to-face or by telephone can effectively correct people's misconceptions and sharpen their understanding of a question under discussion. But formal meetings are necessary when the dispute has solidified and the parties see each other as adversaries. In such situations, formal meetings can promote the exchange of information and provide an arena for negotiation.

People who are quarreling with each other do not respond to new information as they would in less upsetting circumstances. Quite naturally, they often assume that any new development threatens their interests. A common error is to assume that messages can be sent in tense situations with the same content and in the same way as in normal conversation. On the contrary, when adversaries inform each other of new developments, they must be very careful to make their words precise and clear. The other side will interpret vague statements as deliberately misleading.

When people are under stress, both the words used and the regularity of communication will affect efforts to solve a problem. It may be extremely important to schedule regular discussions. If people can count on meeting at predictable intervals and being brought up to date on what is happening, they will be less anxious and less likely to do or say things that will further damage their interests and their relationships with others.

In one controversy, a long period of intense negotiation produced firm agreements between the parties. Then the pace of negotiation slackened while technical data were checked by consulting engineers. The parties had become accustomed to frequent meetings and telephone conversations with each other. Suddenly they found themselves spending little time in negotiations and contact with the other people. The result was dramatic. Rumors began to circulate about secret "deals," although none had been made. People who had trusted each other completely during negotiations two months before began questioning each other's motives. Bridges that had been built between individuals began to fall apart.

Our solution was to resume regular meetings of all working groups to assure predictable opportunities for exchange of information, even when there were no major issues of substance to be discussed. We learned an important lesson: regular, face-to-face contact is important, and the communication network must be sustained throughout the problem-solving process and into the time when agreements are being implemented, regardless of the ebb and flow of negotiation.

Principle 5: Parties must agree on basic data

In complex disputes, disagreements over data can be expected. Growth projections, patterns of use, and levels of production can be ordered into a range of probabilities, but parties in conflict are likely to choose an extreme point in the range, either through fear of what might happen if they change their position at all or as a deliberately chosen bargaining chip.

Most people, especially those with technical training, recognize the importance of agreeing on a single common data base and working out an acceptable range of figures. However, people caught up in the dynamics of conflict resist letting go of figures that seem to support their case even if they are considered unreasonable by other parties. A common, but nonetheless remarkable, phenomenon occurs when each party conducts elaborate statistical studies to justify its position, but never sits down with the other side to see why their figures are contradictory.

Alternative: negotiating assumptions and endorsing the figures People with a problem to solve must be comfortable with the data they use to describe it, not necessarily in single precise figures for every item, but at least in a range from a reasonable low to a reasonable high. Reaching agreement on data is a good way to start negotiations. In reviewing information, the parties may also find erroneous conclusions that demand new information, thus building a more reliable foundation for subsequent agreements. The experience of finding mistakes and jointly agreeing that the figures should be corrected can stimulate cooperation in analyzing the general problem.

A combination of techniques may be used to reach common ground on data. First, all assumptions can be made explicit and carefully examined by the parties. Original sources should be checked when possible. If data discrepancies involve sophisticated computer models, representatives from each party capable of understanding them can negotiate the assumptions and the model, or they may retain an impartial technical expert to review and assess the figures.

In one water dispute, parties disagreed on most of the statistics they were using to describe the issues before them. The annual yield of water from the current system, population projections for the service area, potential gain from conservation, and alternative water storage capacities were all topics of intense disagreement. The parties recognized that they could not find solutions until they reached a common understanding of the dimensions of the problem. Separate task groups were established to deal with each of the major issues. With the help of technical experts, each task group collected, reviewed, and negotiated statistical information. After several months of work, agreements were finally reached, sometimes on specific figures and sometimes on an acceptable range of numbers. Agreement on data enabled the parties to begin exploring acceptable alternatives.

Principle 6: Ownership in the process leads to problem-solving

"I just can't understand why they don't like my proposal. I listened carefully to all the sides and came out with what I think is the best solution possible." Government and industry managers who work closely with a problem as part of their daily responsibilities are likely to see a sensible way to solve it. They are frequently surprised by the diversity and intensity of opposition they face from groups responding to what the managers thought were clearly the right decisions. Sometimes after they have done everything right—consulted with all the people involved and developed a plan that meets the wishes of the parties—everyone attacks them anyway.

It is tempting for a program manager to try to "sell" his or her solution. One federal land manager told us about a dispute over livestock grazing rights on public lands. For more than a decade, ranchers had fought over the control of a tract of land. The land manager had spent several years trying to persuade the parties to adopt a "reasonable" solution—his solution—and was totally frustrated that neither side would accept it. Instead, the parties continued to pursue an exhausting, unproductive quarrel. The irony is that if the manager had brought them together and asked them to work out a proposal for what should be done, they probably would have come up with an answer almost identical to his.

A government or industry manager has final responsibility for finding a solution. But the way he or she approaches the decision may well determine whether or not the solution can be carried out. Asking for opinions and then issuing a directive misses the opportunity to place some of the responsibility for reaching a satisfactory conclusion on the shoulders of the contending parties. And if they do not exchange information with each other, they are unlikely to understand fully what the alternatives may be. As a consequence, they may oppose any reasonable solution proposed by the manager.

Alternative: involving the parties in designing the process and developing the solution   When people are asked to help design the process for resolving a dispute and take an active role in developing a solution, their energies are channeled away from criticism and attack toward constructive problem-solving. Giving ownership to the conflicting parties means allowing them to determine which issues are important and what solution is most desirable. Active involvement builds credibility for the solution and promotes efficient implementation of the agreements.

On the surface it may appear more expedient to have a public or private manager "solve the problem" without involving the affected groups. After all, the clock is running; government is under pressure to promulgate its policies and regulations, and companies view any delay as a costly impediment to project deadlines. A decade or two ago, a manager probably could have succeeded with this approach. Today, however, interest groups that are dissatisfied with either the process used to achieve a resolution or the solution itself can block its implementation for years through litigation. And once established as adversaries, these groups will be even more adamant in their opposition the next time a similar issue appears.

People are more likely to participate in a constructive conflict resolution effort, and stay with it, if they feel that they had a part in designing the program. In one developing controversy, we asked key individuals to specify what must be included in a resolution process to assure their participation. Some wanted access to resource management information. Others recommended that the participants be decision-makers, not technical experts or lawyers. Others said that candid discussions would be essential and suggested that the press be excluded from the deliberations. One person emphasized the importance of each representative at the table staying in close touch with his or her constituents to bring them along and to seek their ideas as the discussion progressed. Each of these concerns was integrated into the design of the negotiation.

Participation in the process design continued after the planning phase was complete. Participants were asked throughout the program for their views on the progress of the discussions and whether any adjustments in the process should be made. When problems arose, the participants were asked how they thought the problem should be solved.

Beyond helping design the program and having responsibility for its effectiveness, people should be directly involved in determining the details of the solution. Public hearings are supposed to bring citizens into the decision-making process, but they rarely produce sufficient information for resolution. In fact, they frequently make matters worse. At hearings, people present their most extreme views in an effort to persuade government decision-makers to swing at least partway toward their position. They do not exchange specific information nor do they usually suggest creative alternatives.

On the other hand, when the parties most directly affected by a disagreement are given an opportunity to work together toward resolution of their problem, they have an incentive to educate themselves thoroughly about the issues, to understand what the interests of the other parties are, and to look for solutions that all the parties can accept.

Both the oil and gas industry representatives and environmental advocacy groups were dissatisfied for different reasons with procedures used by a federal land-management agency to inform citizens of proposed exploration and drilling in wilderness study areas. People were threatening to sue the agency, and both sides were attacking each other publicly. Frustrated by the complaints, the state director of the agency told the two groups that if they could work out a better system for notification, the agency would accept it. Much to the surprise of both groups, after a series of meetings with a mediator they were able to negotiate an alternative procedure and submit it to the state agency director. Similar modifications suggested unilaterally by the agency to the parties almost certainly would not have been accepted by either side.

Principle 7: Lasting solutions are based on interests rather than positions

People will take a stand for all kinds of reasons. Fear of change, fear of loss, anger, resentment, and frustration may be as important as logic in the formation of a position. Sometimes people take irrational positions, but they hold fast to them nevertheless.

Traditionally, negotiators sit around a table and bargain away chips one by one. The side that has the greatest staying power gives away the fewest chips and wins, at least for the moment. Each side progressively gives up things that it had previously insisted it must keep. Each side takes a position knowing that it will not get all that it asks for. The positions, not the problem, determine the direction of the bargaining. Positions become realities separate from the original issue, especially if they have been stated publicly. Since publicly stated positions tend to be narrow and simplistic, they allow little room for maneuvering.

For years a land management agency wanted to place a new ranger station in a remote section of its management area. People in a small community nearby strongly resisted the plan and were able to block it politically. Agency personnel could not understand why the local citizens were so opposed to a proposal intended to protect land that was important to the community. The agency manager happened to meet informally with a town leader over another matter and asked casually why the community had objected so adamantly to the construction of the ranger station. The answer was a shock: "Because you would put in an outsider as the ranger!" Shortly thereafter, the manager promised to appoint a local person and the community dropped its opposition.

In this case, the dispute had come down to a question of which position would win and which would lose, and for a long time both sides lost. Positions are a poor foundation on which to build a successful resolution of differences, composed as they are of anxieties, resentments, desires, public pronouncements, face-saving and playing to constituents. Positions limit the range of opportunities for solution.

Alternative: understanding what people need for a satisfactory solution   A good way to begin a search for solutions is to persuade the parties to disengage for a moment and do something that will be unfamiliar and even uncomfortable at first: talk with each other about their interests and what they need for a satisfactory resolution. Focusing on interests forces contending parties to back off from their stated positions and perform a straightforward task—talking about themselves. When they talk about themselves, they lose their adversarial tone, and their opponents begin to understand why they have taken the positions they have. People in a dispute may have one position but many interests, some more important than others. The stand they take is often determined by a combination of motives rather than a single clear objective.

One of the conflict manager's principal purposes in persuading the parties to discuss interests is to begin the process of building

trust. Most interests are reasonable and can be described. The realization that the other side's needs are not as outrageous as their
position seems to be can awaken hope that there may be a way to
solve the problem. When the list is laid out for the group to review,
and the adversaries hear what is said and consider the list, they
often discover that, in contrast to their stated positions, their interests are different but not mutually exclusive. This happens with
surprising frequency, even in hot disputes. Cooperative efforts to
solve the problem can be built on the realization that interests are
not necessarily in conflict.

The process of listing interests is likely to be successful because
it is uncomplicated, and because talking about what they really need
makes sense to people caught up in a conflict. In listing interests,
the parties should be free to express their thoughts without challenge or criticism. Comments must be limited to clarifying questions.

Interest-based negotiation was used effectively in the Metropolitan Water Roundtable. After adopting a set of ground rules for
behavior, the Roundtable participants were ready and anxious to
resume the many separate battles over water management they had
been fighting for decades. Instead, they were divided into four balanced working groups and asked to develop lists of interests that the
Roundtable must address. These people had fought each other in
innumerable costly battles, but this was the first time that they had
ever listened to each other describe what they needed. The importance of this procedure became evident to everyone as the Roundtable participants developed a set of general principles of agreement that formed the basis for all later negotiations.

Conclusion

Conflict is natural and necessary in a free society. But disputes are
increasingly damaging and costly, and the consequences of not finding wise solutions become more and more grave. In the United
States, we depend on outmoded methods for resolving disputes. The
adversarial approach works in some situations but produces avoid-
able costs and defective conclusions in others. Over the past decade,
a body of theoretical knowledge and practical case experience has
developed that offers better alternatives for managing conflict. The
lessons we have learned are applicable across the full range of multiparty disputes.

Managing conflict does not demand an exotic methodology or
require drastic changes in the ways people do business. We encourage people in a conflict to pause and ask two questions: What is the
real problem? and What is the most sensible way to solve it? Leaping at conclusions and declaring positions usually make matters
worse. Planning a strategy, maintaining relationships, acquiring

and agreeing on essential information, and involving conflicting parties directly in working out solutions are some logical steps toward solving the problem. The seven principles for managing conflict suggested in these pages have been applied successfully in dozens of conflict situations, both simple and complex. They work because they are based on the systematic application of common sense.

1.   ACCORD Associates, based in Boulder, Colorado, is a private, nonprofit organization concerned primarily with mediation in environmental controversies.

Settling Disputes through Mediation

Leah K. Patton

Since 1974, when the phrase "environmental mediation" was coined to describe the negotiated settlement of an environmental dispute with the assistance of a mediator,[1] interest in innovative approaches to the settlement of complex environmental controversies has increased. Leaders of organizations that often are at odds have been brought together for general discussions aimed at improving the climate and tone of the existing dialogue between business, industry, and environmental interests. Leaders of the agricultural chemical industry and of environmental and church groups have met to agree on a voluntary code of standards for American chemical companies that export or market agricultural chemicals to developing countries.[2] There are numerous examples of successful negotiations,[3] leading to binding settlements of complex, multiparty, site-specific disputes.[4] Finally, there is increasing interest in[5] and some experience with[6] negotiating proposed federal regulations to supplement the existing rulemaking procedures which are characterized by delay and expense and often result in rules unsatisfactory to all concerned.

With the possible exception of the general discussions, all of these efforts have involved negotiation, have had as their goal settlement of issues, and often have involved the use of a mediator to help convene or guide the negotiation process. But these three words—negotiation, settlement, and mediator—are often misunderstood. It is useful to begin by discussing the implication of these words in the context of what has been learned about successful settlement of environmental disputes.

Originally published as "Settling Environmental Disputes: The Experience with and Future of Environmental Mediation," by Leah K. Patton, 14 *Environmental Law* 547 (1984). Adapted from a speech given at the National Conference on Dispute Resolution, sponsored by the Conservation Foundation, Washington, D.C., January 24, 1983.

Defining the terms

Negotiation means more than the sort of haggling that goes on over the price of a rug or even the price of a house. It means getting beyond horsetrading over positions to see whether the core interests of each side can be met and integrated. It means looking for areas where mutual gains are possible, or at least areas where one party's gains will not detract in a significant way from the other party's interests. Negotiation also can mean simply discovering some mutually acceptable plan that makes the best of a very bad situation.

The settlement of environmental disputes may take many different forms. The Mediation Institute has been involved in informal, politically based, consensus-building efforts in which the consensus recommendations that resulted from the negotiations were forwarded to an elected body. At the other end of the spectrum have been settlements in the form of consent decrees filed in federal district court. Settlement means that the parties have reached closure on a set of issues, by their own definition. This does not imply that they have resolved the basic differences among their respective interests. The negotiations over water quality, reclamation, and related issues concerning Homestake's uranium mine in the Gunnison National Forest (Colorado) are illustrative of this distinction.[7] Although the Homestake negotiators did a good job of reaching settlement on the issues before them, and although the parties came away from the negotiations with a heightened respect for each other, it was understood that no consensus had been reached on the merits of nuclear power or uranium mining.

Finally, the mediator is an independent third party (in environmental disputes a more accurate term might be seventh or fourteenth party) who helps the disputants reach what they consider to be an acceptable settlement. By definition, the mediator normally has no legal authority to impose a decision, compel a concession, or even require attendance at joint meetings. The specifics of the mediator's role are determined by the particular needs of the parties and their representatives. The mediator can be effective only if the negotiators want her to be. An apt analogy would be the civilian who directs traffic at the scene of an accident. That civilian is respected by the drivers who want to get through the snarl. But if anyone profits from the delay, finds accidents interesting, or is distracted by his own stereo system, he can ignore the would-be traffic director and frustrate everyone else.

Conditions for settlement

Over the past nine years at the Mediation Institute, three conditions consistently have encouraged parties to seek settlement through negotiation: uncertainty, cost, and inadequate forum. Uncertainty exists when no one party holds all the cards or can hope to dictate the outcome of the controversy with any degree of assurance. One side's legal case looks fairly strong, but far from certain. By the time the administrative appeal reaches the office of the Secretary of Interior, there could be a new, unpredictable administration. Current political momentum may strengthen one party's hand, but the potential exists for backlash that can benefit the adversary.

The cost of a dispute, of course, can be measured in dollars. Lawyers fees add up quickly. It may be clear that whoever loses on the final round of administrative appeal will take the matter to federal court, where the drain of financial and human resources will be burdensome. Or perhaps (and this is frequently the case) the cost is not so much in dollars as bad public relations. An environmental group often is seen as always opposing everything, while a company that wants a clean corporate image may be successfully painted by the press with the brush of the "dirty dozen."

Finally, parties frequently seek innovative approaches to dispute resolution because the existing forums (courts, legislative bodies, or regulatory bodies) are not reaching the real issues. The classic circumstance is a suit over some procedure. People care about due process and procedural protections, but that is not what really motivates them to commit the resources to the fight. They are concerned about substantive issues. The procedure is just what they can grab.

These three conditions—uncertainty, cost, and inadequate forum—may not sound altruistic, but the existence of great statesmen who know that this is the right thing to do for the good of some broader public does not appear high on the list of conditions for successful negotiation. This observation does not denigrate the importance of such statesmen, but it points out the need to be realistic about the circumstances in which a statesman can be effective. Individuals who have the potential to be statesmen should not be asked to encourage settlements in situations where settlements are inappropriate or impossible, or in which the troops will not follow their leader. By asking the impossible, the credibility of those valuable individuals is diminished. In the disputes in which the Mediation Institute has been involved, some extremely skilled leaders have worked to achieve settlements. No doubt a large part of their success has been based on the fact that people recognized negotiation as being better than the costly, frustrating, and time-consuming alternatives.

Impediments to negotiation

Uncertainty, cost, and forum problems exist in numerous controversies in which negotiation is never seriously considered because of the many impediments. A few of these impediments are outlined below, together with examples of how mediators have helped parties overcome them.

The first impediment to proposing negotiation is risk, both interest-based and personal. The interest-based risk is that the very offer of negotiation may be seen as an indication of weakness—a sign that one side is not prepared to carry the legal case to the bitter end. An offer of negotiation also may be interpreted as one party succumbing to the public pressure mounted by another party. In this unending poker game, perceptions about one's intentions may be as important as the actual intentions. The personal risk is that by proposing negotiation an individual may lose the ability to lead. A mine manager suggests sitting down with that flaky handful of troublemakers? An environmental leader suggests sitting down with the company that is in the process of despoiling pristine land? Those who advocate negotiation, whether they are working within a corporate hierarchy or the most chaotically democratic of grass-roots groups, run the risk of losing power and status within their own organization by proposing the use of a process that depends equally upon their intentions and behavior and those of their opponents for its success.

Mediators frequently are used to introduce the concept of negotiation in a way that minimizes risk to conflicting parties and their representatives. By definition, mediators to some extent assume the mantle of meddlers. As such, they can begin an informal series of inquiries with persons indirectly connected to the dispute to acquire background information and be introduced to those directly involved; with agency staff who may be caught up in the dispute, but may not have, beyond certain legal requirements, an ax to grind; and with the parties themselves. In these initial conversations, the mediator can describe similar situations in which negotiation proved helpful and can explore whether appropriate conditions exist to make negotiation effective in the current controversy. As these discussions progress, the mediator becomes the principal advocate of negotiation. No other party or person need assume the interest-based or personal risk. Negotiation does not become the idea of one side, thereby arousing the suspicion of the other side. The details of how negotiations may be structured—who would be represented, what issues would be open for discussion, how an agreement would be formalized—can be worked out with the help of the mediator. This allows the parties and their representatives to make a well-informed decision on whether to enter into negotiations, based on the considerable procedural work that already has been completed.

A second impediment to negotiation is the often well-founded skepticism that the opposition can ratify and then abide by an agreement, even if one is reached. Any sophisticated negotiator knows that the health of the other party's internal dynamics are of prime importance in reaching an agreement. How does one know when it is an unwarranted intrusion into the other party's internal affairs to send one's own people out to snoop around? It is not unusual for mediators to be asked to deal with the internal dynamics. For example, the Mediation Institute was asked to assist with a dispute in which the primary parties were an Indian tribe and a county.[8] There were deep and long-lived political divisions within the tribe which called into question in some peoples' minds the ability of the tribe to act as one body in settling this controversial dispute. The leaders on the tribal council recognized the dangers of this division and encouraged the mediators to meet with a variety of individuals on the reservation. Some of the people, though not holding elected or appointed positions, could have had an important influence on peoples' perceptions of the legitimacy of negotiations and any resulting agreement. Not only did the time spent on the reservation serve an important function in developing an understanding of, and support for, negotiations within the tribe, but it also enabled the mediators to credibly reassure the county that the tribe would be able to reach an agreement that would not be vulnerable to shifting political winds.

Regarding the internal dynamics of the opposing party, there is one message which mediators deliver that often is not well-received. That message is that the opposing party has to be organized for the fight in order for them to be organized for the settlement. To put it another way, settling before the opposition has had an opportunity to organize in such a way as to do real damage may affect the durability of the settlement.

A third impediment to negotiation is that people frequently take public positions literally—both their own and their opponent's—so that there appears to be no middle ground. One of the common functions of the mediator is to help the parties reframe the substantive issues for discussion; the parties need not abandon their public positions unless and until an agreement is reached.

In his book, *Settling Things*, Allan Talbot describes such a problem in the dispute over Portage Island.[9] The Indian tribe and the county were adversaries in administrative proceedings. The issue was whether the tribe could legally withdraw the county's right-of-access to the island. The tribe took the position that its action was justified under the terms of its earlier agreement with the county. The county took the position that it was not. There was no middle ground. Either the county did or did not have access. However, the basic issue motivating the parties was the ownership, development, and management of the land. After almost three months of shuttling between the tribe and the county, the mediators had helped define a structure for the negotiations which stipulated that the issues for discussion were ownership, development, and management of the land. The question of denial of access was not "on the table."

Neither party altered its position on the access issue, but everyone recognized that the access issue would be either moot or easy to resolve if the other major issues were settled.

Finally, a fourth impediment (and a frustrating one) exists when the parties want to settle, but do not want to negotiate. The Mediation Institute assisted in one classic case involving a sewage treatment facility that had been built in the meander of a river. Predictably, the river meandered and began to undercut the concrete apron around the sewage lagoon. Because the lagoon was located near the mouth of the river and was affected by the tides, it was clear that the next combination of storm conditions and high tides would wash away the lagoon. This not only would destroy the village's sewage system, but it also would damage the water supply system and aquaculture project.

The United States Army Corps of Engineers was prepared to protect the lagoon with riprap, but there was one problem. In order to reach the lagoon, which was on an Indian reservation, the Corps of Engineers had to pass through land that was within the reservation but owned by a private developer. The private developer was not interested in having the sewage lagoon destroyed. But the developer and the tribe were involved in litigation before the Court of Appeals for the Ninth Circuit concerning the tribe's authority to regulate development and other activities within the reservation. Neither the tribe nor the developer were interested in negotiating a settlement of that issue. Both believed that the issue was properly in the courts. It was most important to each of them that, in addressing the immediate threat to the sewage lagoon, they not take any action that would affect the outcome of the Ninth Circuit case. Therefore, the private developer was not willing to accept the sponsorship of the tribe for the lagoon protection project.

The project had to be sponsored in order for the Corps of Engineers to carry it out, but the tribe and the private developer did not wish to sit down in the same room to address the immediate problem. They did not want to sign the same document. For four weeks a mediator shuttled between the tribe, the developer, the Indian Health Service, the Corps of Engineers, and the county (which became a co-sponsor of the project). Five separate documents were devised that met the Corps of Engineers' legal requirements for sponsorship, but did not require both the tribe and the developer to sign any one document. The day after the fifth document was signed, the Corps of Engineers was on the site with the riprap.

The future

The experiment, which began in the mid-1970's with the use of negotiation to settle environmental disputes, has proved successful. If procedures are developed to show parties that it is legitimate and productive for them jointly to define and settle the issues dividing them, and if these procedures make it safe for the parties to invent new options, they can be remarkably creative and accommodating in devising settlements of the substantive issues.

Important questions remain as to whether the use of negotiation and consensus-building efforts will occur on anything other than an ad-hoc basis and whether financial support will be found to allow mediators to help parties successfully negotiate. Those questions will be answered in the next few years. The answers will determine whether the successes of the last decade were of limited long-term value, or whether they laid the groundwork for a significant change in the process by which parties with conflicting interests come to terms with each other and creatively settle the particular issues facing them.

1. Cormick, "Mediating Environmental Controversies: Perspectives and First Experience," 2 *Earth L.J.* 215, 215 (1976).
2. "Conservation Found.," *Resolve* 8 (Summer 1983).
3. See, e.g., A. Talbot, *Settling Things* (1983).
4. Lempert, "Lawyers Sans Armor Resolve Environmental Clash," *Legal Times*, May 24, 1982, at 1, col. 2.
5. See: Harter, "Negotiating Regula-
tions: A Cure for Malaise," 71 *Geo. L.J.* 1 (1982).
6. "Union and Industry: Still Stalking a Benzene Rule," *Chemical Wk.*, Jan. 11, 1984, at 35. Harter, "Regulatory Negotiation: The Experience So Far," *Resolve* 1 (Winter 1984).
7. Watson and Danielson, "Environmental Mediation," 15 *Nat. Resources Law* 687–723 (1983).
8. A. Talbot, *supra* note 3, at 55–66.
9. *Id.*

Negotiated Investment Strategy: Mediating Intergovernmental Conflict

Christine Carlson

Since the middle 1970s, staff members at the Kettering Foundation have been developing a process that enables representatives from the public and private sectors to address complex intergovernmental issues through the use of mediated negotiation. We have called this process Negotiated Investment Strategy. Unlike traditional approaches to conflict resolution, which resort to mediation *after* impasse occurs, the Negotiated Investment Strategy (NIS) is introduced as discussions begin so that a trained mediator can help guide the parties toward an agreement.

Public- and private-sector interests that elect to use NIS appoint teams which, with the help of a mediator, negotiate a joint strategy for solving selected problems. Their final agreement embodies that strategy and defines the respective roles and commitments of the teams for carrying out the strategy.

As originally conceived, NIS was a process for delivering a coordinated national urban policy to a local community. The idea was that use of NIS could help avoid some of the inadvertent impacts of federal policy on the cities, such as the effects from public works projects, regulatory requirements, business loans and subsidies, and investment tax credits. In addition, those who have helped to develop NIS (including a large number of people from both public and private institutions), were looking for ways to address several other major problems facing the "intergovernmental system."

One of these problems (which has grown more apparent as NIS has evolved), is that of dwindling government resources for meeting social needs. It is becoming obvious that, in the face of reduced government funding, progress in dealing with social issues will depend

Reprinted by permission from *National Forum: The Phi Kappa Phi Journal*, Vol. LXIII, No. 4 (Fall 1983), pp. 28-29.

on better use of existing resources, both public and private. However, when government funds are reduced, conflict among government agencies tends to increase—a situation that works against efficient and effective use of the available resources.

Past efforts to reform the intergovernmental system have been repeatedly hampered by the reformer's inability to appreciate the fact that while there is cooperation within the system, there is also competition, conflict, and even coercion among the various governmental levels. And while negotiations among government agencies are not uncommon, parties often come to and leave the negotiations with very different objectives. Thus, there is an obvious need for a process that facilitates recognition of the complex nature of intergovernmental relations and allows for developing a core of common objectives.

Governmental reorganization—one of the more obvious approaches to government reform—has the disadvantage of causing such dislocation and resistance among bureaucrats that the reform is often delayed or even derailed. With all of these cautions in mind, the advocates of NIS believe that a new approach to problem solving, rather than structural reorganization, offers the most promise for meeting the current and future challenges of effective government at all levels.

Bargaining "legitimate differences" to achieve coordinated policy

Those actively involved in the NIS bargaining process recognize that legitimate differences exist both within and among various levels of government and the private sector. In light of these differences, NIS teams attempt to address problems in the most comprehensive way possible. They are asked to look at the interrelationships between public- and private-sector programs and policies and determine how these resources can be more effectively directed at solving the problems.

Six key elements compose the core of the NIS: (1) an impartial mediator who guides the process; (2) negotiating teams, which are initially small, but which can be expanded to assure representation of all important interests; (3) informal exchange of information before presentation of formal proposals; (4) face-to-face negotiations; (5) a written agreement containing mutual commitments; and (6) public review and adoption of the agreement with monitoring of subsequent performance by the teams.

The Chicago Federal Council, a regional council made up of representatives of ten federal agencies, initiated the first three NIS applications in St. Paul, Minnesota; Columbus, Ohio; and Gary, Indiana. At each of these sites, the federal, state, and local governments were each represented by one team, with the local teams including some representatives from the private sector. Bargaining agenda at the three sites varied considerably—from increasing economic capacity to improving the quality of life. Complex development projects were the focus of most of the attention in St. Paul and Gary, while in Columbus the local team was more concerned with resolving intergovernmental policy differences that were hampering their ability to achieve the city's priorities. But in all three cities, the process opened a way to a new kind of cooperation among levels of government.

Broadening application of NIS

As the NIS negotiations proceeded in the three pilot cities, it became apparent that mediation is an extraordinarily effective new model for doing other kinds of public business—besides developing urban policy—and for dealing with a wide range of problems.

NIS has been used in Connecticut to determine how to allocate the $33 million Social Service Block Grant (SSBG) for fiscal year 1984, which involves many state agencies and a host of municipal and private, human-services agencies.

It is important to note that NIS is not "business as usual": before the NIS process begins, the key decisionmakers must commit themselves to abide by whatever agreement is reached by the teams. The governor's commitment to the NIS process—which was vital to bringing the other parties to the table—was evidenced by his promise to incorporate the resulting agreement in his budget for the state.

The three teams engaged in the Connecticut negotiations were as follows: a team representing eight state agencies eligible for SSBG funds; a team representing Connecticut municipalities; and a team representing many of the state's nonprofit, service-providing agencies. A fourth group, composed of private-sector, social-service funders, was the official observer team. This was the first time that NIS had involved a nongovernmental team. The participation of the private, service-provider team in face-to-face negotiations placed them on an equal footing with representatives of state and local government in allocating public resources. That kind of direct participation is very different from the usual governmental approach to public involvement through public hearings.

Benefits of the team/mediator concept

The most unique part of the NIS process is the team approach, which provides a basis for building better working relationships among groups. Through their interaction as team members, the private, service-providing agencies in Connecticut have forged a new coalition that will monitor the NIS agreement. As a result of this coalition, these agencies expect to present their positions to the state legislature and state agencies more effectively than each alone has been able to do in the past.

The role of the mediator, of course, is central to the NIS process, and it is the teams themselves that select a mediator who is acceptable to all—one who is perceived as impartial to the outcome of the negotiations. The mediator ensures fairness in the process by making certain that all interests receive full representation in the discussions, that needed information is exchanged, and that the process continues to move toward mutually acceptable solutions. In Connecticut, the negotiations were mediated by Joseph B. Stulberg. Stulberg has extensive experience as a mediator and arbitrator and formerly directed the Community Dispute Program of the American Arbitration Association. Financial support of the mediation, as well as the support services for the local and nonprofit teams, came from local foundations and corporations.

The three negotiating teams first met to set ground rules for the negotiations, after which they met in five public meetings to define the services to be funded by the block grant, establish priorities among those services, and allocate funds among the priorities. All of these decisions were incorporated in the final agreement, which also called for establishing a tripartite committee (made up of three members from each team) and an impartial chairman, to monitor the agreement and continue the working relationships that developed during the process. The agreement was presented to the governor, who, after accepting it, created the tripartite committee by executive order.

Prerequisites for successful NIS negotiations

Not all intergovernmental problems can be resolved through application of the NIS. The process obviously will not be successful where the stakeholders will not come to the table to negotiate or where the parties are not willing to bargain in good faith. In addition, some problems may not lend themselves to the NIS process because of time constraints. However, there are a number of situations in which NIS offers potential benefits.

NIS is most likely to be useful as a method of intergovernmental problem solving when: (1) numerous participants from the public and private sectors are involved; (2) authority for committing resources is dispersed among competing agencies and diverse parties; and (3) complex processes and extensive coordination are required.

As Harlan Cleveland, distinguished public servant, has pointed out, public institutions must find ways to "involve all the actors and still get action." Techniques such as NIS, which use negotiation in the development of cooperation, may be one way to rebuild the public decision-making tradition in our pluralistic society.

Negotiated Investment Strategy: Questions and Answers

The Kettering Foundation

Nature of the NIS

When should NIS be used?   NIS is likely to be useful when:

1. Numerous participants with diverse interests are involved
2. Authority for committing resources is dispersed
3. Complex processes and extensive coordination are required
4. Differences of opinion exist, or are likely to arise, among the prospective participants
5. The need to resolve conflicts is strong
6. Time is an important consideration; the parties are motivated to act.

When should NIS not be used?   NIS will likely be more difficult, and not cost-effective, when:

1. Not all who have a substantial stake in the results will be at, or represented at, the negotiating table
2. Those negotiating lack authority to commit resources
3. At least one party has no intention of working toward a mutually-acceptable outcome
4. One or more of the parties requires more time than is likely to be available for the completion of the NIS
5. The issues are not viewed as weighty enough by all the parties to justify the investment of time, energy, and resources.

Who needs to be involved in an NIS?   Early uses of NIS involved representatives of federal, state, and local government agencies, with some representation from the private sector and non-

From *Public Decision Making: Using the Negotiated Investment Strategy,* © 1984 and reprinted with the permission of the Kettering Foundation.

profit organizations. More recent applications of NIS have included direct representation of private sector and community teams. When NIS is used to reach decisions about public policies, all affected interests need to be involved. The private sector needs to be represented so that private and public resources can be coordinated and committed to the agreed upon solutions. Bringing citizens directly into the decision-making process through NIS can be very important in building broad consensus around strategies to address public issues.

Why use negotiations?   Negotiation is widely recognized as a means of resolving disputes. It is also a valuable tool for arriving at agreements over complex public problems. Through negotiation, parties with legitimate differences have the opportunity to advocate their positions in a variety of ways. By communicating and exchanging information, the parties come to a deeper understanding of the issues and each other's interests. Negotiation allows conflicts between parties to be addressed productively, since unlike other decision-making processes, the presence of all the parties encourages the search for common objectives and solutions. At minimum, successful negotiations bring results that satisfy each party to some degree.

Why use mediated negotiations?   A mediator can assure that all important parties take part (or are represented) in the negotiations, that critical information is developed and exchanged, and that important issues are identified and defined. The mediator helps structure the negotiations, functioning as a catalyst by reasoning, persuading, clarifying, or seeking data. Most important, the mediator manages the process so agreement becomes possible. When an experienced mediator directs the negotiation, it is less likely that permanent obstacles to agreement will develop.

What is an investment strategy?   An investment strategy is a plan that targets resources in order to achieve the outcomes the negotiating parties agree have the highest priority. Ideally, an investment strategy would produce coherent actions on the part of both public and private sectors. The parties would "invest" the time and resources of both public and private interests, fully expecting a higher pay-off in the future.

Why develop an investment strategy?   Ideally, an effective investment strategy would direct public resources toward solutions that would reduce the need for government action later. In addition, the investment strategy would make citizens and businesses better able to deal with their own problems and would strengthen the participation of the voluntary and private sectors now and in the future.

Organizing an NIS

How is an NIS started?   The NIS process begins when a person or group becomes interested in and committed to the idea of an NIS and has the time, energy, and influence necessary to promote NIS. That person or group serves as a catalyst by explaining how the NIS can resolve a complex problem and by securing the commitments from key parties to participate. Usually, the person or group has a specific plan for how the NIS will work. While this plan may change as the process develops, it can serve as a framework for securing participation and planning initial activities. Because it may well take potential participants some time to accept the NIS approach, the start-up phase of an NIS may take several months.

What kinds of costs are involved in an NIS?   Costs vary widely, depending on the complexity of issues and number of parties involved. The major cost is that of the mediation team. In addition, the primary parties must support the time, travel, and expenses of their team members and of supporting staff. Money may also be required for meeting space, meals, printing, duplicating, and mailing expenses.

Who pays for an NIS?   The answer to this question has varied. The most important consideration is that all parties believe the process and mediator are neutral. Securing funds from a non-involved source goes farthest in ensuring that neutrality. Alternatively, the parties could decide that money should come from one or more of the parties and be administered by an impartial agent who would hire the mediator.

The mediation role

What is a mediator?   A mediator is a neutral party (that is, someone without a direct stake in the issues) who assists the negotiations. By facilitating interaction, the mediator helps the parties find a mutually satisfactory solution to the issues. The mediator serves at the pleasure of the negotiating parties.

How does a mediator differ from other intervenors?   Unlike an arbitrator or judge, the mediator lacks authority to impose a settlement. Instead, the mediator assists the parties in reaching an agreement. Participants should not look to the mediator as the source of expert, substantive knowledge about questions at issue.

What special qualities should an NIS mediator possess?   An NIS mediator should be knowledgeable about and committed to the NIS process. He or she should have strong facilitative skills, experience working with the kinds of people who will participate in the negotiation, and should understand intergovernmental relations. In addition, the mediator should have general knowledge of the issue likely to be negotiated, access to expert knowledge, and should have the time necessary to mediate the negotiation.

How can one find and select a mediator?   Careful attention is required to find and select a mediator for this newly emerging form of negotiation. Such a mediator can come from a variety of backgrounds. Regional centers are developing across the country that can offer advice on mediator candidates.

NIS mediators have been chosen in two ways—by recommendation or by selection. In the former, a person was recommended and, if no party objected, that person served as mediator. Each team could refuse the recommendation. In the latter, team representatives interviewed prospective mediators, selecting one of them.

When does an NIS need a mediator?   A mediator should be selected as soon as the decision to hold an NIS is made. The mediator can be helpful in many tasks that precede the actual negotiations, including formation of teams, preparation of team positions, and establishment of ground rules. Most important, the mediator can help teams avoid errors that could jeopardize an agreement later.

Should there be one mediator or a mediation team?   There should be one principal mediator. Because of the complexity of negotiations, it is likely that most NISs will be mediated by a team. If so, the mediation team should be chosen by the principal mediator to help round out the skills needed for the particular NIS. At minimum, the team should be skilled in mediation, should have some knowledge of the substantive issues, and should include at least one member who lives in or near the negotiating site.

Is there a preferred mediator style?   A variety of mediating styles are appropriate. A good mediator can be a person with a purely facilitative approach or someone who actively directs each negotiating phase. The important point is that participants are aware of and comfortable with the principal mediator's style.

The negotiation teams

Why teams?   The team approach allows for numerous participants while preventing the process from becoming unwieldy. Teams provide a way to build better working relationships among interdependent agencies, organizations, and groups through the internal negotiations required to arrive at common objectives and positions.

How many teams participate in an NIS? Although three teams have participated in each NIS to date, that is not a magic number. It is essential, however, to have one team for each major sector that will be party to the negotiations.

Who should be on the teams? Teams should include people who represent the parties with a stake in the result of the negotiation, have substantial knowledge about the issues to be negotiated, are skillful negotiators, and, most important, have the authority to make commitments.

Careful consideration needs to be given to such issues as balancing the representation of interests within the involved sector. It is also important to take into account how to maintain continuity should some of the principals be replaced in the course of the negotiations.

How large are the teams? Teams should meet the criteria listed above, while remaining as small as possible. Five to seven is the ideal size for the "core" team that participates in direct negotiations. Each team will have an "expanded" team that provides advice and counsel to the core team prior to and during the negotiations.

What is the role of a team member? Team members should attend and participate in meetings to develop the team's positions and, if they are on the core team, in negotiation sessions with other teams. Additionally, team members may be asked to serve on subcommittees responsible for developing positions along with representatives from other teams and to communicate with superiors, subordinates, and constituents about the NIS and the issues being negotiated.

What is the role of a team captain? The captain is the chief spokesperson for the team, both in negotiations and with groups interested in the negotiation. He or she acts as liaison with the other teams, with the mediator, and with key leaders (e.g., governor, mayor, board member, or legislator). The captain is responsible for seeing that the team performs its work. Finally, the captain administers team affairs, runs the team meetings, facilitates internal negotiations, and oversees development of team positions.

What kind of staff assistance do NIS teams need? NIS teams customarily have a "coordinator," often someone who has a staff relationship to the team captain. The coordinator informs the team members of the schedule, compiles and distributes information, assists in drafting materials, arranges team meetings, makes certain deadlines are met, and provides general staff assistance for the captain.

How does a team prepare for an NIS?   To participate effectively in an NIS, each team needs two things: first, substantive knowledge of the questions at issue; and second, the ability to develop and negotiate positions, both within the team and with the other teams. Therefore, teams must not only conduct research on the issues, but they may also wish to seek training in negotiating skills. In practice, it has proven useful to have the mediator provide such training. An opportune time for the mediator to help the teams is during the initial period, when teams are developing their own positions and establishing ground rules for the meetings.

How does a team get the information it needs?   Negotiation encourages cooperation, in part, by establishing the expectation that each party will freely and fully meet requests for information from any other party. In addition, a key NIS element is that the initial meeting between teams is for informal exchange of information, during which all parties may exchange requested information and raise clarifying questions.

The negotiation process

How long does an NIS take?   Building consensus and working through differences take time. NIS agreements negotiated to date have taken four to eight months. In Connecticut, where the time was shortest—four months—participants sometimes felt they lacked sufficient time to deliberate over issues, develop alternatives, or consult with constituents. Such considerations should be taken into account when the mediator and the teams establish the schedule for negotiations.

How is the agenda set?   One way in which agendas have been set is when one of the teams takes the initiative. In Gary, city officials drafted a Negotiated Investment Strategy that became the initial agenda for meeting. Agendas have also emerged from deliberations. In Columbus, mediators discouraged teams from coming forward with set proposals. Rather, they asked each team to raise independently what it believed were the issues. The mediators prepared a preliminary agenda based on these responses. Another option for setting the agenda would be through a process of community priority setting.

How many NIS meetings are there?   Two major types of meetings occur—the formal negotiating sessions between teams (often scheduled for one or two days) and the team meetings to prepare for negotiations. Typically, three to five formal sessions have been held. The number of other meetings depends on the complexity of the problem and the needs of the participants.

In Connecticut, between the time the teams were selected and the final agreement was signed, the state team held fourteen planning meetings, the municipal team met five times, and the private, non-profit team met nineteen times.

What happens at face-to-face negotiation sessions?   In the formal sessions, the teams meet to exchange information, clarify points, present proposals, react to proposals, and reach agreements. With three teams, the meeting room is typically arranged in an open square, with one team on each side and the mediator(s) sitting on the fourth side. Most communication during the formal sessions is between the team captains and the mediator(s). Occasionally the deliberations are recessed so that a team may caucus, which may occur at the table, in the hallway, or in smaller rooms reserved for that purpose. Caucuses occur more frequently as the teams move toward agreement. The mediator occasionally requests the full group to subdivide and work in committees with representatives from each team.

Where do NIS meetings take place?   The meetings usually take place in a large room with other smaller rooms available for team caucuses. In St. Paul, the city and state provided space in public buildings. All Columbus meetings were held in a city building. The Gary and Connecticut meetings occurred in hotel rooms.

What are the "rules" for the meetings?   Rules varied somewhat from NIS to NIS. Each NIS established ground rules on the mediator's role, communications (including how records were kept), team make-up, an roles of the team captain and members, access of the press and public, time constraints, and meeting location.

How much time is required of each participant?   As an evaluator of the Connecticut NIS observed, "The NIS process is time-consuming. It required about ten person-days per negotiator in joint meetings, plus two to three times that amount of time in intra-team meetings, other meetings, and individual conversations with negotiators, advisors, and other interested persons. Virtually all negotiators feel that while the process is inordinately time-consuming, it was 'worth the results.'"

Negotiations in Public Sector Labor Relations

Randolph J. Forrester

Labor relations is one of the most important components of municipal management because it involves the city's most valuable resource—its employees. Negotiation is regarded as the apex of this ongoing process but unfortunately it is often perceived as a laborious, time-consuming, and highly unpleasant task. This need not be the case. A variety of techniques, strategies, and appropriate management philosophy can help to make the negotiations process one which can be done relatively quickly, be beneficial to both management and the union and entail mutual respect.

What I would like to relate are some of the techniques, strategies, and approaches which I have found quite useful in negotiations during my local government career. Numerous examples and anecdotes will help illustrate the major points.

Preparing for negotiations

Guidelines from the council   Thorough and comprehensive preparation prior to actual negotiations is critical to successful collective bargaining. The first, and most important step, is to have clear direction from your council as to acceptable parameters for cost-of-living adjustments (COLA) and fringe benefits. Even obtaining specific percentage limits sometimes may not be a clear enough understanding. In one city, for example, I went back to the council with a proposed settlement which came in exactly on the limit the council had given me. One of the councilmembers recommended, however, that the employees be given *more* than what the

Reprinted with permission from *Municipal Management*, vol. 5 (1982-83), pp. 181–190. *Municipal Management* is published by the Department of Public Administration, University of Hartford, W. Hartford, CT 06117.

settlement called for. I indicated that while the city employees would certainly appreciate the extra money, it would definitely not help my credibility in future negotiations. Another councilmember also indicated his willingness to go along with a larger post facto settlement. The majority of the council, however, agreed to the settlement as proposed within the original guidelines. After the fact, of course, I realized the original guidelines given by the council were conservative and in fact they would probably have been willing to approve a larger settlement.

Review   The next important step is to thoroughly review the collective bargaining agreement or contract, personnel policies and procedures, or ordinances dealing with personnel matters. This should be done in order to note any items which have been causing problems for management during the past year or since the last time negotiations took place. These items should be reviewed with other department heads, as well as the city manager (if he or she is not the chief negotiator). The chief negotiator should solicit any other suggestions they have relating to problems which have occurred during the year which could be addressed in the collective bargaining process. These items will become "management proposals," which will be covered in another section.

Composition of management team   Composition of the management team is important, and should consist of someone from finance, personnel, the department with whose employees you are negotiating, as well as a general management employee. This way financial proposals can be quickly costed out; impact on personnel matters will be known; departmental practices and procedures will be known (thus precluding the possibility of the union or departmental employees pulling the wool over one's eyes); and the general management representative helps keep the overall organizational perspective.

Site visits   Something else which can be done prior to, or at the beginning of, negotiations is to visit the work site of the bargaining unit. In one city, management team members visited the new wastewater treatment plant which was alleged to have some safety problems. The reception the team received was a pleasant surprise. Apparently no one from management had been to the plant for some time. The employees were very grateful that we had taken the effort to become acquainted, on a firsthand basis, with their work site. They wanted to show us every facet of their operation. This information and the concern it demonstrated proved very helpful in the ensuing successful negotiations.

Strategies

Management proposals As noted earlier, by reviewing the collective bargaining agreement, personnel policies and procedures, personnel ordinances, and seeking advice from department heads as to operational problems they have had, a number of issues can be pulled together which will constitute "management proposals." Management proposals are important because they constitute "bargaining chips" which can be used in the collective bargaining game, when the union puts its proposals (chips) on the table.

Years ago management used to enter negotiations and accept the list of proposals from the union and then negotiate to limit the number of concessions. In other words, it was a holding strategy to minimize, if possible, the losses which could be incurred, be they salary, fringe benefits, management control, or other matters. Meeting the union with a list of your own demands starts negotiations off on an equal basis. Management proposals can be anything from "buy back" recommendations (reducing existing compensation/benefits), language improvements, policy changes, to any creative suggestions you may have. One year I recommended a "management grievance procedure" to deal with violations of the collective bargaining agreement by union members. While the union representative informed me that he had never heard of anything like this anywhere across the country, it nevertheless did serve as a good bargaining chip and was eventually adopted in modified form.

Turf While a fairness argument can be made for alternating negotiating sessions between city facilities and union sites, practicality as well as management advantages accrue to remaining on city turf. It is certainly more convenient for all city employees to meet at a city building. This also gives management the opportunity to have easy access to telephones, calculators, food, restrooms and so on. One exception to utilizing a city site, however, is when marathon negotiating sessions are taking place. In this case, negotiating at a hotel or motel is preferable because it gives ready access to sleeping quarters as well.

Equal treatment A tangential element of fairness and equality to consider is ensuring that union employees are given similar status to the members of the management team. In one city, for example, the sanitation and street division employees were not required to work on their routes for several hours before coming into a morning negotiating session. Instead, they would come into work for the morning negotiating session and then change into their work clothes for their afternoon assignments (if sessions were not all day). This is a matter of treating both sides of the negotiating table as fellow professionals, which I believe is fair, and contributes to harmonious labor relations in the long run.

Issues and techniques

Ground rules   Now that the preparation and strategy stages have been completed, negotiations proceed. At the first meeting, after the customary introduction of all team members, the first order of business should be the establishment of ground rules. These should include any and all procedural and logistical matters or any other items not immediately related to the proposals themselves. These may include days and times of sessions, work schedules or time off for union employees, contact with the media, location of negotiations, sign-off procedure on agreed-to items, notification of agreement procedures, designation of chief negotiator or spokesman, deadline for completion of negotiations and designation of official notetaker.

On stage   The theatrical aspect of negotiations is an integral element of this process. It is a drama which will unfold with expected roles to be played by the union and management. The roles or "on-stage" personalities should not interfere with the real issues which will soon be broached. Part of the drama may include unpleasant accusations and/or name-calling. Union members have been paying dues for a year since the last negotiations and they expect their union representative to bellow forth some fire and brimstone about the terrible misdeeds of management, onerous and unsafe working conditions, and poorly paid employees toiling in highly dangerous jobs. Management, in turn, may expound about tales of budget woes, insufficient revenues, references to the employees being the highest paid for miles around, and usurpation of traditional management rights. It's all rhetoric but necessary for the drama of negotiations. Most of this should occur in the early part of negotiations with it popping up only periodically thereafter. It is necessary to recognize this theatrical component for what it is, get through it as quickly as possible and move on to the heart of the negotiations.

Surprise   Using the unexpected introduces an element of surprise which is a strategy to get one up on the other side or to put them off guard. Both sides may use this. I once heard of a police union which brought in two of their K-9 officers and German shepherds as part of their negotiating team. Management proposals, when being used for the first time, can also be a major surprise. The first time I employed them at an opening negotiating session was also the first time this particular union representative had ever seen any. To make matters worse, he only had 7 proposals that particular year while I had submitted a list of 18 management proposals. Besides the shock of a new concept he was also left in the unenviable position of being far outweighed in bargaining chips. At the next bargaining session this particular union spokesman said that after receiving the management proposals at the first session, he went home and put a "buzz on for a week."

Timeliness and timing   Timeliness and timing are crucial parts of collective bargaining and can be part of the strategy leading to a successful completion of negotiations. One aspect of negotiations I initially found very frustrating was the drawn-out nature of negotiations, where sessions would drag on for months or even years. I made a vow to myself that if I ever became a chief negotiator I would do my best to keep this from occurring. Fortunately, one can develop techniques and use contract language which result in negotiations being completed in a timely manner. Some of the proudest moments in my local government career have been the rapid conclusions of negotiations with bargaining units with good settlements reached. In my last formal negotiations, agreement was reached within 10 days; and the year before within 18 days.

Attitudes, techniques, and contract language contribute to quick resolution of negotiations. Part of this is a mind set which needs to be transmitted to the union's chief negotiator, which goes along the lines of "I want to get down to serious business, work hard, and knock this agreement out quickly. Let's keep to a minimum the dramatics, quickly get to the important issues and reach a resolution, so that we can get back to other pressing items on the job." I have found union reps very amenable to this approach, since it also saves them time, eliminates a lot of unnecessary theatrics and verbiage, yet still gives them time to air all their serious issues and concerns. In order for this quick resolution mind set to work, it is also necessary for management to have an open mind and be willing to compromise and meet in the middle, which is what negotiations are all about.

Contract language can also facilitate this process. One city's agreement with AFSCME had two of the best provisions along these lines that I have seen anywhere. They were as follows. "Negotiations must be completed no later than March 30th of each year, unless mutually extended by both parties. [This city was on a July 1st to June 30th fiscal year.] The union must notify management in writing no later than 60 days prior to March 30th if it wishes to change any provisions in the collective bargaining agreement. If such notice is not received, the contract will automatically renew for an additional one year period."

This is excellent language to facilitate a rapid completion of negotiations, and I use it to the fullest extent possible. At the opening session, during the establishment of ground rules, I would always reiterate the collective bargaining provision requiring that negotiations be completed prior to March 30, and officially note that under no circumstances would I agree to an extension of negotiations if they were not completed by that date. This essentially closed the only loophole available to the union and dictated completion within this time frame. Not to complete negotiations within the limits would mean that the contract would automatically renew with no salary or fringe benefit increases, changes in contract language, and so on. Since this was a provision of the contract, the union would not have any recourse to appeals, since they also have to live by the provisions of the agreement. A strong reiteration of this provision at the first session always had a sobering impact on the union and helped set the stage for rapid completion.

The latter part of this language can also be very important, particularly if the union representative is lax or a bit careless as this mandated deadline for notification approaches. This procedural oversight, in fact, was made by the AFSCME representative one year. The request for changing provisions of the collective bargaining agreement (request to negotiate) was received on February 11, rather than by the January 30 deadline. I informed the union representative that the deadline had been missed and that the contract had automatically renewed itself for another year. Needless to say, the union representatives and other union officials were very angry and quickly made many trips to my office in an effort to permit negotiations to proceed. I reminded them that the language in the contract was approved by both parties and both parties therefore had to live up to all provisions of the contract. That was the end of the union's involvement that year and, in fact, no negotiations took place. Thereafter, management always referred to that year as "The year the union forgot to negotiate." Again, since this was a contract provision, the union had no course of appeal. As a result of this union oversight, the union representative was reassigned to another part of the state. Within the year city employees had initiated an effort to find a new collective bargaining agent, or decertify AFSCME.

I must note, however, that management was not so insensitive as to not consider compensation increases for the employees for that year. Instead, we used this hiatus as an opportunity to poll the employees as to what compensation or working conditions the employees really wanted (and not just what the union represented). The results of the survey indicated that salary was their primary concern, increased annual leave was second, and a variety of miscellaneous matters ranked much further below. We compiled this information, made it available to all employees, and then had several meetings with the employees we usually negotiated with (minus the union rep). As a result we granted a salary adjustment, an increase in annual leave, and some other minor changes which was a better package than what the union had won for the employees the year before. I also took the additional step of making some professional courtesy phone calls to our newly assigned union representative to keep him informed of what we were doing and soliciting his informal advice and suggestions. After all, a year from now we would almost assuredly be meeting and a professional courtesy like this will almost always pay dividends later. The union, at this point, obviously didn't need any more embarrassment.

Timing, that knowledge or instinct of knowing when the time is right to resolve a certain matter, is also a very important part of negotiations and can help facilitate reaching an earlier agreement. Being alert to the union negotiator's words, actions, or situations which may be occurring elsewhere will often reveal when he or she is willing to drop an item from the original list of requests or come to resolution on a COLA. A union rep will normally be negotiating several contracts concurrently and may be having much worse problems in another jurisdiction. It's an ability to detect that moment of weakness, hesitation, or perception that the "time" is right to make your move, proposal, or trade off.

All items on the table   After proposals have been exchanged, and each item explained by the respective sides, it is important for management to ask the union: "Are these all the items that are on the table?" When they say "yes," management can similarly say "These are all our items." What this does is limit negotiations to these proposals "on the table," and precludes either party from bringing up new items for negotiation at a later session.

Shaking the issue tree   Proposals from both the union and management will contain a wide variety of items, constituting what may be called the "issue tree." Only a minority of the proposals from either party will be serious issues which they want or expect to be achieved. It is necessary, therefore, to "shake the issue tree" as soon as possible in order to get rid of the spurious issues (closed shop, 5 personal leave days, 15 holidays, etc.), and ascertain what are the serious issues about which the union really wants to negotiate. This is done by questioning the union negotiator, general probing, trading "drop off" for "drop off" items ("I'll drop these two, if you drop those two"), reviewing the proposals and their importance or necessity. In other words, both parties should strive to reduce the issues to those proposals that are really important to the other side. You don't want to waste time on minor or spurious items when the "meat and potatoes" items are where the real negotiating will take place.

Official note taker   One member of the management negotiating team should be designated as the "official note taker." The chief negotiator never assumes this role, because he must have the time and freedom to manage the negotiations, and cannot afford to be hampered with keeping an official record of the proceedings. It is important, however, that the official record of the proceedings be kept (as to issues dropped, agreed upon, modified, etc.) and this is what the official note taker does. Any time both parties agree on issues from the original list of proposals, both chief negotiators should initial the agreement to preclude any questions or doubts later on.

Caucuses   Caucuses are the traditional mechanism utilized by both parties to leave the negotiating room in order to devise counterproposals, changes in strategy, seek approval on certain items, or inculcate some dramatic flair. Caucuses are used so that a team can talk and strategize among themselves or with others but not in front of the other team. Caucuses can also be used, as previously indicated, for dramatic effect. The first individual under whom I negotiated once related to me that on one occasion he had been negotiating for several hours, when all of a sudden he bolted up from his chair, and said "That does it; I'm leaving." He thereupon left the room and his team members sheepishly followed him. When he got outside the room he indicated to his team members that he just had to go to the bathroom but thought it might be a good idea to see what effect this approach might have on the union, since they were beginning to approach settlement. When the management team returned they found the union team somewhat flustered and wanting to know what they had done to irritate the management team, especially when things seemed to have been going so well. The ploy paid off and settlement was reached shortly thereafter.

Similarly, toward the end of negotiations one time, the union finally made a counterproposal that fell within our parameters of acceptable settlement but fell outside of what we had been parroting as possible. I thereupon said, "I don't know if I can sell this, but give me a chance and I'll call the city manager and see if I can get him to accept this." Our team thereupon left the room and adjourned to an adjacent office. I sat at a desk for about a minute, not doing anything, when a team member finally asked, "Aren't you going to call the city manager?" I said, "No. The proposal's acceptable. But all along I've been telling them that we couldn't accept anything that high. So, I've got to tell them I'll see if the city manager might accept this rather 'high' proposal, so that I can maintain my credibility!" So, we sat around another two minutes without doing anything, then went back to the negotiating room with smiles on our faces and indicated that the city manager had accepted their proposal. All parties were happy and negotiations were completed.

Side bar   The side bar is a technique whereby the chief negotiators for both sides will leave the room to talk about a matter between themselves, without any other members of the negotiating team present. This technique is utilized for clarifying items, to clear up a confusing matter, to ascertain why certain actions are being taken, or to try to package the final agreement which can be sold to all parties. During side bars both chief negotiators are very honest with each other and true professionalism for both parties comes into play. The side bar is utilized when some behavior from the other side of the table doesn't make sense or is out of character with the chief negotiator. The chief negotiator will honestly explain his actions which can vary from "I've got to break off negotiations now, because I've got to get to another city"; "The guys in the shop wanted me to play this one up"; to "We're close enough now that we can reach agreement; let's put together the package we can both sell"; "I need a face saver." This will also be the only time you can be somewhat honest with the other party as to what your *realistic* parameters or guidelines are. Knowing the union representative well also helps facilitate successful side bars. While side bars are used only a few times during the negotiating process and thus may comprise only 0.5% or less of the actual negotiating time, they can constitute up to 60% to 70% of the final negotiated settlement as to major items. Thus, the side bar is a very important element in collective bargaining. It can resolve confusion and be the medium for putting together the final settlement out of the limelight of the labor relations stage.

Face saver   The management chief negotiator must be alert and sensitive to the need for a "face saver" by the union chief negotiator. The need for this comes about when the union has misestimated what the city can do in terms of wages or benefits and thus the union rep has overcommitted himself to the union employees as to what can be achieved during negotiations. The union representative can extricate himself from this dilemma with a "face saver." This is a relatively small item or matter which the rep will request from management, but which he will parlay to his members as a major item or concession, which will serve as the icing on the cake for settlement. Face savers may be anything from language changes, minor fringe benefits with little if any fiscal impact, to joint management-union committees to study a certain matter. The union rep will relate the need for a face saver through a side bar meeting with you, or calling you between negotiating sessions. It is only necessary that management be aware and sensitive to this need which is perfectly acceptable.

Get to know the union rep   Successful negotiations are facilitated by getting to know the union representative who will be the chief negotiator during collective bargaining. You will be seeing this individual during the year on official business but make sure you take time to get to know him also on an informal or unofficial basis. Take time to just sit down and "chew the fat." Find out about each other's backgrounds, general management/union beliefs, family, career plans, general condition of the union, and so on. With most labor relations negotiators there is a great deal of mutual respect between management and labor negotiators. Most good union and management negotiators actually share a common approach and interest about public sector employment, namely, that there should be good delivery of public services, with a day's pay for a day's work.

Another advantage of personally knowing the union rep is that this provides a medium and opportunity to do professional or administrative favors for each other. In one city, for example, the AFSCME rep called me up one time and said, "Randy, I need you to do a favor for me. It's not required anywhere, but if you could do this for me, I'd really appreciate it." Well, his request involved some minor inconvenience but it was nothing major so I obliged him. I asked him to keep me in mind if I ever had a similar need which he said he would be glad to do. A year and a half passed before I ever had occasion to request a similar favor. But that type of situation did occur where I needed to take some administrative action but it only could be carried out if there would be no opposition from the union. So I called up the union rep and said, "Paul, remember that favor I did for you a while back? Well, here's a situation I'm in and I need your help." His response, "Well, I don't like that, but you're right, I owe you one, and I'll go along with you." Having a relationship with the union rep where this can be done can be of immeasurable assistance.

No elected officials   It should probably go without saying that no elected officials should be directly involved in the negotiations process. I have only heard of unpleasant or non-beneficial results when having an elected official directly involved in negotiations. This is due to the fact that it is not their proper role and that they may have a different agenda from yours. Their role is to set the negotiation and compensation parameters and to approve the agreement that comes within or near those parameters. It is useful and appropriate, however, to keep the council informed of how negotiations are proceeding while these are under way. This should be done in executive session.

No end runs   On the other end of the spectrum, it is important to ensure that no employees or bargaining agents "end run" you by going directly to the council. This can only lead to disruption and confusion of a delicately balanced process and should always be precluded. Within my first week of arriving on the job in one city, the police chief sent a letter to the council requesting additional salary compensation due to the fact that the city had received some unanticipated revenues after compensation considerations had already been approved. It was an unpleasant but also very necessary step which I took the first week on the job to inform the police chief that his bypassing me on this matter was improper and was not to be repeated again while I was city manager. Incidentally, it was not repeated by him or any other city employee.

Strike plan   If there ever has been or there is a possibility of a strike it is important to develop a "strike plan." This is an extremely detailed, logistical plan of actions which will be taken in the event of a strike. Some items included are replacement of strikers, subcontractors, mutual aid pacts, fringe benefits of employees during strikes, media contact, communication, legal remedies and provision of public services. Much has been written about this elsewhere and I will not go into any further detail about it here.

Celebrate   When agreement has finally been reached, I believe it is appropriate and very useful to celebrate the successful conclusion of negotiation with all parties involved in the negotiations. This helps to bridge some of the organizational or job roles which are usually present, makes for a more human and informal understanding of each other, helps smooth over any wounds or hurt feelings which may have occurred in negotiations and helps build camaraderie. If both parties can't celebrate together, treat the management team to a celebration. They have undoubtedly worked hard and deserve a little celebration now that they are out of the pressure cooker of the negotiating room.

Conclusion

It is important to keep in mind that the conclusion of the negotiations process is actually just the beginning of having to live with and administer the collective bargaining agreement for the upcoming year or years. Labor relations, of which negotiations is only a part, is a year-round activity. That is part of the reason why union representatives and unionized employees must be treated with respect—you must work with them during the coming year.

On a career and personal basis, labor relations, and particularly negotiations, when carried out in an atmosphere of mutual respect and professionalism, done in a timely manner, and looking to the welfare of the employees, as well as the public at large, can be very personally rewarding. Some of the most satisfying moments in my city management career have revolved about the successful completion of negotiations and maintaining a positive labor relations attitude during the ensuing year.

Collective Bargaining: Questions and Answers

Organization for bargaining

Q: Is it important for public sector management to prepare for negotiations?

A: Yes. Management should prepare its attitudes, its organization, and its information before going to the bargaining table. Too often this is not done in the public sector. If managment is not prepared, negotiations become merely a series of reactions by management to union proposals with the union backing up its proposals with information. If the union fails to cost out its proposals adequately, many hours can be spent debating over whether proper figures and formulae are being used. The same is true for contract language. If no research has been conducted by either party on sample contract clauses, many unnecessary hours can be spent "reinventing the wheel," laboriously drafting new language to cover common problems.

Q: How should management prepare for negotiations?

A: By preparing specific proposals and gathering the data necessary for explaining proposals, as well as costing out counterproposals. Local government is complex and such preparation cannot be left to one or two individuals working in the office independently of the rest of management. Preparing for bargaining must be a team effort. Experts at all levels of management—the personnel officer, the budget director, the legal coun-

From "Questions and Answers on Collective Bargaining: A Practitioner's Guide," prepared by the Midwest Center for Public Sector Labor Relations, Indiana University, reprinted with permission from *Current Municipal Problems*, (pp. 83-112, 1978-79, Vol. 5), published by Callaghan & Co., 3201 Old Glenview Rd., Wilmette, IL 60091.

sel—should all be involved. Preparation may include surveys of other local governments and private employers, surveys of line supervisors, and discussions among the top level administrators in the governmental unit. Contacting all levels of management in the city or county is especially important.

Q: Who should coordinate the efforts of preparing for negotiations?

A: The person selected to be chief spokesperson at the bargaining table.

Q: How does extensive preparation by management for negotiations benefit management?

A: By preparing for negotiations, management avoids agreeing to a proposal which has hidden costs that significantly change its value. Management can present its own proposals for consideration by the union instead of merely reacting to union proposals. This gives management a positive position to take in negotiations. Extensive preparation lays a better groundwork for informed compromise; it saves hours of time in negotiations that would otherwise be spent in last minute research. Preparing sample contract language saves both parties from arduously constructing acceptable language for each new non-economic item in the contract. Preparation gives the parties an understanding of how other jurisdictions handled the same problems they're having.

Q: Who should be on management's negotiating team?

A: This is one of the most important decisions for management in the whole collective bargaining process. A mix of representatives from the personnel and budget offices with representatives from the departments with the biggest operations, such as the Sanitation Department or the Department of Public Works, is the most common choice. Often the city attorney will be on the negotiating team and may act as chief spokesperson.

Q: What is the advantage of putting in-house staff on management's negotiating team?

A: The value of having the city attorney and representatives from the budget office, the personnel office, and departments with the largest operations lies in their expertise. The responsibilities these people will have in bargaining come from their individual areas of experience. The personnel officer will examine employee records for information on types of employees, age and seniority distribution, and grievances on file. The budget officer will prepare data on expected revenues, priority allocations, operating costs, and other finances. The department heads will provide background on difficulties within their operation that stem from the present contract. They know which management prerogatives they would like to see protected. They are familiar with the causes of employee dissatisfaction within their departments. The city attorney will provide advice on contractual language and the legality of union and management proposals.

Q: Is it necessary for members of management to be on management's actual negotiating team or can they merely act as advisers?

A: No, it is not necessary for these members of management to appear at the bargaining table. They must, however, do the preparatory research necessary to carry out informed bargaining. They should be available to the negotiators to answer questions and evaluate proposals if problems arise.

Q: Should the chief executive of the local government be a member of management's negotiating team?

A: No. This is not usually done. As the final authority responsible for binding management to an agreement, the mayor, the county commissioner, or the town manager may be placed under extreme pressure during negotiations to agree on the spot to union proposals, when reflection and consultation are necessary. Another reason is that the chief executive is often an elected official. It is better to staff the negotiating team with appointed officials to keep bargaining centered on issues rather than political personalities. Elected officials may be pressured to repay labor for its support during the official's political campaign by conceding to labor at the bargaining table. Finally, chief executives are usually unable to commit themselves fully to negotiations because of time constraints. Bargaining is a time-consuming process demanding a concentrated effort. Local government officials usually have many other demands on their time. In addition, much of bargaining concerns detailed construction of language calling for a level of expertise the chief executive usually does not have nor need to attain.

Q: Should members of the city or county council be included on management's negotiating team?

A: No. They are usually removed from the negotiating team for much the same reasons as the chief executive is. Elected officials may be pressured into responding to political favors that had been granted by unions earlier. They don't have the time to participate, and they lack the expertise to be valuable in collective bargaining. The political problems of elected officials are exacerbated by the bipartisan nature of most councils. As the funding body, the council will have to ratify the contract in most cases anyway. This is the time for council involvement. Because it must ratify the contract, the council should be kept informed of the progress of negotiations on a periodic basis, and the executive branch should know the approximate range of wage increases that the council will fund.

Q: Should management hire a professional negotiator to be its chief spokesperson at the bargaining table?

A: It should be considered. A professional negotiator brings immediate expertise on strategy and contract language. The hiring of a professional makes participation by city officials unnecessary, thus leaving them to their normal duties. The professional provides an example to in-house staff who then can develop expertise of their own. The short-term expense may be outweighed by the value of the professional negotiator's experience, particularly if management is negotiating its first contract. Hiring a professional just for negotiations provides expertise to small jurisdictions at less cost than hiring a permanent staff person.

Q: Are there any disadvantages in hiring a professional negotiator to serve as chief spokesperson for management at the bargaining table?

A: Yes. The professional does not stay to enforce the contract once it is negotiated. If the city has not been closely involved in bargaining, it may be left with a contract it does not understand. The professional often is resented by the union and considered a "hired gun" brought in by management to overwhelm them with legalisms and tactical maneuvering. If the jurisdiction has a personnel office, it might be more beneficial to hire or train a personnel officer as a specialist in labor relations. Hiring a professional negotiator creates a dependency on outside experts that curtails the development of in-house expertise and removes the bargaining responsibility from persons directly accountable to the public.

Q: If management decides to hire a professional negotiator, should it allow the professional to work independently or should management work with the professional?

A: Local officials should work closely with the professional negotiator because they are the ones who will have to live with the agreement. They must not remain aloof from the negotiations. They should view it as a learning experience, and be aware that it will be their responsibility to administer the contract after the negotiations end.

Q: *What should management do after selecting its negotiating team?*

A: Several arrangements must be made. Authority to bargain must be granted to the bargaining team. A chief spokesperson must be appointed. Department heads and other officials who are affected by the negotiations but not on the bargaining team should be made available for consultation when needed to supply the pertinent information in their area of expertise, and to consider union proposals directly related to their operations. Line and middle managers must be kept generally aware of the progress of negotiations in terms of settlement on certain issues, progress on other issues, and deadlock if it occurs.

Q: *What is meant by* authority to bargain?

A: The negotiators should be able to bargain with the authority to settle. The chief negotiator should not be perceived by the union as a "walking memo" to and from the mayor. If this is the union's perception, the chief negotiator cannot bargain effectively. Guidelines should be set beforehand by the policymakers in local government on the range of wage increases, benefits, and non-economic concessions possible. After this initial agreement, the negotiators should be able to proceed independently, with periodic reports to the elected officials and consultation with them if an alteration in the settlement seems necessary.

Q: *Is the chief spokesperson merely a figurehead or does that person really speak for the whole negotiating team?*

A: This person is definitely not a figurehead. It is essential that the team members understand that only this person is to speak during negotiations, unless it is agreed before each session begins that other members will address certain issues within their area of expertise. If the union team notices dissension within the management team, it will try to exploit that dissension and play one side of management against the other. Committee members other than the spokesperson are there to evaluate union proposals that fall within their fields of knowledge, to offer advice, and to give another perspective during caucuses.

Q: Why must management keep middle managers and line managers informed during negotiations?

A: Management needs their feedback about the outcome of ongoing negotiations. Management should try to make all levels of management feel involved in negotiations to foster their understanding of the collective bargaining process. It is particularly important that these middle and line managers be committed to the collective bargaining agreement that is made.

Procedures for collective bargaining
Physical setting and scheduling

Q: In what physical setting should collective bargaining be carried out?

A: Bargaining should be carried out in a room located near the offices of the management negotiators. It must be free from unnecessary interruptions. This means there should be no telephone. However, there must be a way to get emergency messages to negotiators. The room should be large enough to be airy and comfortable, but not so large that negotiators feel dwarfed by the surroundings. The following items should be in the room: blackboard, chalk, conference table, a sufficient number of chairs, coffee, soft drinks, ashtrays.

Q: What other space is needed to carry out collective bargaining besides the actual negotiations room?

A: Caucus rooms for both parties. Each negotiating team will need a room to discuss proposals and counterproposals privately during negotiations. If caucus rooms near the negotiations room are available, the team can have private discussions without ending that particular bargaining session. The caucus rooms should have blackboards and chalk as well. These same rooms may be used during the mediation process, if the negotiations end in impasse and mediation is necessary. These caucus rooms are essential for successful mediation.

Q: How should the negotiating sessions be scheduled to produce the best results?

A: Begin negotiations with short, relatively infrequent meetings to give the parties time to consider the proposals and to prepare counterproposals. As negotiations progress and the date for agreement nears, negotiating sessions should be scheduled twice a week. The deadline for agreement will depend on the deadline for budget submission, the end of the legislative session, or the expiration date of the present contract.

Q: Why is the negotiating process so frequently marked by extended, climactic meetings as the deadline for agreement approaches? Are such long, drawn out sessions productive?

A: Such continuous bargaining is not particularly conducive to reasoned debate and the drafting of precise contract language, but it often occurs. The reasons for these extended, climactic meetings at the end of negotiations is found in the nature of bargaining. Neither party wants to settle at less than the best position, and by delaying agreement until the last possible moment, the other side will be forced to make its best offer. These long sessions are often inevitable and should not be perceived as bad faith bargaining. Management negotiators must be prepared for such sessions as the deadline for agreement approaches. Management negotiators should use these sessions as productively as possible. If a mediator enters the bargaining due to impasse, these sessions will only be drawn out longer.

Q: At what time of the day should negotiations between labor and management be scheduled?

A: Bargaining can be held during working hours or after the employees have finished their shifts. This scheduling is negotiable, and it is not considered bad faith bargaining for management to insist that all negotiations take place in the evening when the employee representatives are on their own time. The number of employees involved in negotiations is primarily a union matter. The employer, however, can refuse to allow an unreasonably large number of employees to remain on the clock, collecting regular wages, when they are acting as part of the union negotiating team.

Q: How do the union and management settle on such questions as scheduling negotiations and location of bargaining?

A: A meeting prior to negotiations is often held between the spokespersons to reach agreement on scheduling, location, and the number of persons to be on each negotiating team.

Initiation of bargaining
Q: What is usually discussed at the first negotiating session?

A: Three items are commonly covered. The parties agree on a bargaining format. They discuss the principles of negotiations, particularly the concept of good faith bargaining in order to establish a climate for constructive work. The management negotiators receive the union's proposals in writing, and the union runs through these proposals, clarifying any if necessary. It is desirable for management to fully understand the goals of the union, especially the relative importance of the various union demands. Management can then prepare adequate counterproposals. Management's attitude at this time can affect the willingness of the union to compromise and settle as much as management's actual proposals.

Q: One of the purposes of the first negotiation session is to settle on a bargaining format. What is a good format?

A: To discuss individual proposals and counterproposals either as separate items or as packages, and to resolve them in one of three ways:

1. Come to a tentative agreement, contingent upon the final contract package, and its ratification by the union membership, and if necessary, ratification by elected officials.
2. Agree to drop the item or package.
3. Agree to set the issue aside temporarily and to return to it later in negotiations.

Q: What should be the topics of discussion at the second bargaining session?

A: The agenda at the second session should contain management's proposals and the union's proposals as rewritten by management based upon the discussions at the first session. The agenda should list the proposals in the order they will be discussed. A safe procedure is to first negotiate those non-economic items which are less significant to either party, such as the location and number of union bulletin boards, parking lot privileges, and so forth. Save the more important non-economic items such as grievance arbitration and management rights for later to be considered along with economic issues. Management and labor should discuss the new management proposals on the agenda at this second session and management's goals for the negotiations should be clarified at this time. The contents of the agenda as proposed by management will have to be discussed, particularly the order in which proposals are to be negotiated. The management versions of the union proposals should be discussed if they have been changed substantially. After these discussions, the agenda must be agreed upon by both labor and management. The closing of the agenda at this time precludes any additions later in negotiations. This does not mean, however, that new alternatives cannot be offered during negotiations to resolve a deadlock.

Q: Why are non-economic proposals usually discussed first in negotiations?

A: They are usually easier to agree on. Early agreement on non-economic items sets a tone of cooperation for later negotiations on the tougher money issues. If the parties cannot agree, these non-economic items can be dropped, expediting negotiations. These items are more difficult to settle at the last minute. As the deadline for contract settlement nears and there are only hours or minutes left before settlement, it is easier to agree upon the simple dollars and cents involved in wage increases than to rewrite complicated contract language necessary for non-economic items.

Q: Is it generally agreed that non-economic items should be settled first in negotiations?

A: No. Many negotiators object to this format on two grounds. First, they argue that very few issues in negotiations are really non-economic ones. For instance, seniority systems, union security arrangements, and grievance arbitration have no measurable costs but each can substantially affect the efficiency of a public operation, and each has a real although indirect cost. Thus, the negotiators argue that these items must be treated seriously by the negotiating teams. The other argument against settling non-economic issues first concerns trading. Many non-economic items can be traded during negotiations for cost items, and therefore should not be considered as a separate category. For instance, a strong management rights clause about overtime assignments and filling vacancies may be obtained only in exchange for a substantial wage increase, particularly if the desired flexibility was lost in a previous agreement. On the other side of the table, a union security arrangement, which costs the employer nothing, is extremely valuable to some unions, and can be traded for a significant decrease in the union's wage demand.

Subsequent bargaining sessions

Q: After the first two negotiating sessions, how should subsequent sessions be organized?

A: All subsequent negotiating sessions should follow the agenda in the following manner:

1. Discuss a specific proposal.
2. Ascertain the areas of agreement and put them in writing. Even if the parties only agree on the principle of the proposal, that agreement should be formalized by putting it in writing.
3. Specify the areas of disagreement and the rationale of each side.
4. Begin negotiations on each area of disagreement, continuing until agreement, with specific language then drafted and initialed, contingent upon the final contract package. If there is still disagreement, perhaps the item should be discarded as unnecessary or impossible to resolve, or set aside for further discussion later in the negotiations. This should help avoid impasse early in negotiations and permit significant agreement to occur fairly rapidly.

At the bargaining table

Bargaining power

Q: Is the purpose of bargaining to arrive at a "fair" level of wages and benefits for employees?

A: No. It is a mistake to think of collective bargaining as a process for arriving at a "fair" level of wages and benefits. Fairness cannot be defined, and no two reasonable people, much less the negotiating teams for labor and management, will ever agree on a "fair" and just wage. The outcome of bargaining depends wholly upon the bargaining power of the two parties involved. Bargaining is a process in which each of the two parties has particular and often contradictory interests. Each party tries to persuade, cajole, and force the other into accepting the position most favorable to its interests. Bargaining power is the ability to secure the other party's agreement on one's own terms.

Q: What factors determine the strength of the union's bargaining power?

A: The more able employees are to strike, the greater is the union's bargaining power and the less is management's bargaining power. Factors affecting the ability of the union to strike include:

1. The time the present contract expires. Teacher strikes are most effective in the fall; police and sanitation worker strikes would be more effective during the summer. Nobody likes to walk a picket line in the winter.
2. Local economic conditions. High unemployment decreases the likelihood of employees securing supplemental income

during a strike. It also decreases the likelihood that another member of the household is a wage earner.

3. Local employment conditions of the public employees covered by the contract. Are their benefits equal to other local public employees? Are their benefits comparable with local private sector employees and with public employees in similar jurisdictions?
4. The willingness of the local union membership to strike.
5. The severity of the statutory penalties for public employee strikes.
6. The nature and scope of support that state and national union affiliates give the local union.

Q: What factors determine the strength of management's bargaining power?

A: External factors affecting the bargaining power of management include the environment of the local community, the local political situation, the organizational and administrative leadership, and the skill and preparation of negotiators. Community sentiment has a large effect. If the public vocally expresses its opposition to rising taxes and the poor quality of government services, management's bargaining power is increased. If the city is highly unionized and supportive of the public employee position, management loses bargaining power. A local government which has reached the ceiling on tax rates set by state law has a strong justification for limiting wage increases during bargaining. Bargaining power is greatly influenced by the degree of unification among the labor faction and the management faction. A high degree of unification within the leadership consolidates the support of their constituencies.

Communicating for effectiveness

Q: How can the management negotiating team best communicate with union negotiators at the bargaining table?

A: The following suggestions for management are based upon the comments of professional trainers and negotiators. Their value in a particular situation depends on the specific circumstances and personalities involved. The following suggestions should be kept in mind during negotiations:

1. Don't agree to a proposal unless you can live with it in the agreement and sell it to the elected officials who must ratify it.
2. Explain why you are rejecting a proposal. Never flatly refuse to consider proposals offered by the union.

3. Ask open-ended questions about the union proposals to
    maintain the momentum of negotiations. Questions that
    can be answered with a "yes" or a "no" tend to bog down
    negotiations and stall constructive bargaining.
4. Change the topic if no progress is made, or if, given the
    priorities of management, there can be no concessions or
    progress on a particular issue.
5. Assume that your proposals will be accepted during your
    presentations. An attitude or comment indicating they
    are throw-away items will immediately be recognized by a
    skilled negotiator on the other side.
6. Assume a positive attitude during negotiations and ad-
    dress the issues as problems to be solved.
7. Avoid discussing personalities whether the individuals are
    at the bargaining table or away from it.
8. Be careful that your mannerisms or body language do not
    display disdain for the union negotiators when your state-
    ments are meant to be conciliatory.
9. Recognize the point of view of the union bargaining team
    and tell the team you understand it, even if you cannot
    make a concession on the particular point.
10. View the union team as individuals and recognize that in
    order to secure agreement on management's terms, these
    individuals must change their opinions.
11. Allow the other side to save face. Never put the other
    party in a tight corner from which they cannot back out
    gracefully with their pride intact. The goal is to solve
    problems and to establish a workable relationship, not to
    destroy the other side.

**Q: *Is timing important for management in making propos-
als at the bargaining table?***

A: Timing is very important in making a proposal. Making a firm
or final offer early in negotiations may seem reasonable on its
face but it will probably be construed by the union membership
as less than the best that management is really willing to concede. The union negotiators may also see this early offer as just
a minimum offer that can be raised through traditional bargaining tactics. Even worse, the union could consider an early
firm offer as an insult, a rejection of the collective bargaining
process and of the union's legal rights to participate in settling
wages and working conditions. The most unnecessary crisis in
bargaining occurs when the public management negotiator, in a
good faith effort to avoid the conflict and antagonism that often
arises in negotiations, lays all the cards on the table in the second negotiating session and makes a "firm, fair, and final offer."

Proper timing, with a consideration for the human and organizational side of bargaining, can avoid this problem. It is important to remember that the presentation of proposals, particularly wage proposals, should always be timed according to the organizational needs of the union and the personal needs of the union negotiators.

Q: *Does it benefit management to delay on making a wage offer?*

A: Yes. Delaying a serious wage offer until late in bargaining, thereby drawing out negotiations for weeks or months, presents the union negotiating team with convincing evidence for its membership that they have been properly represented at the bargaining table. This delay makes the employer's offer more acceptable to the union negotiators and the union membership. A delayed offer is more convincing to the union negotiators. Elected officials have similar reactions. Extended negotiations indicate a serious effort has been made by management negotiators to protect the public interest. Elected officials may distrust negotiations that are settled without the customary expenditure of time and energy. Delaying the offer also protects management from conceding more than is necessary. By slowly feeling out the union as its first proposals are whittled down to more realistic ones, concessions more generous than are necessary to reach an agreement are avoided. During this process, management can make small adjustments in its initial offer. Finally, by delaying, management can save its final wage offer as a sweetener for the time when the negotiations deadline is drawing near. The wage offer at this time will sweeten a package that contains otherwise unacceptable provisions, and make the union much more likely to agree to it.

Q: *How can the management negotiating team convince the union negotiators as individuals to change their opinions about a settlement?*

A: If agreement is desired, emphasize the positive. Describe the proposal as an efficient and logical resolution of the problem at hand. If disagreement is desired, emphasize the negative. Describe the proposal in terms of its costs to both sides and how it will jeopardize the rest of the agreement. Personalize the acceptable aspects of the union proposal, and depersonalize the unacceptable aspects. Don't ever misrepresent the facts, play tricks, or indulge in name-calling, even in retaliation. Such tactics constitute bad faith bargaining and are illegal as well as impractical.

Q: How should the management negotiating team go about rejecting a union proposal during negotiations?

A: Saying "no" to certain union proposals is inevitable and should not come as a surprise to the union. Bargaining in good faith does not mean that management must concede to every union demand. Still, no union proposal should ever be rejected by management until it has been carefully considered, both in terms of its unacceptability to management and its importance to the union. Rashly rejecting a union demand, no matter how ridiculous that claim appears on its face, will offend the union negotiators and may force them into a defensive and immovable position. A history of cooperation, reasoned discussion, and full consideration of the union's proposals and goals will make rejecting a union proposal much more acceptable. This is because management builds up its credibility through cooperation and loses its credibility through misrepresenting its interests or bluffing. If it has gained a history of misrepresentation, management may appear to be bluffing when it is honestly taking a firm position.

Q: What is the most important rule management should follow in rejecting a union demand?

A: Never say "never" to a union proposal unless you are rejecting an illegal item of bargaining. The relationship between labor and management evolves and changes. As the parties grow to trust and respect each other, what was inconceivable in one contract becomes a reasonable problem to be resolved in the next. Take supplemental unemployment benefits (SUB plans) as an example. When these benefits were first proposed by unions, most managers laughed at the proposition. Now many contracts provide for such benefits. This illustrates why every union proposal should be considered a legitimate interest of the union. Every union proposal should therefore be treated courteously, even if management plans to firmly reject it.

Recognizing the inevitable: conflict

Q: American labor relations attempts to channel conflict between labor and management in the most productive direction possible. What is the source of this seemingly inevitable conflict?

A: There is a basic conflict of interests between union and management. The needs and desires of the union and the needs and desires of management are often irreconcilable. The statements of one party can be misinterpreted by the other, because the points of view of management and labor are so different. Another cause of conflict in negotiations is the show of bad temper by union members who decide they can let off steam at the bargaining table without jeopardizing their jobs. Personal animosity against management for real or imagined wrongs is often voiced at the bargaining table.

Q: *How should management react if one of the union negotiators uses the bargaining session to let off steam?*

A: Every labor union trainer will instruct local union leaders never to lose their tempers during negotiations. Nonetheless, it occurs. Management should bear with such outbursts if possible. It is up to the members of the union team to control each other. If such disruptions begin to bog down negotiations, management should address the problem firmly but tactfully, emphasizing that "the goal is to reach an agreement. Let's get back to the issues."

Q: *Why do union negotiating teams sometimes make "pie in the sky" demands during collective bargaining?*

A: Such demands are so inflated that inexperienced management negotiators find them ridiculous and often tell the union team so. This is a mistake. Each union demand should be considered a legitimate interest of employees. Such inflated union demands are presented for several reasons. They give the union room to make trade-offs with management during negotiations. They meet the demands of the various factions within the union. By merely presenting the demand from a special interest group within the union, unity can be maintained among the employee ranks, even if the demand is given little consideration thereafter. Inflated demands at the beginning set the stage for more serious talks on that topic in future contract negotiations. For instance, the union may propose a fundamental change in employee benefits, such as supplemental unemployment benefit plans (SUB plans) or guaranteed annual income plans, year after year with the hope that eventually the plan will sound less radical and be seriously considered by management during negotiations. Finally, inflated demands ensure that the union will not settle for less than the best possible deal. This is probably the most important reason for the union to make initial "pie in the sky" proposals. Never knowing in advance at what point the employer will settle, the union starts high and slowly comes down, hoping to reach agreement at the highest possible point, which is the employer's maximum possible offer and therefore management's least desirable position.

PART 3

The Psychology of Negotiation

Negotiation: An Introduction to Some Issues and Themes

Jeffrey Z. Rubin

It has been said that conflict is a growth industry. If so, then negotiation can help. Instead of attempting to club an adversary into submission, running away from the scene of conflict, giving up, or appealing to some higher authority, people in conflict can often negotiate their differences. The process is a familiar one. Typically, each side begins by asking for more than it expects to get, and through a series of offers and counteroffers in a stepwise concession process, a mutually acceptable agreement is ultimately reached.

The fact that virtually all of us frequently engage in negotiation does not make us effective negotiators; nor for that matter does it make negotiation an appropriate tool for the resolution of all conflicts. All too often negotiation has been used not in the service of moving toward the genuine reduction of differences but as a device for engineering artifice: a Trojan horse of sorts that—in the name of an amicable exchange of views—resorts to bluff, deceit, and threat in order to "sucker" an unsuspecting foe into a personally advantageous agreement.

Moreover, despite the promises of a spate of recent pop books on the subject,[1] one cannot negotiate everything. Deeply cherished beliefs and values are simply not negotiable; there is no give here, no possibility for concession-making. Either we believe in God, capital punishment, and a woman's right to have an abortion or we do not. These views may change, but they are not negotiable. You are not likely to modify your outlook if I agree to change my own.

Similarly, not all conflicts *should* be settled through negotia-

Jeffrey Z. Rubin, "Negotiation: An Introduction to Some Issues and Themes," *American Behavioral Scientist*, Vol. 27, No. 2 (November/December 1983), pp. 135–147. Copyright © 1983 by Sage Publications, Inc. Reprinted by permission of Sage Publications, Inc.

tion. Too often people regard conflict as a disease that must be eradicated at all cost. Some conflicts exist for good reason; they reflect differences that are genuine and profound. Rather than try to use negotiation in order to homogenize these differences—in the service, for example, of preserving a marriage that is foundering because of deep-rooted, chronic sources of conflict—it may make a great deal more sense to allow such relationships to terminate. It is perfectly appropriate for some relationships to end not with a bang, a whimper, or a negotiated settlement but with a farewell. To be sure, most conflicts can and should be settled through negotiation, and to this end we need all the ingenuity we can collectively muster. Some conflicts, however, may best be left to find their own eventual resting place.

Over the last several years, social scientists have begun to take the formal study of the negotiation process seriously. Witness, for example, the range and number of scholarly books on the subject.[2] Although no grand theory of negotiation—one that applies with equal facility to conflicts between individuals, groups, and nations—yet exists, we nevertheless know a fair amount about how the process works. More precisely, social scientists know far better now than they once did when negotiation is likely to lend a genuinely helping hand, and when it is instead likely to make a bad situation even worse. Here, then, is a listing of some of the major themes and issues in effective negotiation, many of which have emerged as the result of psychological research.

Negotiation tightropes

Negotiators are continually pulled in a number of extreme directions among which they must attempt to walk a tightrope. First, as researchers[3] have pointed out, negotiators are confronted with a pull toward the extremes of cooperation and competition. It is tempting to be tough and demanding in an effort to acquire the personally most favorable agreement possible, in doing so, however, we run the risk of driving the other party away from the negotiating table. It is also tempting to be entirely cooperative and accommodating in an effort to reach a fair agreement; but in doing so, we run the risk of yielding more resources than absolutely necessary and of settling for less than we might have obtained otherwise.

Second, negotiators must walk the tightrope between complete honesty and openness and total misrepresentation.[4] To be completely open and honest—that is, invariably to say what you mean and mean what you say—is to run the risk of being exploited by the other party. One of the hallmarks of negotiation is that neither party can know for sure what the other player's cards really are— only what the other *says* they are. If you in fact disclose the true identity of your cards, then I will probably be able to pick your pocket as cleanly as a cheating poker player. On the other hand, if you completely withhold, invariably keeping your hand close to your vest and your cards under the table, you run the risk of engendering so much distrust that I will be unwilling to negotiate at all.

Third, effective negotiators must be able and willing to walk the tightrope between short-term gain and gain in the long run. If one pushes hard enough, it is possible to come up with a quick killing in negotiation, albeit at the other's expense; such short-term personal gain, however, is often acquired at the sacrifice of mutual gain in the long haul. Especially in relationships that tend to be ongoing—as in marriage or labor negotiations between regularly appointed spokespersons—the short-term gains that we reap through a quick betrayal of trust or a quick "shot at the jugular" are apt to sow the seeds of distrust that reduce the chances of *any* agreement in the future. Conversely, research[5] has made abundantly clear that it is short-term sacrifice—a willingness to accept just a bit less than the very most one might have obtained—that tends to engender mutual gain and satisfaction in the long run.

The three preceding tightropes of negotiation may be summarized in the general observation that negotiation is a quintessential illustration of interdependence. Just as clapping requires two hands working in synchrony, so does negotiation require two parties moving to a common center. Negotiators must be willing to give up more than they would like in order to get more than would have been possible in the absence of this process. In negotiation, as in life, we each tend to end up with less than our wildest dreams, but with a great deal more than is provided by the next-best alternative.

The need to impress others

Each of us, in our own way, craves the approval of others. As a result we are inclined to say or do those things that we believe will generate this approval. If such concerns are with us in all aspects of our daily lives, they are particularly poignant in negotiation. Here, after all, we perform on a stage of sorts, where our toughness and mettle are the objects of considerable interest to our adversary, and various constituencies, as well as ourselves.

Brown has demonstrated experimentally the considerable lengths to which negotiators will go in an effort to maintain an appearance of strength.[6] In one of these studies, participants negotiated against an adversary who was in league with the experimenter and who was instructed to behave in ways that resulted in the systematic exploitation of the participant. During the second half of the negotiation session, the participant was given an opportunity to retaliate. Retaliation involved levying a monetary fine against the adversary at increasing monetary cost to self. Brown's negotiators were so eager to restore face once it had been lost or damaged that they went out of their way to punish their adversary as strenuously as the negotiation context allowed—even though such punishment required that they absorb more of a financial beating themselves than they could impose on the other.

It is under precisely such circumstances—when negotiators are unwilling to make even the slightest gesture of conciliation for fear of losing face—that the door can and should be opened to the intervention of third parties. Because they are external to the conflict and are of sufficiently high status such that the disputants wish to make a favorable impression, these third parties are often able to facilitate concession-making *without* loss of face. Consider: If I, a third party, ask you to make a concession and you agree to do so (perhaps you think highly of me, or perhaps you regard a concession as inevitable in the long run), your concession is likely to be construed by the other person as a sign of strength rather than weakness. You have compromised not because you were bullied by your adversary but because I, the third party, have requested your assistance. Should your concession-making lead to an agreement that you like, you can take credit for having been sufficiently prescient to know what to do and when. On the other hand, should your concessions result in exploitation by the other person, you can always blame me, the third party, for this failure.

The preceding observation regarding the face-saving function of third parties has been supported by the results of a number of laboratory investigations;[7] even a minimally involved third party (someone who is labeled merely as an outside observer, and in no way attempts to bring about a settlement of differences) may be sufficient to facilitate more rapid conflict resolution than occurs in the absence of this individual. The face-saving function of third parties can also be seen in countless real-world examples: couples counselors, divorce mediators, President Carter at Camp David in 1978, Kenneth Moffatt during the 1981 baseball strike, and so forth.

Interpersonal sensitivity

We all know the virtues of being tuned to the behavior of another, and these same virtues obtain in negotiation as well. Such sensitivity promotes effective negotiation in several ways. Negotiators are able to do a better job of anticipating and evaluating how the other person is likely to respond to the offers of that are made. Similarly, attentiveness and sensitivity enable negotiators to read the difference between what the other person says and what the other really means. Again, in negotiation one does not get to see the other's cards but only what the other says these cards are. An effective negotiator must therefore be able to decipher the language of an opponent's offers and demands, translating what is said into what is really meant. The more sensitive one is to the other's behavior, the easier this is.

Psychological research indicates that interpersonal sensitivity may help increase negotiating effectiveness but only up to a point. To be unduly sensitive to the other's behavior is to risk two kinds of problems. First, negotiators may end up being inappropriately and excessively reactive to everything the other says and does. Given conciliatory gestures by the adversary, they are likely to be cooperative and conciliatory in return; but given the slightest hint of intransigence or exploitiveness on the part of the other, these inordinately sensitive negotiators are likely to react quite viciously and with considerable vengeance.[8] If it is counterproductive to ignore everything another negotiator says and does, then it is also just as problematic to develop a "knee-jerk" response to each jowl jiggle that inevitably occurs during the transaction.

The second and more important problem with undue interpersonal sensitivity is that it may lead negotiators to forge an agreement that is less than optimal. Consider in this regard the plight of cooperative negotiators who are forever concerned about placing themselves in the other's shoes. Intuitively it might seem that people with a cooperative outlook would do a better job of reaching a jointly attractive solution than would those who are simply out to maximize their own gain. Research by Kelley and Schenitzki has indicated exactly the reverse.[9] Negotiators who are overly eager to cooperate, it appears, spend too much time and effort trying to get inside the opponent's head. Instead of beginning by making extreme initial demands, such cooperative negotiators try to be "nice guys"; they initially demand far less than their wildest dreams, and may even circumvent the negotiation process altogether by asking precisely what they will settle for. The problem with beginning by demanding less than the maximum is that the other negotiator is likely to assume (typically quite correctly) that one's opening demand is far in excess of what one will eventually accept. Cooperators, in their great concern to put themselves in their adversary's place, may thus develop and act on incorrect expectations of the other's preferences and intentions. In contrast, report Kelley and Schenitzki, more individualistic negotiators do a better job of stating extreme opening demands up front, thereby providing their opponent with the information necessary to move toward a mutually advantageous solution.

Affecting the other's sense of competence

As indicated in the section on impressing others, negotiators are reluctant to make concessions when they believe these moves imply loss of face. Negotiators want to believe that their concessions will be construed not as weakness but as a sign of their willingness to deal from a position of strength. I have made a conciliatory move not because you forced me to do so but because my competence as a negotiator has led to the development of a mutually satisfactory quid pro quo. If this line of reasoning is correct, then, paradoxically, the key to inducing conciliatory behavior is not coercion and intimidation but a set of moves that encourage the other negotiator to feel competent and effective.

Psychological research on the various strategies for inducing cooperation in an adversary lends general support to the importance of perceived competence. Participants in these laboratory experiments[10] are typically pitted against a simulated adversary who has been programmed to adhere to one of a number of different strategies. These include noncontingent cooperation (that is, concession-making that is entirely independent of anything the participant may say or do), noncontingent competition, and a contingent arrangement known as "tit-for-tat" (in which the participant's cooperative or competitive moves are matched by the programs' identical behavior on the immediately subsequent turn).

As you might expect, negotiators are more conciliatory when faced with an adversary who is consistently (noncontingently) cooperative rather than competitive.[11] Interestingly, the greatest cooperation of all is induced when the programmed adversary adheres to a tit-for-tat strategy.[12] To understand why, consider the message implicit in either of the two extreme noncontingent strategies: "Regardless of what you do and regardless of how you do it, I am going to cooperate (or compete); nothing you can do will get me to change my stance." In contrast, the implicit message conveyed by the tit-for-tat strategy reads something like this: "My behavior is dependent upon your own. You are capable of making me shift from a pattern of competition to one of cooperation, and vice versa; you have the wherewithal to bring about such change."

Negotiators want to believe that they are capable of influencing their adversary's behavior. If you negotiate with someone who appears to ignore your fiercest threats or kindest conciliatory gestures, and instead persists in a course of consistent cooperation or competition, you are likely to conclude that you have been pitted against a saint, a devil, or a fool—in any event, surely an adversary who has not the slightest interest in, let alone respect for, your negotiating skill. In contrast, an adversary whose behavior is contingent upon your own is letting you know that you have the skill and competence necessary to shape his or her behavior. The bottom line, then, is that negotiators are more likely to make concessions when they feel competent. So if ways can be found to let the other negotiators know that they are regarded as tough and worthy negotiators—perhaps by coordinating a few concessions on relatively minor issues with some of your adversary's moves—then it may be possible to induce even greater concessions on those issues that really count.

Avoiding commitments to intransigence

Negotiators often find it tempting, particularly when discussions bog down and things appear not to be going the way they would like, to commit themselves to tough negotiating positions from which they swear they will never retreat. Like the players in the proverbial game of "chicken,"[13] each negotiator threatens not to turn aside (to concede) until the other does so first. There are several problems with such bold, seemingly irrevocable commitments. First, if they work—that is, if they succeed in eliciting some long-sought concession—the adversary is likely to think twice before sitting down to negotiate again. Why deliberately elect to walk into a buzz saw if one can help it? On the other hand, should the negotiation commitment *fail* to work—that is, should the adversary refuse to knuckle under—then the perpetrator is likely to be confronted with a nasty choice: To go back on one's stated commitment is to run the risk of losing credibility in the eyes of the adversary, while opening the way to subsequent exploitation by the other; on the other hand, to carry through a commitment to intransigence, in light of the adversary's determination to resist concession, is in turn to run the risk of engineering unnecessary havoc for both sides.

The reason negotiators commit themselves to standing pat and budging no further, presumably, is because they assume that their threatened intransigence will impose so considerable a cost upon their adversary that he or she will yield rather than suffer the consequences. The problem with this assumption is that it is often wrong. It is a mistake to assume that if only the costs of not reaching an agreement are great enough (whether these costs are bilaterally or unilaterally imposed) negotiators may be pressured into arriving at a settlement. The costly possibility that time will expire and an impasse will be reached may have the effect of inducing movement toward agreement; but this threat, like many others, may instead push the negotiators into a rather dangerous game of chicken. The problem with negotiation gambits in which some sword of Damocles is deliberately or inadvertently suspended over the bargainers' heads is that each side, as in the game of chicken, may be sorely tempted to conclude that the other will give in first. If each side reasons this way, the result is likely to be a collective disaster.

Conflict intensity

Many of the moves, gestures, and gambits that work quite well when conflict is relatively low in intensity may prove ineffective or may even backfire in conflict-intensified circumstances. Consider a few research-documented examples of this generalization.

In the spirit of being sensitive (but not overly sensitive) negotiators, it seemingly makes good sense for people to place themselves in their adversary's shoes as best they can in an effort to see the world as the adversary sees it. Research has indicated that this technique of role reversal is likely to work well, so long as the dispute in question is based on illusory rather than real differences.[14] In the midst of a genuinely tough issue, however, the kind in which face-saving concerns are likely to crop up, role reversal is likely to produce a most unwanted effect: As a result of efforts to see the world as the other sees it, each negotiator is likely to be reminded of precisely how very different this world looks. If negotiators are far apart on every issue that confronts them, then efforts to take the other's part are likely to serve only as a painful reminder of the shared hopelessness of their situation.

Similarly, standard armchair psychologese dictates that we should never let the sun set on our anger. If we have some gripe, we should let the other person know about it, venting our spleen in the service of giving all feelings an open airing. The problem with this advice is that it is only half right. Negotiators in the midst of relatively small-scale conflicts do fine when encouraged to talk with each other about how they're feeling; communication is used to identify points of overlapping interest, of which there are many, and the chances of agreement are thereby increased. Research has indicated, however, that things go rather differently under conditions of intense conflict.

Pairs of negotiators in one series of experiments were first placed in a situation in which each could threaten the other at will: This had the effect of engendering intense conflict. Deutsch and Krauss[15] then set out to see how communication could be used to reduce conflict. The researchers gave negotiators the opportunity to communicate with each other if they wished. Nothing happened; although a channel of communication was made available, it was not used, and the conflict remained unabated. Deutsch and Krauss next tried requiring communication: The negotiators now had to say something, no matter what, on each turn in the negotiation game. As before, communication did little to help. In fact, the requirement of communication led negotiators to heap abuse on each other, hurling insults, threats, and lies. Rather than facilitating the reduction of intense conflict, compulsory communication only made things worse.

In general, then, the intensity of conflict must be taken into careful account as negotiators plot their moves and countermoves. It is particularly important not to assume automatically that the techniques that prove effective under conditions of low conflict intensity will continue to work well when conflict is protracted or exacerbated.[16] In the throes of a conflict that appears to be deteriorating into rancor, it may make sense to adhere to a general "rule of change": If the negotiators have been talking a blue streak, perhaps they should consider taking a breather for a while; if they've gone through a period of stony silence, perhaps they need some vehicle for getting communication going again. Negotiators stuck in hostility may need to shake things loose by experimenting with different arrangements: where they sit, what they talk about, whether they talk at all, whose turf they negotiate on, and so forth—anything that may help break the negative momentum the disputants have generated.

Summary and conclusion

In the preceding pages I have attempted to highlight a few of the major themes and issues in the study of negotiation. This list is by no means complete, nor has it been constructed in such a way as to invite the formulation of a general theory of negotiation. This listing of issues and themes, however, is suggestive of several prescriptions for effective negotiation. Thus, the implication of this article is that to be an effective negotiator, it is important (1) to be aware of the tightropes that confront both parties; (2) to avoid being seduced by the shared need to look good in the eyes of others; (3) to be sensitive—but not overly so—to the other's moves and gestures; (4) to help induce in the other a sense of negotiating competence; (5) to avoid commitments to positions of intransigence; and (6) to be sensitive to the intensity of conflict and the different coping strategies such intensity may necessitate.

Negotiation is not a nostrum for the common cold; there are conflicts that cannot, and should not, be resolved through negotiation. Even when such situations have been carefully parsed, however, what remains is the ubiquitous terrain in which negotiation makes good sense. People are remarkably ingenious at inventing new and better ways of creating a morass for themselves. Negotiation remains one of the best human inventions in response to this condition, a technique that promises less than one might like but a great deal more than typically can be obtained without it.

1. S. Chastain, *Winning the Salary Game: Salary Negotiation for Women* (New York: John Wiley, 1980); H. Cohen, *You Can Negotiate Anything* (New York: Bantam, 1980); F. Greenberger and T. Kiernan, *How to Ask for More and Get It: The Art of Creative Negotiation* (New York: Doubleday, 1978); J.

Ilich and B. Jones, *Successful Negotiation Skills for Women* (Reading, Mass.: Addison-Wesley, 1981); G. I. Nierenberg, *Fundamentals of Negotiating* (New York: Hawthorn, 1973); M. Schatzki, *Negotiation: The Art of Getting What You Want* (New York: Signet, 1981).

2. S. B. Bacharach and E. J. Lawler,

Bargaining: Power, Tactics and Outcomes (San Francisco: Jossey-Bass, 1981); D. Druckman, *Negotiations: Social-Psychological Perspectives* (Beverly Hills, Calif.: Sage, 1977); R. Fisher and W. Ury, *Getting to Yes: Negotiating Agreement without Giving In* (Boston: Houghton Mifflin, 1981); I. E. Morley and G. M. Stephenson, *The Social Psychology of Bargaining* (London: Allen & Unwin, 1977); D. G. Pruitt, *Negotiation Behavior* (New York: Academic, 1981); H. Raiffa, *The Art and Science of Negotiation* (Cambridge, Mass.: Harvard University Press, 1982); J. Z. Rubin and B. R. Brown, *The Social Psychology of Bargaining and Negotiation* (New York: Academic, 1975); I. W. Zartman, ed., *The Negotiation Process: Theories and Applications* (Beverly Hills, Calif.: Sage, 1978); I. W. Zartman and M. R. Berman, *The Practical Negotiator* (New Haven, Conn.: Yale University Press, 1982).

3. M. Deutsch, *The Resolution of Conflict* (New Haven, Conn.: Yale University Press, 1982); H. H. Kelley, "A classroom study of the dilemmas in interpersonal negotiations," in K. Archibald, ed., *Strategic Interaction and Conflict: Original Papers and Discussion* (Berkeley: Institute of International Studies, 1966); Pruitt, *Negotiation Behavior.*

4. Kelley, "A classroom study."

5. For example, J. G. Cross and M. J. Guyer, *Social Traps* (Ann Arbor: University of Michigan Press, 1980); J. Platt, "Social traps," *American Psychologist* 28 (1973): 641-651.

6. B. R. Brown, "Face saving following experimentally induced embarrassment," *Journal of Experimental Social Psychology* 6 (1970): 255-271; B. R. Brown, "The effects of need to maintain face on interpersonal bargaining," *Journal of Experimental Social Psychology* 4 (1968): 107-122.

7. R. J. Meeker and G. H. Shure, "Pacifist bargaining tactics: some 'outsider' influences," *Journal of Conflict Resolution* 13 (1969): 487-493; J. E. Podell and W. M. Knapp, "The

effect of mediation on the perceived firmness of the opponent," *Journal of Conflict Resolution* 13 (1969): 511-520; D. G. Pruitt and D. F. Johnson, "Mediation as an aid to face saving in negotiation," *Journal of Personality and Social Psychology* 14 (1970): 239-246.

8. Rubin and Brown, *Social Psychology;* W. C. Swap and J. Z. Rubin, "Measurement of interpersonal orientation," *Journal of Personality and Social Psychology* 44 (1983): 208-219.

9. H. H. Kelley and D. P. Schenitzki, "Bargaining," in C. G. McClintock, ed., *Experimental Social Psychology* (New York: Holt, Rinehart & Winston, 1972).

10. S. Oskamp and D. Perlman, "Factors affecting cooperation in a prisoner's dilemma game," *Journal of Conflict Resolution* 9 (1965): 359-374; Rubin and Brown, *Social Psychology.*

11. M. Deutsch, "Trust and suspicion," *Journal of Conflict Resolution* 2 (1958): 265-279; S. S. Komorita, "Cooperative choice in a prisoner's dilemma game," *Journal of Personality and Social Psychology* 2 (1965): 741-745; L. Solomon, "The influence of some types of power relationships and game strategies upon the development of interpersonal trust," *Journal of Abnormal and Social Psychology* 61 (1960): 223-230.

12. T. A. Baranowski and D. A. Summers, "Perception of response alternatives in a prisoner's dilemma game," *Journal of Personality and Social Psychology* 2 (1972): 35-40; C. L. Gruder and R. J. Duslak, "Elicitation of cooperation by retaliatory and nonretaliatory strategies in a mixed motive game," *Journal of Conflict Resolution* 17 (1973): 162-174; A. Kahn, J. Hottes, and W. L. Davis, "Cooperation and optimal responding in the prisoner's dilemma game: effects of sex and physical attractiveness," *Journal of Personality and Social Psychology* 17 (1971): 267-279; W. Wilson, "Reciprocation and other techniques for

inducing cooperation in the prisoner's dilemma game," *Journal of Conflict Resolution* 15 (1971): 167-195.

13. T. C. Schelling, *The Strategy of Conflict* (Cambridge, Mass.: Harvard University Press, 1960).

14. D. W. Johnson, "Role reversal: a summary and review of the literature," *International Journal of Group Tensions* 1 (1971): 318-334; D. W. Johnson, "Use of role reversal in intergroup competition," *Journal of Personality and Social Psychology* 7 (1967): 135-141.

15. M. Deutsch and R. M. Krauss, "The effect of threat upon interpersonal bargaining," *Journal of Abnormal and Social Psychology* 61 (1960): 181-189; R. M. Krauss and M. Deutsch, "Communication in interpersonal bargaining," *Journal of Personality and Social Psychology* 4 (1966): 572-577.

16. J. Z. Rubin, "Experimental research on third party intervention in conflict: toward some generalizations," *Psychological Bulletin* 87 (1980): 379-391.

Negotiating Power: Getting and Using Influence

——————————————— Roger Fisher

Getting to Yes[1] has been justly criticized as devoting insufficient attention to the issue of power. It is all very well, it is said, to tell people how they might jointly produce wise outcomes efficiently and amicably, but in the real world people don't behave that way; results are determined by power—by who is holding the cards, by who has more clout.

At the international level, negotiating power is typically equated with military power. The United States is urged to develop and deploy more nuclear missiles so that it can negotiate from a position of strength. Threats and warnings also play an important role in the popular concept of power, as do resolve and commitment. In the game of chicken, victory goes to the side that more successfully demonstrates that it will not yield.

There is obviously some merit in the notion that physical force, and an apparent willingness to use it, can affect the outcome of a negotiation. How does that square with the suggestion that negotiators ought to focus on the interests of the parties, on the generating of alternatives, and on objective standards to which both sides might defer?

This article is a brief report on the present status of some thinking about negotiating power. It represents work in progress. After briefly suggesting a definition of negotiating power, and the kind of theory for which we should be looking, I set up two straw men—that are perhaps not made wholly of straw: (1) the basic way to acquire real power in a negotiation is to acquire the capacity to impose unpleasant physical results on the other side; and (2) an ef-

Roger Fisher, "Negotiating Power: Getting and Using Influence," *American Behavioral Scientist*, Vol. 27, No. 2 (November/December 1983), pp. 149–166. Copyright © 1983 by Sage Publications, Inc. Reprinted by permission of Sage Publications, Inc.

fective way to exercise negotiating power is to start off by letting the other side know of your capacity to hurt them and of your willingness to do so. Both propositions seem wrong. In the central body of the article, I discuss six elements of negotiating power that can be acquired before and during negotiation, only one of which is the capacity to make a credible threat. Finally, I consider the sequence in which those different elements of power are best used to maximize their cumulative impact, and explore the debilitating effect of making threats at an early stage.

How should we define negotiating power?

It seems best to define "negotiation" as including all cases in which two or more parties are communicating, each for the purpose of influencing the other's decision. Nothing seems to be gained by limiting the concept to formal negotiations taking place at a table, and much to be gained by defining the subject broadly. Many actions taken away from a table—ranging from making political speeches to building nuclear missiles—are taken for the purpose of "sending a message" to affect decisions of the other side.

The concept of "negotiating power" is more difficult. If I have negotiating power, I have the ability to affect favorably someone else's decision. This being so, one can argue that my power depends upon someone else's perception of my strength, so it is what they *think* that matters, not what I actually have. The other side may be as much influenced by a row of cardboard tanks as by a battalion of real tanks. One can then say that negotiating power is all a matter of perception.

A general who commands a real tank battalion, however, is in a far stronger position than one in charge of a row of cardboard tanks. A false impression of power is extremely vulnerable, capable of being destroyed by a word. In order to avoid focusing our attention on how to deceive other people, it seems best at the outset to identify what constitutes "real" negotiating power—an ability to influence the decisions of others assuming they know the truth. We can then go on to recognize that, in addition, it will be possible at times to influence others through deception, through creating an illusion of power. Even for that purpose, we will need to know what illusion we wish to create. If we are bluffing, what are we bluffing about?

What kind of theory are we looking for?

An infinite number of truths exist about the negotiation process, just as an infinite number of maps can be drawn of a city. It is easy to conclude that negotiators who are more powerful fare better in negotiations. By and large, negotiators who have more wealth, more friends and connections, good jobs, and more time will fare better in negotiations than will those who are penniless, friendless, unemployed, and in a hurry. Such statements, like the statement that women live longer than men, are true—but they are of little help to someone who wants to negotiate, or to someone who wants to live longer. Similarly, the statement that power plays an important role in negotiation is true—but irrelevant.

As negotiators we want to understand power in some way that helps us. We want diagnostic truths that point toward prescriptive action. The statement that women live longer than men points toward no remedial action. I am unable to live longer by choosing to become a woman. On the other hand, the statement that people who don't smoke live longer than people who do smoke is no truer, but it is far more helpful since I can decide not to smoke.

Thus a lively interplay exists between descriptive and prescriptive theory. The pure scientist may not care whether his truths have any relevance to the world of action; he leaves that to others. But those of us who are primarily concerned with change (one hopes, for the better) are searching for descriptive categories that have prescriptive significance. We are looking for ideas that will help us make better choices. We are not simply trying to describe accurately what happens in a negotiation; we are trying to produce advice of use to negotiators, advice that will help them negotiate better. We need to say something other than that powerful princes tend to dominate less power princes, as true as that may be. We are looking for the kind of theory that will help a prince. He, presumably, has two key questions with respect to negotiating power: how to enhance negotiating power and how to use such power as he may have.

Mistaken views of negotiating power

"Physical force = negotiating power"   It is widely believed that in order to enhance our negotiating power we should acquire those assets like a strike-fund, a band of terrorists, or 100 MX missiles, which convey an implicit or explicit threat to harm the other side physically if it fails to agree with us. This belief is based on the assumption that, since threats of physical force undoubtedly exert influence, the ability to make such threats is the essence of negotiating power. Force is seen as the necessary and sufficient element of negotiating power.

Negotiating power is the ability to influence others. The pain that we threaten to inflict if the other side does not decide as we like is simply one factor among many. And as I have written elsewhere, making threats is a particularly expensive and dangerous way of trying to exert influence.[2]

Total negotiating power depends upon many factors. Enhancing negotiating power means building up the combined potential of them all. Exercising negotiating power effectively means orchestrating them in a way that maximizes their cumulative impact.

And this is where a second, widely held assumption about negotiating power appears to be mistaken and dangerous.

"Start tough, you can always get soft later"   There is a widespread belief that the best way to start a negotiation is with a hard line. "Let them know early who's in charge." The thought is that since, in the last analysis, physical power may be the decisive factor, the entire negotiation should take place governed by its shadow. Conventional wisdom insists that it is easier to soften one's position than to harden it. A negotiator is encouraged to start off flexing his muscles.

Alan Berger, reviewing Seymour Hersh's *Kissinger in the White House*, emphasized this feature of Nixon's foreign policy. "Nixon's first impulse was to attempt to intimidate his adversaries." He was anxious to "get tough," to "seem tough," to "be tough." "'The nuclear option was not an ultimate recourse to be considered only *in extremis*; it was, as Hersh persuasively demonstrates, the point of departure. . . .'"[3]

President Reagan appears to be operating on a similar assumption with respect to negotiating power. We began with a threat. We sought to influence the Soviet Union with respect to intermediate-range nuclear missiles in Europe by starting off with a public commitment that U.S. Pershing II missiles would be deployed in Europe before the end of 1983 unless by that time the Soviet Union had agreed to withdraw all its missiles from Europe, on terms acceptable to us.

The notion that it is best to start off a negotiation with a warning or threat of the consequences of nonagreement may result from a false analogy. Other things being equal, it is true that in purely positional bargaining the more extreme one's initial position (the higher a price one demands or the lower a price one offers), the more favorable an agreed result is likely to be. But opening with a very low substantive offer is quite different from opening with a threat of painful consequences if that offer is not accepted. The more firmly one is committed at an early stage to carrying out a threat, the more damaging that threat is to one's negotiating power.

If these two propositions are wrong, how should someone enhance and exercise negotiating power?

Categories of power

My ability to exert influence depends upon the combined total of a number of different factors. As a first approximation, the following six kinds of power appear to provide useful categories for generating prescriptive advice:

1.   The power of skill and knowledge
2.   The power of a good relationship

3. The power of a good alternative to negotiating
4. The power of an elegant solution
5. The power of legitimacy
6. The power of commitment.

Here is a checklist for would-be negotiators of what they can do in advance of any particular negotiation to enhance their negotiating power. The sequence in which these elements of power are listed is also important.

1. The power of skill and knowledge   All things being equal, a skilled negotiator is better able to influence the decision of others than is an unskilled negotiator. Strong evidence suggests that negotiating skills can be both learned and taught. One way to become a more powerful negotiator is to become a more skillful one. Some of these skills are those of dealing with people: the ability to listen, to become aware of the emotions and psychological concerns of others, to empathize, to be sensitive to their feelings and one's own, to speak different languages, to communicate clearly and effectively, to become integrated so that one's words and nonverbal behavior are congruent and reenforce each other, and so forth.

Other skills are those of analysis, logic, quantitative assessment, and the organization of ideas. The more skill one acquires, the more power one will have as a negotiator. These skills can be acquired at any time, often far in advance of any particular negotiation.

Knowledge also is power. Some knowledge is general and of use in many negotiations, such as familiarity with a wide range of procedural options and awareness of national negotiating styles and cultural differences. A repertoire of examples, precedents, and illustrations can also add to one's persuasive abilities.

Knowledge relevant to a particular negotiation in which one is about to engage is even more powerful. The more information one can gather about the parties and issues in an upcoming negotiation, the stronger one's entering posture. The following categories of knowledge, for example, are likely to strengthen one's ability to exert influence:

Knowledge about the people involved   What are the other negotiators' personal concerns, backgrounds, interests, prejudices, values, habits, career hopes, and so forth? How would we answer the same questions with respect to those on our side?

Knowledge about the interests involved   In addition to the personal concerns of the negotiators, what additional interests are involved on the other side? What are their hopes, their fears, their needs? And what are the interests of our side?

Knowledge about the facts It is impossible to appreciate the importance of unknown facts. Time permitting, it is usually worthwhile to gather a great deal of unnecessary information about the subject under negotiation in order to gather a few highly relevant facts. The more one knows about the history, geography, economics, and scientific background of a problem, as well as its legal, social, and political implications, the more likely it is that one can invent creative solutions.

It takes time and resources to acquire skill and knowledge; it also takes initiative and hard work. Lawyers who would never think of walking into a trial without weeks of preparation will walk into a negotiation with almost none: "Let's see what they have to say." Yet the lawyer would help his client more in persuading the other side next week than in persuading a judge next year. The first way to enhance one's negotiating power is to acquire in advance all the skill and knowledge that one reasonably can.

2. The power of a good relationship The better a working relationship I establish in advance with those with whom I will be negotiating, the more powerful I am. A good working relationship does not necessarily imply approval of each other's conduct, though mutual respect and even mutual affection—when it exists—may help. The two most critical elements of a working relationship are, first, trust, and second, the ability to communicate easily and effectively.

Trust Although I am likely to focus my attention in a given negotiation on the question of whether or not I can trust those on the other side, my power depends upon whether they can trust me. If over time I have been able to establish a well-deserved reputation for candor, honesty, integrity, and commitment to any promise I make, my capacity to exert influence is significantly enhanced.

Communication The negotiation process is one of communication. If I am trying to persuade some people to change their minds, I want to know where their minds are; otherwise, I am shooting in the dark. If my messages are going to have their intended impact, they need to be understood as I would have them understood. At best, interpersonal communication is difficult and often generates misunderstanding. When the parties see each other as adversaries, the risk of miscommunication and misunderstanding is greatly increased. The longer two people have known each other, and the more broadly and deeply each understands the point of view and context from which the other is operating, the more likely they can communicate with each other easily and with a minimum of misunderstanding.

Each side benefits from this ability to communicate. We may have interests that conflict, but our ability to deal with those conflicting interests at minimum risk and minimum cost is enhanced by a good working relationship. Two men in a lifeboat at sea quarreling over limited rations have sharply conflicting interests. But the longer they have known each other, the more dealings they have had, and the more they speak the same language, the more likely they are to be able to divide the rations without tipping over the boat. The ability of each to affect favorably the other's decision is enhanced by an ability to communicate. More power for one is consistent with more power for the other.

A good working relationship is so helpful to the negotiation of satisfactory outcomes that it is often more important than any particular outcome itself. A banker, for example, is often like a person courting. The prospect of a satisfactory relationship is far more important that the terms of a particular loan or a particular date. A relationship which provides a means for happily resolving one transaction after another, becomes an end in itself. Particular substantive negotiations become opportunities for cooperative activity that builds the relationship.

The same is true internationally. A better working relationship between the Soviet Union and the United States would facilitate the negotiation of particular arms control agreements. Even more important, having a better working relationship would enhance the security of each country more than would the outcome of any particular treaty. The better the working relationship we develop with the Soviet Union, the more likely they are to heed what we say.

3. The power of a good alternative to negotiation   To a significant extent, my power in a negotiation depends upon how well I can do for myself if I walk away. In *Getting to Yes*, we urge a negotiator to develop and improve his "BATNA"—his Best Alternative To a Negotiated Agreement. One kind of preparation for negotiation that enhances one's negotiating power is to consider the alternatives to reaching agreement with this particular negotiating partner, to select the most promising, and to improve it to the extent possible. This alternative sets a floor. If I follow this practice, every negotiation will lead to a successful outcome in the sense that any result I accept is bound to be better than anything else I could do.

In the case of buying or selling, my best alternative is likely to result from dealing with a competitor. Obtaining a firm offer from such a competitor in advance of a proposed negotiation strengthens my hand in that negotiation. The better the competing offer, the more my hand is strengthened.

In other cases, my best alternative may be self-help. What is the best I can do on my own? If the two boys offering to shovel the snow off the front walk are asking an exorbitant price, my best alternative may be to shovel the walk myself. To think about that option, and to have a snow shovel in the basement, strengthens my hand in trying to negotiate a fair price with the boys.

The less attractive the other side's BATNA is to them, the stronger my negotiating position. In negotiating with my son to cut the lawn, I may discover that he lacks interest in earning a little pocket money: "Dad," he says, "you leave your wallet on your bureau and if I need a little money I always borrow some." My son's best alternative to a negotiated agreement to cut the lawn is to get the same amount or even more for doing nothing. To enhance my negotiating power, I will want to make his BATNA less attractive by removing that alternative. With my wallet elsewhere, he may be induced to earn some money by cutting the lawn.

Conventional military weapons typically enhance a country's negotiating power by making a nonnegotiated solution less attractive to a hostile neighbor. With adequate defense forces, Country A can say to Country B: "Let's settle our boundary dispute by negotiation; if you try to settle it by military force, you will fail." With sufficient military force, Country A may be able to improve its alternative to negotiation enough that it will be in an extremely strong negotiating position: "We hope you will agree through negotiation to withdraw your forces to the boundary which has been recommended by impartial experts; if you do not agree to withdraw your forces voluntarily, we may force them to withdraw."

The better an alternative one can develop outside the negotiation, the greater one's power to affect favorably a negotiated outcome.

4. The power of an elegant solution   In any negotiation, there is a melange of shared and conflicting interests. The parties face a problem. One way to influence the other side in a negotiation is to invent a good solution to that problem. The more complex the problem, the more influential an elegant answer. Too often negotiators battle like litigators in court. Each side advances arguments, for a result that would take care of its interests but would do nothing for the other side. The power of a mediator often comes from working out an ingenious solution that reconciles reasonably well the legitimate interests of both sides. Either negotiator has similar power to effect an agreement that takes care of his or her interests by generating an option that also takes care of some or most of the interests on the other side.

A wise negotiator includes in his or her preparatory work the generation of many options designed to meet as well as possible the legitimate interests of both sides. Brainstorming enhances my negotiating power by enhancing the chance that I will be able to devise a solution that amply satisfies my interests and also meets enough of your interests to be acceptable to you.

In complicated negotiations, and even in some fairly simple ones, there is usually a shortage of options on the table. The United States and the Soviet Union would presumably welcome a plan that left them at the same level of insecurity at substantially less cost, but no one has yet been able to devise one. In any negotiation, generating a range of options in advance, some of which may later be put on the table, is another way to increase the chance that I will affect the outcome favorably.

5. The power of legitimacy   Each of us is subject to being persuaded by becoming convinced that a particular result *ought* to be accepted because it is fair; because the law requires it; because it is consistent with precedent, industry practice, or sound policy considerations; or because it is legitimate as measured by some other objective standard. I can substantially enhance my negotiating power by searching for and developing various objective criteria and potential standards of legitimacy, and by shaping proposed solutions so that they are legitimate in the eyes of the other side.

Every negotiator is both a partisan and one of those who must be persuaded if any agreement is to be reached. To be persuasive, a good negotiator should speak like an advocate who is seeking to convince an able and honest arbitrator, and should listen like such an arbitrator, always open to being persuaded by reason. Being open to persuasion is itself persuasive.

Like a lawyer preparing a case, a negotiator will discover quite a few different principles of fairness for which plausible arguments can be advanced, and often quite a few different ways of interpreting or applying each principle. A tension exists between advancing a highly favorable principle that appears less legitimate to the other side and a less favorable principle that appears more legitimate. Typically, there is a range within which reasonable people could differ. To retain his power, a wise negotiator avoids advancing a proposition that is so extreme that it damages his credibility. He also avoids so locking himself into the first principle he advances that he will lose face in disentangling himself from that principle and moving on to one that has a greater chance of persuading the other side. In advance of this process, a negotiator will want to have researched precedents, expert opinion, and other objective criteria, and to have worked on various theories of what ought to be done, so as to harness the power of legitimacy—a power to which each of us is vulnerable.

6. The power of commitment   The five kinds of power previously mentioned can each be enhanced by work undertaken in advance of formal negotiations. The planning of commitments and making arrangements for them can also be undertaken in advance, but making commitments takes place only during what everyone thinks of as negotiation itself.

There are two quite different kinds of commitments—affirmative and negative:

a. Affirmative commitments
    (1) An offer of what I am willing to agree to
    (2) An offer of what, failing agreement, I am willing to do under certain conditions
b. Negative commitments
    (1) A commitment that I am unwilling to make certain agreements (even though they would be better for me than no agreement)
    (2) A commitment or threat that, failing agreement, I will engage in certain negative conduct (even though to do so would be worse for me than a simple absence of agreement).

Every commitment involves a decision. Let's first look at affirmative commitments. An affirmative commitment is a decision about what one is willing to do. It is an offer. Every offer ties the negotiator's hands to some extent. It says, "This, I am willing to do." The offer may expire or later be withdrawn, but while open it carries some persuasive power. It is no longer just an idea or a possibility that the parties are discussing. Like a proposal of marriage or a job offer, it is operational. It says, "I am willing to do this. If you agree, we have a deal."

We have all felt the power of a positive commitment—the power of an invitation. (We are not here concerned with the degree of commitment, or with various techniques for making a constraint more binding, but only with the content of the commitment itself. Advance planning can enhance my power by enabling me to demonstrate convincingly that a commitment is unbreakable. This subject, like all of those concerned with the difference between appearance and reality, is left for another day.) The one who makes the offer takes a risk. If he had waited, he might have gotten better terms. But in exchange for taking that risk, he has increased his chance of affecting the outcome.

A wise negotiator will formulate an offer in ways that maximize the cumulative impact of the different categories of negotiating power. The terms of an affirmative commitment will benefit from all the skill and knowledge that has been developed; the commitment benefits from the relationship and is consistent with it; it takes into account the walk-away alternatives each side has; the offer will constitute a reasonably elegant solution to the problem of reconciling conflicting interests; and the offer will be legitimate—it will take into account considerations of legitimacy.

With all this power in its favor, there is a chance the offer will be accepted. No other form of negotiating power may be needed. But as a last resort the negotiator has one other form of power; that of a negative commitment, or threat.

A negative commitment is the most controversial and troublesome element of negotiating power. No doubt, by tying my own hands I may be able to influence you to accept something more favorable to me than you otherwise would. The theory is simple. For almost every potential agreement, there is a range within which each of us is better off having an agreement than walking away. Suppose that you would be willing to pay $75,000 for a house if you had to; but for a price above that figure you would rather buy a different house. The best offer I have received from someone else is $62,000, and I will accept that offer unless you give me a better one. At any price between $62,000 and $75,000 we are both better off than if no agreement is reached. If you offer me $62,100, and so tie your hands by a negative commitment that you cannot raise your offer, presumably, I will accept it since it is better than $62,000. On the other hand, if I can commit myself not to drop the price below $75,000, you presumably will buy the house at that price. This logic may lead us to engage in a battle of negative commitments. Logic suggests that "victory" goes to the one who first and most convincingly ties his own hands at an appropriate figure. Other things being equal, an early and rigid negative commitment at the right point should prove persuasive.

Other things, however, are not likely to be equal.

The earlier I make a negative commitment—the earlier I announce a take-it-or-leave-it position—the less likely I am to have maximized the cumulative total of the various elements of my negotiating power.

The power of knowledge   I probably acted before knowing as much as I could have learned. The longer I postpone making a negative commitment, the more likely I am to know the best proposition to which to commit myself.

The power of a good relationship   Being quick to advance a take-it-or-leave-it position is likely to prejudice a good working relationship and to damage the trust you might otherwise place in what I say. The more quickly I confront you with a rigid position on my part, the more likely I am to make you so angry that you will refuse an agreement you might otherwise accept.

The power of a good alternative   There is a subtle but significant difference between communicating a warning of the course of action that I believe it will be in my interest to take should we fail to reach agreement (my BATNA), and locking myself in to precise terms that you must accept in order to avoid my taking that course of action. Extending a warning is not the same as making a negative commitment. If the United States honestly believes that deploying one hundred MX missiles is a vital part of its national security, then letting the Soviet Union know that in the absence of a negotiated agreement we intend to deploy them would appear to be a sound way to exerting influence. In these circumstances, the United States remains open to considering any negotiated agreement that would be better for us than the MX deployment. We are not trying to influence the Soviet Union by committing ourselves to refuse to accept an agreement that would in fact be in our interest (in hopes of getting one even more favorable to us). We are simply trying to influence them with the objective reality that deployment seems to be our best option in the absence of agreement.

Two kinds of negative commitments are illustrated by the MX case. One is the example of Mr. Adelman's letter, which apparently described the only possible agreement that the United States was willing to accept. His letter appeared to commit the United States to refusing to agree to any treaty that did not commit the Soviet Union "to forego their heavy and medium ICBM's."[4] This was an apparent attempt to influence the Soviet Union by making a public commitment about what the United States would not do—we would not take anything less than a Soviet agreement to dismantle all its heavy and medium missiles in exchange for a United States promise not to add one hundred MX missiles to our arsenal.

The second kind of negative commitment is illustrated by the MX case if one assumes, as many of us believe, that deploying one hundred MX missiles does not really enhance U.S. security but rather damages it. The proposed deployment is bad for us; perhaps worse for the Soviet Union. On this assumption, the threat to deploy the MX missiles is like my trying to influence a fellow passenger by threatening to tip over a boat whether or not I am the better swimmer. Tipping over the boat will be bad for both of us, perhaps worse for him. I am committing myself to do something negative to both of us in the hope of exerting influence. If I make such a commitment, it is because I hope that by precluding myself from acting in some ways that would be in my interest, I will be able to achieve a result that is even more favorable.

To make either kind of negative commitment at an early stage of the negotiation is likely to reduce the negotiating power of a good BATNA. It shifts the other side's attention from the objective reality of my most attractive alternative to a subjective statement that I won't do things that (except for my having made the commitment) would be in my interest to do. Such negative commitments invite the other side to engage in a contest of will by making commitments that are even more negative, and even more difficult to get out of. Whatever negotiating impact my BATNA may have, it is likely to be lessened by clouding it with negative commitments. This is demonstrated by Deputy Secretary of State Kenneth Dam's insistence (following Mr. Adelman's ill-fated letter) that the MX "is not a bargaining chip in the sense that we are just deploying it for purposes of negotiation. It is a vital part of our national security." That statement implicitly recognizes that a statement made for negotiating reasons is likely to exert less influence at the negotiating table than would a good alternative away from the table. Mr. Dam's statement also reflects recognition on the part of the United States that a premature negative commitment weakens rather than strengthens our negotiating power.

The power of an elegant solution   The early use of a negative commitment reduces the likelihood that the choice being considered by the other side is one that best meets its interests consistent with any given degree of meeting our interests. If we announce early in the negotiation process that we will accept no agreement other than Plan X, Plan X probably takes care of most of our interests. But it is quite likely that Plan X could be improved. With further study and time, it may be possible to modify Plan X so that it serves our interests even better at little or no cost to the interests of the other side.

Second, it may be possible to modify Plan X in ways that make it more attractive to the other side without in any way making it less attractive to us. To do so would not serve merely the other side but would serve us also by making it more likely that the other side will accept a plan that so well serves our interests.

Third, it may be possible to modify Plan X in ways that make it much more attractive to the other side at a cost of making it only slightly less attractive to us. The increase in total benefits and the increased likelihood of quickly reaching agreement may outweigh the modest cost involved.

Premature closure on an option is almost certain to reduce our ability to exert the influence that comes from having an option well crafted to reconcile, to the extent possible, the conflicting interests of the two sides. In multilateral negotiations it is even less likely that an early option will be well designed to take into account the plurality of divergent interests involved.

The power of legitimacy   The most serious damage to negotiating power that results from an early negative commitment is likely to result from its damage to the influence that comes from legitimacy. Legitimacy depends upon both process and substance. As with an arbitrator, the legitimacy of a negotiator's decision depends upon having accorded the other side "due process." The persuasive power of my decision depends in part on my having fully heard your views, your suggestions, and your notions of what is fair before committing myself. And my decision will have increased persuasiveness for you to the extent that I am able to justify it by reference to objective standards of fairness that you have indicated you consider appropriate. That factor, again, urges me to withhold making any negative commitment until I fully understand your views on fairness.

The power of an affirmative commitment   Negative commitments are often made when no affirmative commitment is on the table. The Iranian holders of the hostages in Tehran said for months that they would not release the hostages until the United States had adequately atoned for its sins and had met an ambiguous set of additional demands. No clear offer was given by Iran, and the United States, accordingly, was under no great pressure to do any particular thing. During the Vietnam War, the United States similarly failed to offer those on the other side any clear proposition. We would not leave, we said, until North Vietnam agreed "to leave its neighbors alone"—but no terms were on the table; no offer, no affirmative commitment was given.

Once an affirmative commitment is on the table, the negotiators must make sure that the varied elements of the communication are consistent with each other. No matter what the magnitude of a threat, it will have little effect unless it is constructed so that the sum total of the consequences of acceptance are more beneficial to the other side than is the sum total of the consequences of rejection. While negotiators frequently try to increase power by increasing the magnitude of a threat, they often overlook the fact that increasing the favorable consequences of acceptance can be equally important.

But no matter how favorable the consequences of acceptance are to the other side, and how distasteful the consequences of rejection, the proposition will carry little impact if the various implications of timing have not been thought through as well. Just as my son will look at me askance if I tell him that unless he behaves next week he will not be permitted to watch television tonight, so the North Vietnamese were unable to comply when the United States said, in effect, "If over the next few weeks you haven't reduced support for opponents of South Vietnam, we will bomb you tomorrow." The grammar must parse.[5]

To make a negative commitment either as to what we will not do or to impose harsh consequences unless the other side reaches agreement with us, without having previously made a firm and clear offer, substantially lessens our ability to exert influence. An offer may not be enough, but a threat is almost certainly not enough unless there is a "yesable" proposition on the table—a clear statement of the action desired and a commitment as to the favorable consequences which would follow.

This analysis of negotiating power suggests that in most cases it is a mistake to attempt to influence the other side by making a negative commitment of any kind[6] at the outset of the negotiations, and that it is a mistake to do so until one has first made the most of every other element of negotiating power.

This analysis also suggests that when as a last resort threats or other negative commitments are used, they should be so formulated as to complement and reinforce other elements of negotiating power, not undercut them. In particular, any statement to the effect that we have finally reached a take-it-or-leave-it position should be made in a way that is consistent with maintaining a good working relationship, and consistent with the concepts of legitimacy with which we are trying to persuade the other side. I might say:

"Bill, I appreciate your patience. We have been a long time discussing the sale of my house, and I believe that we each fully understand the other's concerns. We have devised a draft contract which elegantly reconciles my interest in a firm deal, adequate security, and reasonable restrictions to protect the neighbors, with your interest in being able to move in early, to stretch out the payments, and to have your professional office in the house. The only open issue is price. On that, we have discussed various criteria, such as market value based on recent sales, providing me a fair return on my investment, and value based on professional estimates of replacement cost depreciated for wear and tear. These criteria produce figures ranging from $73,000 down to $68,000. I have offered to sell you the house for $70,000.

"Your response, as I understand it, is to say that you will pay no more than $100 above the best written offer I have from another potential buyer, now $62,000. Knowing that you would pay $75,000 if you had to, I am unable to understand why you should get all but $100 of the advantage of our shared interest in my selling and your buying the house. Nor, as we have discussed, do I think it a wise practice for me to defer to what looks to me like an arbitrary commitment.

"The transaction costs of further discussion would appear to outweigh any potential advantage. Unless you have something further you would like me to say now, or unless you would like to try to convince me that this procedure is unfair, I hereby make a final offer of $68,000, the lowest figure I believe justified by objective criteria. Let me confirm that offer now in writing and commit myself to leaving that offer open for three days. Unless something wholly unexpected comes up, I will not sell the house to you for less. Please think it over.

"In any event, let's plan to play golf on Saturday afternoon if you are free."

A great deal of work remains to be done toward formulating the best general advice that can be given to help a negotiator increase his or her ability to influence others. Some of that work relates to what can be done to acquire power in advance of a negotiation; much relates to how best to use such power as one has. No attempt has been made to advance propositions that will be true in every case, only to advance rules of thumb that should be helpful in many cases. So far, I have been unable to come up with any better rules of thumb covering the same ground.

As indicated at the outset, this article does not cover the kind of negotiating power that comes from creating in the mind of others an impression that is false—from bluffing, deceit, misrepresentation, or other such act or omission. For the moment, I remain unconvinced that the best advice for a negotiator would include suggestions of how to create a false impression in the mind of the other side, any more than I would advise young lawyers on how best to create a false impression in the mind of a judge or arbitrator. But that is a subject for another day.

1. R. Fisher, *International Conflict for Beginners* (New York: Harper & Row, 1969); R. Fisher and W. Ury, *Getting to Yes: Negotiating Agreement without Giving in* (Boston: Houghton-Mifflin, 1981).
2. See: "Making Threats Is Not Enough," chapter 3 in Fisher, *International Conflict for Beginners*.
3. A. Berger, "Hersh probes Nixon years relentlessly," *Boston Globe*, June 19, 1983, pp. B-10, B-12.
4. M. Freudenheim and H. Giniger, "Adelman Gets a Lesson in Letter Writing," *New York Times*, June 26, 1983, p. 2E.
5. See: Fisher, *International Conflict for Beginners*.
6. On reading this article, Douglas Stone of the Harvard Law School suggested that there may be one kind of negative commitment that could be made at the outset of negotiations without damage to the relationship, to legitimacy, or to other elements of one's total power. This might be done by establishing an early commitment never to yield to unprincipled threats. I might, for example, make a negative commitment that I would not respond to negative commitments but only to facts, objective criteria, offers, and reasoned argument. Like an advance commitment not to pay blackmail, such a negative commitment is consistent with legitimacy. In fact, one might propose that both sides make mutual commitments not to respond to threats. An early commitment not to respond to threats might, if convincingly made, preemptively foreclose threats from the other side.

Negotiation: A Look at Decision Making

Lawrence S. Bacow and Michael Wheeler

Negotiation is a fundamental method of dispute resolution. After all, even most lawsuits are not decided by judges or juries. Instead, they are settled out of court by the parties themselves. Negotiation is also central to other forms of dispute resolution. For example, mediation (a device sometimes used for settling environmental disputes) is basically negotiation that is carried out with the assistance of a third party.

On one level, all of us are familiar with negotiation. We may bargain over trivial things, like what to order at a Chinese restaurant, or we may haggle over important items, such as the price of a house. Sometimes we bargain for ourselves; in other cases, we may represent clients or organizations. This sort of firsthand knowledge of bargaining is supplemented by observing negotiations that are carried out in the public arena. The bargaining over the hostages in Iran, the battle over the nuclear power plant in Seabrook, New Hampshire, the air controllers' strike in 1981—all such exchanges regularly provide us with lessons in how (and how not) to negotiate.

Yet, as commonplace as negotiation is in our personal and professional lives, few people have a coherent understanding of the negotiation process. Bargaining often is seen as an art—not a science—and perhaps a "black" art at that. Until very recently, only a handful of law, business, and planning schools have offered courses in the theory and practice of negotiation. Serious interest in negotiation is on the increase, however, and there is now a substantial scholarly literature on the subject. Economists, psychologists, and policy analysts have long studied negotiation, and they have been

This article is an abridged version of "Dispute Resolution Theory," Chapter 2 in *Environmental Dispute Resolution*, by Lawrence S. Bacow and Michael Wheeler (New York: Plenum, 1985). Reprinted with permission of Plenum Publishing Corp.

joined, if belatedly, by lawyers and other professionals whose work brings them into the field. This article provides a brief introduction to some of the fundamental concepts and analytic tools of negotiation theory, using examples from environmental negotiations.

Negotiation analysis

There are several perspectives from which negotiation can be studied. For example, much can be learned from careful descriptions of negotiation experiences. Negotiation can also be studied experimentally. Over the years, behavioral psychologists have conducted revealing research into the way in which people act when they negotiate. Negotiation is also studied from an institutional perspective. Laws can be analyzed to see how they encourage—or discourage—consensual dispute resolution. In litigation, for example, the consent decree serves as a mechanism that enables parties to give greater force to their agreements. Similarly, the social and political contexts in which negotiations take place are significant. The perspective may be broad (national political agendas are relevant) or narrow (a young lawyer, eager to make his or her mark, may be intent on litigating rather than negotiating a case). Institutional analysis is emphasized in this book.

All of these methods have value, but at the outset we wish to introduce another approach that may not be as familiar: *decision analysis*, the application of which can greatly clarify complex negotiation situations. Decision analysis grew out of game theory, an abstract but informative examination of the strategy of competitive choices. In its purest form, decision theory can be highly mathematical and removed from common experience; yet its applications have been felt in economics, management, and foreign policy.[1]

A negotiation presents an intricate sequence of choices. Initially, a prospective negotiator must decide whether bargaining is likely to be worth the effort, and if so, when it should begin. A negotiator also must select a basic strategy; for example, should one be competitive or cooperative? Once negotiation is under way, a participant must make countless tactical decisions: Should an offer be made? Is it necessary to gather more information? Is it time for a caucus? Finally, the parties must decide if they should settle.

Because at least two parties are involved in any negotiation, the process is all the more complex. A negotiator's fate is never completely in his or her own hands. The results of whatever decisions are made depend also on the decisions of the other parties. To take the simplest of examples, two pedestrians "negotiating" their way down a crowded sidewalk will collide unless each moves in a different direction. A prospective buyer of real estate may make a reasonable offer but does not have a deal unless the seller independently decides to accept it. A negotiator who is considering demanding the inclusion of a particular term in the settlement agreement must weigh whether this will provoke the other party into insisting on something else.

In negotiation, the decisions of all the parties interlock, and outcomes are interdependent. If any one party could unilaterally control his or her destiny in all respects, he or she would have no need to negotiate. Instead, however, negotiators have to practice what game theorists call *reflexive reasoning*; that is, when they are contemplating an action, they have to gauge the other parties' reactions. This is the heart of strategic thinking.

Decision analysis requires several steps. First, the parties must be identified. Next, the range of choices they confront must be defined; in all but the simplest situations, choices may be linked in a lengthy chain. Finally, the consequences of those choices must be estimated.

In environmental disputes, as in other negotiations, identifying the parties can be somewhat difficult.

As to the second consideration, *options*, the parties usually face different choices. And often, none of the parties can be absolutely sure of the consequences of their decisions. Negotiators, then, must make decisions in an atmosphere of some uncertainty. Their attitudes toward risk, whether they can afford to take chances or need to be cautious, can shape their negotiation strategy.

In addition to identifying the parties, their interests, the choices they must make, and the outcomes they confront, it is important to understand the context of the negotiation. Two-party bargaining can differ markedly from multiparty negotiation. Likewise, bargaining over one issue often puts the parties in an adversary stance, whereas the presence of a number of items on the agenda may open opportunities for joint problem solving. A negotiation may be independent of other problems or it may be linked to other disputes. The environmental controls the government requires in one instance may establish a precedent of sorts for other situations. Negotiation is quite different when it is between strangers from when it is between people who know one another. Similarly, the style and substance of bargaining usually is different if the negotiation is conducted privately instead of publicly.

The rest of this article will present several different applications of decision analysis to negotiation. Readers should be aware, however, of the limits of decision analysis. It is primarily a prescriptive tool; that is, it identifies how people should act, not how they really behave. Moreover, it is premised on rationality in this context—the notion that people act so as to promote their own interests. These interests, of course, need not be narrowly selfish. A negotiator may be more interested in being thought of as being open and fair than in maximizing his or her financial position; nevertheless, he or she may still be regarded as trying to promote self-interest, albeit in the currency of reputation. In truth, of course, many people are irrational and engage in conduct quite contrary to their stated interests. Sometimes, such people have not fathomed the consequences of their actions; strong emotions may have overwhelmed their intellectual capacities. One who is irrational, however, is not always at a disadvantage in negotiation. A rational person, after all, is vulnerable to threats. The madman or the dunce cannot be reasoned with. In a hostage dispute between cool professionals in the state department and religious fanatics, who wins?

Decision analysis is sometimes attacked for allegedly depicting negotiation as strictly an adversary process rather than one in which joint problem solving may be central. This criticism is misplaced. It is true that much of the early game theory literature, from which decision analysis evolved, set out problems in which the participants are labeled *party* and *opponent*, designations that certainly suggested competition instead of cooperation. In certain zero-sum games, moreover, the race goes to the individual who can commit himself or herself quickly, or who can use a forcing move to limit the other side's options. Even in certain nonzero-sum games, the game theorists seemed to be saying that rational strategies must be pursued, even though they would lead to mutually undesired outcomes. There are also, however, bargaining games that have been developed to demonstrate the dynamics of cooperative behavior. Where parties ultimately do come to a settlement that gives some advantage to all, their individual decisions to agree can be reasonably interpreted as advancing self-interest, whether that interest is mercenary or highly principled, manipulative or altruistic.

Decision theory is sometimes wrongly faulted for suggesting a static rather than a dynamic approach. If this is ever true, however, it is only for the simplest, most abstract of the classic two-party games. Indeed, one of the great virtues of applying decision analysis to negotiation is that it takes into account the important variables of uncertainty and time. The choices that a negotiator faces at the beginning of bargaining may change significantly before the process is over. Opportunities may develop or be foreclosed. A strategy that made sense at the start may later have to be abandoned lest it prove fatal. This is particularly true in the environmental arena. Coalitions of interests may come together and then drift apart. Technological developments, the passage of revised laws, and changing economic conditions may radically alter the possible outcomes.

In sum, negotiation is ultimately a consensual process: There can be no settlement if the parties do not all choose to agree. By identifying the choices that parties confront and the incentives and disincentives that constrain them, we can see negotiation from the parties' points of view and from a broader perspective. In addition to clarifying complex relationships, decision analysis teaches two important lessons. First, if one wishes to change the likely result of a negotiation, one must alter the incentives of one or more of the parties in order to encourage different bargaining decisions. Second, decision theory provides a basis for understanding reflexive reasoning and the strategic thinking on which it is based. Third, decision theory illustrates some important paradoxes of bargaining. As we shall shortly see, for example, even if all the parties in a negotiation behave rationally so as to promote their own particular interest, the collective result may be harmful to all. As Thomas Schelling has provocatively demonstrated, the pursuit of self-interest, though utterly rational, may lead to an unwanted outcome.[2] Finally, decision theory enables us to better understand the importance of the manner and context of negotiation. The parties' capacities to communicate with one another can be an important determinant of negotiation. The key to resolution may sometimes be to get the parties to communicate less, not more.[3]

Incentives to negotiate

Negotiation is a consensual process from beginning to end. Any party can elect not to participate, or, having once entered negotiations, any party can drop out. Moreover, a negotiator does not settle a case out of compulsion. One settles because settlement appears better on balance than nonagreement. That does not necessarily mean that the negotiator is pleased by the outcome; it may simply be the least of a variety of evils.

In their book *Getting to Yes: Negotiating Agreement without Giving in*,[4] Roger Fisher and William Ury introduce the concept of a negotiator's BATNA—the best alternative to a negotiated agreement. To be acceptable, any proposed settlement must be at least a little bit better than the alternative of not settling. This should be self-evident. But what does *better* mean? In practice, *better* can mean a variety of things. People who live near a factory and bring a nuisance suit seeking recovery for the damage done by its pollution may settle out of court if the company offers more money than they expect to get from a jury; for such plaintiffs *better* also could mean more significant actions to abate the nuisance. Other plaintiffs, however, may rationally agree to settle for *less* than they think they will win in court. Dockets in many states are crowded, and it can be years before a case will come to trial. It may be necessary financially to accept less now rather than waiting years for more. Likewise, people may be very optimistic about winning a lawsuit; yet, there is almost always some uncertainty. Judges and juries can err and unexpected evidence may appear. Some plaintiffs may be reluctant to take chances, even if the odds are very much in their favor.

Better thus can mean more, sooner, or with less risk. It can also mean *cheaper*. Lawsuits are expensive. Lawyers must be paid, investigations conducted, and expert witnesses obtained. Different phases of litigation bear different costs. It is not very expensive to file a lawsuit, but discovery—the taking of depositions and the production of documents—can be costly, particularly in suits where the facts are complex and disputed, as if often true in environmental cases. A person who can afford to start a suit may not necessarily have the means to keep it going.

Negotiations may be expensive as well. At the very least, the time of the participants should be regarded as an expense, a considerable one in protracted cases. In highly technical cases, it may be costly but essential to gather relevant scientific information. (If the case is being litigated at the same time, this may not necessarily be an added cost.) Environmental groups may find it expensive to inform and organize their constituencies. A party may avoid negotiating with a long-time adversary, not wishing to give them or their claims any implicit legitimacy. On the other hand, the very process of negotiating sometimes may carry a positive value that is wholly apart from any agreements that may be reached. Good will may be important. A negotiation, though failing to produce agreement, may establish a useful precedent for the handling of future disputes.

It is important to remember that the factors that induce a person to come to the bargaining table may not be precisely the same as those that induce settlement. A person may rationally agree to negotiate, even though she or he sees no hope of reaching agreement. By the same token, a person conceivably may decline to negotiate even if there is an acknowledged possibility of settlement if the costs of negotiating seem too high. Focusing on incentives (and disincentives) is central to understanding negotiation. It helps explain the actions of individual negotiators. It also underscores the factors that must be manipulated if we wish to encourage people to seek consensual resolution of their differences. Incentives to negotiate are thus a central theme of this book.

We shall encounter two different sorts of negotiations. In one, if the parties do not settle, then a court, an arbitrator, or some other official will impose a resolution. This occurs in any lawsuit in which at least one of the litigants is intent on seeing it through. There is a second category of cases, however, in which the consequence of nonagreement simply is that there is no deal. If a conservation group is trying to buy a tract of beautiful land from a developer, the parties either will be able to come to terms or not. If they cannot agree, then the developer will look for or find other potential purchasers, and the conservation group will explore other ways of using its resources.

How are the incentives to negotiate—and to settle—different in these two different kinds of cases?

Obstacles to consensus

People may decline to negotiate because they do not wish to recognize the legitimacy of other parties, because they seek delay, or because the costs of negotiating seem to outweigh any expected benefits. There are also instances in which people may be able to see the great need for consensus. Yet, a divergence between individual and collective incentives prevents them from reaching accord.

The "commons problem," described by Garrett Hardin in "The Tragedy of the Commons," is the classic example of this type of situation. *Tragedy*, as he uses the term, is not necessarily intended to connote sadness; rather, it connotes "the remorseless workings of things." In Hardin's view of the commons, of course, there is also a strong sense of doom:

Picture a pasture open to all. It is to be expected that each herdsman will try to keep as many cattle as possible on the commons. Such an arrangement may work reasonably satisfactorily for centuries because tribal wars, poaching, and disease keep the numbers of both man and beast well below the carrying capacity of the land. Finally, however, comes the day of reckoning, that is, the day when the long-desired goal of social stability becomes a reality. At this point, the inherent logic of the commons remorselessly generates tragedy.

As a rational being, each herdsman seeks to maximize his gain. Explicitly or implicitly, more or less consciously, he asks, "What is the utility *to me* of adding one more animal to my herd?" This utility has one negative and one positive component.

1. The positive component is a function of the increment of one animal. Since the herdsman receives all of the proceeds from the sale of the additional animal, the positive utility is nearly +1.

2. The negative component is a function of the additional grazing created by one more animal. Since, however, the effects of over-grazing are shared by all the herdsmen, the negative utility for any particular decision-making herdsman is only a fraction of −1.

Adding together the component partial utilities, the rational herdsman concludes that the only sensible course for him to pursue is to add another animal to his herd. And another; and another.... But this is the conclusion reached by each and every rational herdsman sharing a commons. Therein lies the tragedy. Each man is locked into a system that compels him to increase his herd without limit—in a world that is limited. Ruin is the destination toward which all men rush, each pursuing his own best interest in a society that believes in the freedom of the commons. Freedom in the commons brings ruin to all.[5]

One need not ransack history to find examples of the commons problem at work. In the nineteenth century, frontiersmen slaughtered countless American bison, often taking only the highly prized tongues and leaving the rest of the carcass to rot on the prairie. Within several decades, the vast herd was reduced from many millions to just a few dozen. Perhaps some of the more perceptive hunters saw that they were both decimating the bison and eliminating their own occupation. Yet, there was nothing that any one individual could do to halt the trend. The exhaustion of the whale fishery is another example of the same phenomenon.

Hardin recognized that the commons problem applies not only to the consumption of resources like pasture land, bison, and whales but also the pollution of air and water.

Here it is not a question of taking something out of the commons, but of putting something in—sewage, or chemical, radioactive, and heat wastes into water; noxious and dangerous fumes into the air; and distracting and unpleasant advertising signs into the line of sight. The calculations of utility are much the same as before. The rational man finds that his share of the cost of the wastes he discharges into the commons is less than the cost of purifying his wastes before releasing them.[6]

The multiperson prisoners' dilemma is a revealing variant of the commons problem. It succinctly illustrates the obstacles that can exist to negotiation, even, in cases in which all the parties can see the benefits of agreement. The best known of all game theory exercises, it draws its name from its two-person version in which two defendants involved in the same crime must independently choose between confessing and remaining silent. Their best collective outcome occurs if they both are silent; their worst, if they confess. Although it would seem obvious for the prisoners to conspire to be silent, under the terms of the game, the prosecutor can induce each of them to breach any bargain by the offer of a little leniency in sentencing.[7]

The multiperson prisoners' dilemma describes a range of situations in which each party wants to pursue one course of action but hopes that everybody else will do the opposite. The polluter who breathes dirty air most likely wishes everyone else would buy scrubbers and converters; then his foul contribution would not be noticeable. The apartment dweller who shares the building's heating bill wishes his neighbors would turn down their own thermostats but does not obtain much savings if he does so himself. The owner of a house in a blighted neighborhood may understandably be reluctant to invest in improvements if others on the street are going to let their property deteriorate. If, however, they fix up their houses, the parcel will increase in value even if nothing is done.

In all such cases the payoff to an individual depends largely on what all the other parties choose to do. The so-called dilemma arises because it is never in any one person's interest to take the step that will lead to improving joint welfare. It is not a true dilemma because rational choice always dictates one decision: confession, consuming, or polluting. Perhaps the phrase *prisoners' paradox* better captures the fact that rational individual action can produce an outcome that is preferred neither by the group nor the individual.

Whatever the game is called, it also illustrates the importance in negotiation of communication, promises, and the capacity to ensure future compliance. The inability to guarantee future performance is often a major obstacle to consensus. The issue is not merely whether you can trust the other side to live up to the agreement, but how to get them to trust you.

Problem 1

You are the owner of a vacation house on a quiet lake in rural New England. Your property is presently worth $75 thousand. It would be worth $100 thousand were it not for the fact that the lake is so seriously polluted that it cannot be used for fishing or swimming. This pollution is caused solely by the antiquated septic systems of the hundred houses—yours included—that ring the lake. The problem could be eliminated totally if all the residents were to install new holding tanks. The cost of installing and operating a single tank is $10 thousand. Everyone who lives around the lake is distressed by its condition, yet even though everyone realizes that all would be much better off if the tanks were installed, nothing has happened. Why?

For the sake of simplicity, you may make the following assumptions: Everyone's house and lot is identical; the installation of any one tank reduces the original pollution in the entire lake by 1 percent; and a partial reduction of the pollution increases the value of all the houses accordingly. For example, if half the homeowners install tanks, the value of everybody's property increases from $75,000 to $87,500.

1. What solutions can you invent to break the impasse?
2. If 40 owners go ahead and install tanks, will that be enough to induce the others to join in?
3. What kind of private agreements could the parties fashion in order to ensure compliance with an agreement to install the tanks?
4. If none of the homeowners has the incentive to install tanks unilaterally, how would you expect them to vote on the referendum to require such installation? Would it make any difference whether the voting was at an open town meeting or was by secret ballot?
5. Is this a matter that is best addressed by private agreement or by government regulation? Is the level of the government relevant to your answer?
6. Finally, how do your answers change if we remove the simplifying assumptions, that is, that we acknowledge that some people contribute more to the pollution than do others, that some people feel the cost of the pollution more than do others, and that benefits of pollution control are unlikely to increase proportionately to expenditures?

In the problem example, people pollute the lake because the cost to them of doing so is less than the cost (to them) of not polluting. Because others also feel that cost, however, everybody is worse off collectively. Some economists have argued that pollution occurs because, until recently at least, the price for using the environment has been less (often nothing) than its true value. The best-known expression of this view is the Coase theorem:

Drawing on an analogy between environmental problems and other over-uses of common property, Ronald H. Coase attributes the undervaluing of environmental quality to the state's failure to define property rights clearly. He suggests that definition of property right (whether these rights were given to the sources of pollution or to the recipients) would permit bargaining between pollution sources and recipients that would lead to an optimal price for environmental damage. If the source were given the right to pollute, recipients of the pollution would be willing to compensate the source for reducing pollution at a rate equal to the value of the cost of the marginal damage from the pollution. If the amount of compensation exceeded the benefit of pollution, the source would accept the payment and reduce waste discharge. If the recipients held the property rights, the process would be similar: recipients would demand payment equal to their value of the cost of the marginal damage, and the source would be willing to pay for the right to discharge wastes until the fee exceeded the benefit from discharging wastes. Economists regard this result as optimal, since the marginal private benefit from the discharge equals the marginal cost of pollution to society.[8]

The application of the Coase theorem can be illustrated by the following example. Visualize a neighborhood divided into a 3 × 3 grid of 9 parcels, an acre each. As a house lot, each parcel is worth $25 thousand. The owner of the central lot, however, is planning to establish a piggery, and there is no zoning regulation in place to stop him. Used in this manner, his property will increase in value to $100 thousand, but the smell and noise will decrease the value of each of his neighbors' parcels to $10 thousand. Thus, from a collective viewpoint, the farmer's gain of $75 thousand is more than offset by the neighbors' loss of $120 thousand (8 × $15 thousand). In economic terms, the external costs imposed on the neighbors make the proposed use inefficient. If the owner of the central parcel does have the right to go ahead, then, according to Coase, the neighbors should pay him to stop. They should be willing to offer more than $75 thousand (but less than $120 thousand). Everyone would therefore be better off than if the piggery was established. Alternatively, if the law gives the neighbors the right to veto pollution (through a nuisance suit, for example), then the farmer can operate only if he can buy the neighbors out. Because the proposed use is inefficient in this example, he will not be able to offer enough money to induce the neighbors to waive their rights. If the piggery is to be much more profitable, however, the farmer would be able to offer more than the $120 thousand it would take to compensate the neighbors for their losses.

Although the Coase theorem yields interesting insights about property rights and efficiency, it does not address, let alone answer, other important issues, most of which are central to negotiation. First, although it posits negotiation among the neighbors, it does not determine how negotiation will proceed. As we shall see in the next section, the mere fact that there is a potential bargaining range does not necessarily mean that the parties will be able to agree on a settlement figure. Second, the illustration speaks of bargaining between the developer and the affected neighbors, but it does not consider the implications of the bargaining among the neighbors themselves. As in the multiperson prisoners' dilemma, each of the neighbors may look to the others to solve the pollution problem. For any individual, the best solution is to get the benefit of the bargain without having to pay for it. The free-ride factor may cause potential agreements to unravel. Third, the Coase theorem does not speak to questions of equity. What, for example, if the neighbors lack the liquid assets to buy out the developer? In any event, where does the private bargaining end and extortion begin? Finally, there is the matter of transaction costs. It may be difficult and time-consuming to get all the neighbors together and work out an agreement.

In recent years antiregulatory advocates have invoked the Coase theorem in support of allowing the free market to set the price of pollution. Whatever the merits of deregulation, however, this argument ignores the considerable obstacles to negotiation. Transaction costs frequently are significant, and in cases in which each of us feels the effects of a particular polluter only slightly, it is unlikely that we shall band together to negotiate a more efficient use of environmental resources. Government regulation is, in part, a mechanism for working around the problem of transaction costs. Regulation does not, of course, eliminate the need for negotiation; rather, it reconfigures the context in which negotiation occurs.

Zero-sum and nonzero-sum disputes

It is common to think of bargaining as a process of haggling back and forth in a situation in which one person's gain necessarily means an equivalent loss for the other side. Whatever goes into the rug merchant's till comes out of the customer's pocket. Such exchanges are called zero-sum games because the gains and losses of the bargainers exactly offset each other; that is, they add up to zero.

In practice, however, there are few conflicts that are purely zero-sum. A man who must pay alimony to his former wife at least can reduce the bite by claiming a federal tax deduction; if the wife is in a lower bracket, even after she pays taxes, she will effectively receive more than he has paid out of his pocket. (The alimony game is zero-sum if the United States Treasury is considered a player.) In labor disputes, a union may value particular fringe benefits more highly than a straight raise, whereas management may be preoccupied with preserving its control over the workplace. Environmental disputes almost always involve a range of issues, the importance of which may vary among the parties. For example, if the battle is over the development of a tract of land, the environmentalists may feel that a certain portion of it is especially fragile and needs protection. Carrying high-interest costs, the developer may be under greater pressure to come to any reasonable accord. If the negotiators are perceptive enough to recognize their contrasting priorities, they may be able to trade concessions in such a way that the gains far exceed the losses. This is a nonzero-sum game.

There is nothing inherent in the *structure* of zero and nonzero-sum games that makes one more difficult to negotiate and settle than the other. Stalemate may occur in both instances, even when there are possible settlements that all the parties would prefer to impasse. It is possible, however, as Lester Thurow argues in his provocative book *The Zero-Sum Society*,[9] that our political system is poorly equipped to reach resolutions where gain to one segment of society must impose some loss on another. As Thurow demonstrates, the calculation of benefits and the allocation of costs of environmental protection is exceedingly complex, particularly when citizens attach markedly different preferences for clean air and water, jobs, energy costs, and transportation. He contends that environmentalism in general is closely linked to fundamental choices of income distribution, and thus it tends to be zero-sum in nature—at least in a stagnated economy. Even if this is true for general policy, however, specific disputes can be decidedly nonzero-sum.

In any event, it is important to understand that although zero-sum and nonzero-sum disputes are amenable to settlement, they differ somewhat in their underlying dynamics. Consider first a zero-sum game.

Problem 2

Assume that a farmer is about to retire and sell his beautiful tract of land. A real estate developer who plans to build a subdivision has made a bid that the farmer is inclined to accept, but a local greenbelt group has organized a serious effort to buy the land in order to preserve it in its present state. The farmer knows he can sell the property to the developer for $300 thousand. The conservationists have raised $400 thousand to purchase the land.

1. What price do you expect the farmer and the conservationists to settle on? Why? If you were either party, would you be completely satisfied with this price? What might you do in

order to make it even more attractive from your point of view?

2. Should the fact that there is a clear bargaining range (see Figure 1) facilitate a prompt resolution, or will it tend to prolong negotiations?

3. Would it facilitate settlement if each side knew the other side's "bottom line?" (One's bottom line—or resistance point or reservation level, as it is called in the economic literature—is usually calculated with reference to the BATNA, Fisher and Ury's acronym for the best alternative to a negotiated agreement. Here the farmer's bottom line is determined by the competing offer of the developer; if the deal falls through, the farmer can still realize $300 thousand by selling to him or her. Fisher and Ury caution against setting a rigid bottom line, noting that, in the course of negotiating, the parties may discover other terms or compensation that can be incorporated into a deal to make it more attractive even if the dollar amount proves less than the other offer.

4. Deadlocks are sometimes broken when negotiators agree to apply some "fair" principle, such as splitting the difference. Do you have enough information to decide whether that would be a fair resolution in this case? To the extent that splitting the difference is common practice, how does the principle affect the overall strategy of the negotiator?

5. What outcome would you expect if the conservationists knew the farmer's bottom line, but he was in the dark about theirs? What does your answer tell you about the way in which negotiations are then likely to proceed?

6. As posed, this is strictly a zero-sum dispute, but are there other issues that can be introduced to give the matter a non-zero-sum quality. What such issues might be latent here? What other parties might be interested in the outcome of the negotiations. What influence might they be able to exert?

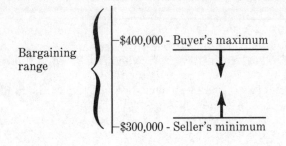

Figure 1. Single issue bargaining range.

Problem 3

When there is just one issue in contention, a dispute can be illustrated in a simple two-dimensional diagram. In Problem 2 that issue was defined simply as how many dollars would it take to buy the farm. The resistance points of the buyer and seller constitute the end points of the bargaining range. In cases in which the seller demands more than the buyer can afford to pay, obviously there is no figure acceptable to both of them; hence there can be no deal.

If there are more issues involved, the model must become more intricate. Consider a case in which the environmental group wants a power plant to reduce its pollution of the air; specifically, its emissions of sulfur dioxide (SO_2) and particulates. From the environmental group's point of view, the ideal resolution would be total elimination of each pollutant. The worst of all worlds would be no reduction of either one. For the environmentalists to establish an agenda for settling a suit against the company, however, they must clarify their attitudes about the host of possible outcomes between the two extremes.

In Figure 2 the two axes represent the percentage reduction of the respective pollutants. The worst outcome is at 0,0 in the lower left; the best, at 100,100 in the upper right. The environmentalists will likely prefer outcomes closer to the latter over those near the former.

Were they asked, moreover, the environmentalists could probably identify a specific point as being marginally superior to taking their chances in the lawsuit. For example, they might draw the line at a promise by the company to reduce each pollutant by 40%; anything less than that would not be acceptable. On further reflection, they should be able to identify other potential solutions that they regard as no better but no worse. They might, for example, be will-

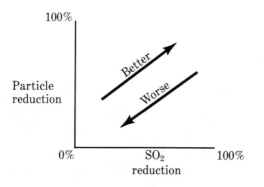

Figure 2. Two-dimensional bargaining.

ing to surrender some improvement in sulfur dioxide pollution for a still greater reduction in particulate pollution. As between their original 40,40 resistance point and a 35,50 outcome, they might be indifferent. Indeed, there should be a number of such combinations that are regarded as no better but no worse than one another. The line connecting all such points is called an indifference curve, and is indicated in Figure 3.

As defined here, the indifference curve also happens to be the environmentalists' reservation level. In the diagram, the environmentalists would ultimately accept any proposed settlement that lies on that curve but would prefer settlements located above and to the right. We can imagine a second indifference curve connecting points that are equally attractive among themselves but that are all preferable to an outcome on the reservation level. Indeed, there may be an infinity of such curves. Proposals below and to the left of the reservation level would not be acceptable.

1. In such a case, what shape do you expect the environmentalists' indifference curves to take: straight, convex, concave, or irregular? (By definition, indifference curves can never intersect.)
2. The owners of the power plant, mindful of the expense of reducing air pollution, likely will want to be obligated to reduce particulates and sulfur dioxide as little as possible. Assume that, if pushed to the wall, they would accept a 65,50 solution. Anything more stringent would be less desirable than fighting the environmentalists in court. How might the technology and economies of pollution control affect the shape of the company's indifference curves?
3. In the same way that the resistance points of the farmer and

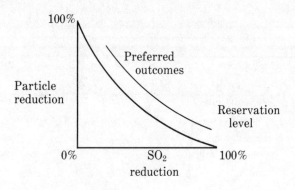

Figure 3. Reservation level with two issues.

the conservation group defined the bargaining in the zero-sum example, can you conceive of a way in which the reservation levels of the environmentalists and the power company here can be merged to define an area of possible settlement? You may find it helpful to sketch a resistance curve for the company, but keep in mind that it regards the status quo (0,0) as the best outcome and total elimination of pollution (100,100) as the worst.

4. Imagine that the parties reach tentative agreement on a solution that falls on the intersection of their resistance levels: How might *both* parties do better? In such a case must there always be a better outcome?

5. We have moved from one-dimensional bargaining to two. In many instances, of course, there will be far more than two issues. It is hard for most of us to think in more than three, or at the most, four dimensions, so we will excuse you from drawing a descriptive diagram of such cases. We have seen that two-dimensional bargaining often offers opportunities for joint gains not possible in one-dimensional situations. Do you suspect that this opportunity is present in multidimensional cases?

Bargaining strength

Bargaining strength is a familiar but poorly understood commodity, largely because it sometimes works exactly the opposite from what we might suspect intuitively. A negotiator with limited authority usually has more power than one with complete discretion. A negotiator who does not have the capacity to receive messages from the other side may find that this is an advantage, not a shortcoming. The irrational negotiator may prevail over the rational one. This section will briefly explore these seeming paradoxes.

The source of bargaining strength usually lies outside the negotiation itself: one's power within the negotiation depends on the impact of possible failure of the negotiations. As Fisher and Ury stress, the consequences of nonagreement determine the relative attractiveness of settlement.[10] To enhance your bargaining power, then, work to improve the consequences of nonagreement. For example, the farmer in Problem 2 will strengthen his bargaining hand with the conservationists if he can get the developer to up his bid to $350 thousand. The competing conservationists will now have to meet or exceed that offer. Note that the farmer has enhanced his bargaining strength by pursuing a deal he really does not want to make; moreover, he has done so outside the negotiation with the conservationists. Bargaining strength thus is not necessarily a constant. It can be manipulated by the parties in some cases. In others, it may be affected by events beyond their control. The farmer's position will be significantly changed if the developer independently decides to drop out of the bidding.

Thomas Schelling explains bargaining strength as a function of commitment.[11] Drawing on Schelling's example, picture two teenage drivers barreling down the road at each other, playing the deadly game of chicken. The first to swerve saves his neck but at the price of appearing cowardly. A driver who can wrench his steering wheel off and heave it out the window commits himself to going straight ahead. By committing himself, he forces the other driver to swerve, and he wins the game.

Commitment can take many forms. It may be aggressive, as in the game of chicken, or it may be decidedly conciliatory. The soldier who lowers his gun or the potential litigant who lets the deadline for filing suit pass has made commitments that may be small or large, depending on the circumstances. Commitment to one road is often made by deliberately burning bridges to others.

Making commitments can involve risk. The soldier who lowers his or her gun is exposed to the enemy who does not. People who forfeit their right to go to court may have their rights exploited. There are also significant risks to committing oneself to an aggressive strategy. The driver who tries to win the game of chicken by throwing the steering wheel out the window is doomed if the opponent does the same thing simultaneously. Likewise, the gambit is useless if the opponent does not see it or concludes that the driver has some other way of controlling the car.

The game of chicken may seem far removed from most of our lives (though there are chilling parallels to some international confrontations), but the lessons have broad application to everyday negotiation.

Bargaining strength is related to the options each party faces and to the parties' abilities to commit themselves to act (or to refrain from acting) on them. Commitment, in turn, often is dependent on the parties' capacities to communicate. Making a commitment of any sort is unlikely to affect the negotiation strategy of the other parties if they are unaware of the step that has been taken. A negotiator who cannot receive messages may be immune from threats (but he or she is also deaf to promises).

Commitment also raises the question of the first move. There are negotiations in which the race goes to the swiftest. The first party that can commit itself to a course of action preempts all the others. Some unscrupulous developers have been known to dump fill in wetlands before seeking conservation commission approval. Such a tactic can breed ill will, but it often moots the question of protecting fragile ecosystems. Developers may have to pay a fine for illegal dumping, but they will get a permit. Had the developer asked first, he or she might have been denied permission. There are also conflicts, of course, in cases in which each side tries to wait for the other side to make the first move.

Commitment can also be affected by whether the negotiation is public or private. One common form of commitment is public declaration. The environmental group that proclaims that it will never accede to the development of a particular tract seeks to enhance its bargaining power by tying its own hands. If the group is later pressed to compromise, it must take into account the loss of credibility that will come with retreating from its prior stand.

Commitment is not always self-imposed. The lawyer or executive representing a company may profess sympathy with neighbors who are claiming damages for air pollution, but truthfully state that she or he has no authority to settle for more than a given amount. The client or employer has, in effect, been committed to a low settlement by refusing to give the authority to agree to a higher one.

In sum, commitment is one of the tools that a negotiator may use to increase bargaining strength. Even if one objects to the manipulative aspects of using commitment in this way, negotiators must understand how others may seek to use it against them.

Problem 4

Assume six identical apartment houses sit on six lots of equal size on a city block. The most profitable use for each lot is multifamily housing; each property is worth $500 thousand. If a developer could assemble all six parcels as a site for an office building, however, they would be worth $5 million in toto; that is, $2 million more than they are worth separately. Keep the concept of bargaining strength in mind as you consider the following questions.

1. How should a prospective developer approach the six owners of the apartment buildings: individually or collectively?
2. Given that the developer could sell the six lots as a single parcel for $5 million, how much should she or he be willing to pay for each one? If the developer has paid $600 thousand for the first five of the parcels, how much should she or he be willing to pay for the sixth, to complete the deal? Who is in the position of bargaining strength in this situation: the developer or the last owner? Can you imagine a situation in which the developer would rationally, if regretfully, agree to pay more than $5 million for the six?
3. Do your answers to the first two questions give you any guidance about whether as an apartment house owner you would want to be the first to deal with the developer or the last? What risks go with the strategy of waiting to be the last?

4. As the developer, what strategies can you devise to protect yourself from possible exploitation?[12]

5. In one environmental case, the EPA negotiated a pollution discharge permit with a company. One of the issues was the capacity of the river to absorb the pollutants; there were other companies that discharged their waste into the river. The EPA had to allocate the carrying capacity of the river among the various dischargers. In this circumstance, if you represented one of these other companies, would you want to be the first to negotiate with the agency or the last?

1. The best introduction to this discipline remains: Howard Raiffa, *Decision Analysis* (Reading, Mass.: Addison-Wesley, 1968).

2. Thomas Schelling, *Micromotives and Macrobehavior* (New York: W. W. Norton, 1978).

3. Those interested in a far more extensive introduction to the rigorous study of negotiation are encouraged to read Howard Raiffa's *The Art and Science of Negotiation* (Cambridge: Harvard University Press, 1982).

4. Roger Fisher and William Ury, *Getting to Yes: Negotiating Agreement without Giving In* (Boston: Houghton Mifflin, 1981).

5. Garrett Hardin, "The Tragedy of the Commons," *Science* 162 (1960):1244.

6. *Ibid.*, p. 1245.

7. The prisoners' dilemma and some of its implications are discussed more fully in chapter 2 of Thomas Schelling's *The Strategy of Conflict* (Oxford: Oxford University Press, 1960). Lest you think that the prisoners' dilemma is wholly an abstract exercise, read George V. Higgin's description of the strategy of Watergate prosecutor Earl Silbert: "The Judge Who Tried Harder," *The Atlantic Monthly*, April 1974, pp. 83, 90-92.

8. William B. Marcus and Laurence E. Lynn, Jr., "Note on Environmental Enforcement Program," *Kennedy School of Government Note*, 1977:1.

9. Lester Thurow, *The Zero-Sum Society* (New York: Basic Books, 1980).

10. Fisher and Ury, *Getting to Yes.*

11. Schelling, *Strategy of Conflict.*

12. For a description of negotiation strategy and land assembly, see: C. Trillin, "U.S. Journal: Atlantic City, New Jersey," *New Yorker*, January 8, 1979, p. 4; and P. Hellman, "How They Assembled the Most Expensive Block in New York History," *New York*, February 25, 1974, p. 31.

The Dynamics of Negotiations

Orion White, Jr.

The great paradox of the mediation role is that, while negotiation is universally considered to be highly *rational*, it is in fact driven by nonrational dynamics. The dominant impression is that, when people sit down to negotiate something, they are focused and centered on their *self-interest*—that is, on their immediate *stakes* in the matter under consideration. They are, we tend to think, calculating how they can best serve their own interests through the negotiation process. This description suggests a highly *calculated, cognitive, emotionally cool* image of negotiation. We speak of people as being "shrewd negotiators," implying a sharp awareness and weighing of the outcomes that result from negotiated deals.

In fact, however, anyone who has participated in negotiations, either as party to them or as a mediator, has probably found that the process seldom fits this rational image. Affective, emotional factors frequently form the baseline along which negotiations proceed. The interpersonal dynamics between the parties can sometimes be the critical factor that turns the process toward successful settlement or toward breakdown and, in many cases, the courtroom. One consequence of this gap between the image and reality of negotiations is that the mediator on the one hand must appear as a hardheaded realist who is oriented toward the stakes for which the parties are playing, and on the other hand must have the skills to intervene in the "softer," affective side of the process—that is, to effectively deal with the emotions and interpersonal tangles that can snarl and stop negotiations.

From *Intergovernmental Mediation: Negotiations in Local Government Disputes*, by Roger Richman, Orion F. White, Jr., and Michaux H. Wilkinson. Published in 1985 by Westview Press, Boulder, Colorado.

A conceptual model

This article presents a conceptual model of the dynamics of the negotiation process as it has operated in city-county boundary disputes in Virginia. Its purpose is to show the complex interplay of cognitive and emotional elements that occur in negotiations and that place the mediator in the paradoxical position suggested above. Although the examples here involve boundary dispute negotiations, they provide insights to help mediators in other negotiations be more effective in moving disputes toward successful, nonlitigious resolutions.

The conceptual model presented here is based on the sequence of presentation of positions of each negotiating party. That is, the model shows what happens at each stage as the parties formulate a presentation of what they seek from the negotiations. As might be surmised, this sequence of events begins "inside" each party—in the intrapsychic realm—and moves through interpersonal exchanges into public pronouncements that become the substance of the negotiation talks. The course of the presentations is affected by myriad structural and more capricious influences. The road from "wants" to stated positions is a rather long and tortuous one. Figure 1 summarizes the concepts of the model.

The source point: vital interests or wants

Clinical psychologists are known to remark that if God had given people the capacity to know what they wanted all the time, therapists and counselors could not stay in business. This point is relevant for understanding negotiations. At the very core of negotiations is a sense of vital interests, desires, or wants. It is the satisfaction or achievement of these that each side is seeking through the vehicle of negotiation. These wants make up the "psychological bottom line" of each party. This term "bottom line" captures the essence of stakes as they are felt at the psychological level —namely, that there is a point past which each party will not go in making concessions, a hard and fast limit to compromise that bounds the negotiation talks.

Nonetheless, while stakes are felt to be immutable, it is almost always difficult if not impossible for the parties in a dispute to translate these vital interests into concrete negotiational positions. As the psychologists' remark implies, what people must often do in their personal lives is conduct nonfocused discussions (sometimes with therapists) through which psychologically felt wants or interests can be recognized and stated as practical agendas. The same is true in negotiated disputes. The parties definitely have "bottom lines," but they are generally ambiguous and vague. Indeed, it is when the parties can carry their discussion to the level of vital interests that negotiations acquire the special texture so vital to con-

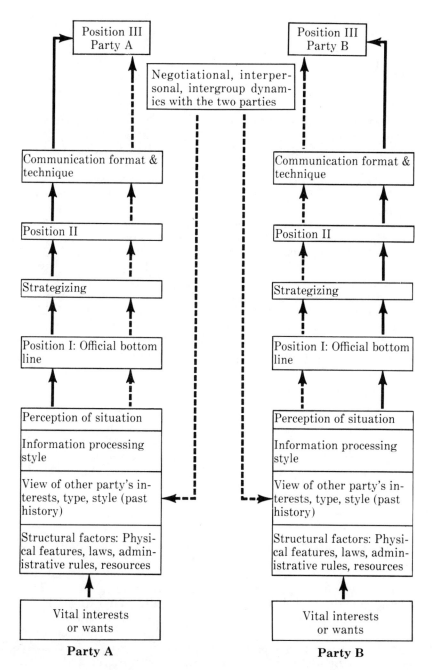

Figure 1. Negotiation dynamics.

structing the "package" of payoffs to each side that makes for settlement. Again, in negotiations we are faced with a paradox: we would expect the parties to become most rigid when they get down to discussing their bottom-line interests, but it is at that point that the process maximizes potential for creative dialogue.

This is why identification with and dialogue around positions, while probably inevitable, are so difficult and progress so haltingly. While the stereotype of negotiation is "splitting the difference," few disputes of any complexity or scale ever get settled in this way; such matters require the synergy of true negotiation, a synergy that occurs only when authentic contact about vital interests is achieved.

The lack of clarity with which a party perceives of its own stakes derives from a number of sources. One is that the situation being addressed is seldom clear. Usually several alternatives are available. Apart from extreme choices, the decision among options may be ambiguous, affected more by sentiments about what other parties are doing than by the merits of each alternative.

Second, as a culture we are not attuned to looking at wants; rather, we are more oriented toward "oughts" and "shoulds." Hence, we often seek to define wants in terms of "rights" or other imperatives. There may or may not be a correspondence between the underlying psychological want and the externally defined value. People sometimes change homes because they "ought to" now that they have achieved a certain status in life. They consider a new home as more appropriate to their position, even though they may not actually *want* (or be happier in) the new home.

The third and most powerful reason that our wants are so obscure to us is that our culture—capitalistic and competitive as it is—teaches us not to identify and seek *what we want* but to get *as much as we can*. As E. L. Doctorow put it in his novel *Ragtime*: in America, it is not enough to win, others must lose. Given this orientation, it is irrelevant to specify one's underlying vital interests. Since the objective is to best the other party, attention is turned outward, toward the situation (or game), and energy becomes focused on how to outdo the other side. Some observers of mediated settlements—especially attorneys—have wondered how the parties involved can be happy with the outcome, since there can always be a nagging feeling that "more could have been gotten in court." Even if this is true and the parties suspect it, mediated settlements probably still produce a curious type of satisfaction—that is, for our culture. Both parties are almost always relieved to have the dispute done with—this is a clear mutual payoff—and they often do "get what they wanted." While they do not know how to appreciate this fully, sometimes, it is a fully satisfactory outcome at a psychological level.

Unfortunately, this attitude seems to structure conflicts so that things must get worse before they can get better. That is, parties initiate their discussions by stating positions—positions that they claim are reasonable and "as far as they can possibly go" but that are in truth inflated grossly in preparation for "horsetrading." Parties almost always feel this process is beneath them, but they do not know any alternative; nor can they envision one, so strong are our cultural images about how negotiations proceed. As a consequence, the present model of negotiation dynamics begins where vague psychological "wants" begin interacting with external considerations. It is here that a party to a dispute begins to formulate a position that can be brought to the negotiating table.

Structural factors

The conscious formation of a negotiational position starts with the structure of the external situation as perceived by the attorneys, professional staff, and politicians. It is against "reality" that the desired outcome of "getting as much as we can" is initially reflected. It is typical in decision situations in this culture for the parties involved to turn first to the "facts" and proceed from there; parties to annexation-immunity disputes are no exception. In these cases, for example, attention is often focused on the physical setting, the actual topography of the land involved. In some instances, topographical or physical features, such as watershed lines, riverbeds, interstate highways, or mountains, indicate definite limitations or opportunities in the formation of a position. Another aspect of the external situation is the relevant laws and administrative rules. This is the major factor conditioning the process of these disputes. The money available for litigating the dispute is a third substantial element bearing on the parties' concept of what position they are to take.

A second consideration is each side's view of the other side—particularly the people who make up the governing board. Here, assessments of character come in, and the necessity or possibility for reason, persuasion, intimidation, or dismay is weighed. The one side attempts to read the other side's interests and get a sense of what they are up to. These judgments typically are rather personal, and past experiences with the people involved are inevitably brought up. At this point the emotional postures of each side toward the other are set, and they become the ones that will be carried into the negotiation sessions.

This set of information and perceptions is worked through, in a context that is structured by the personal styles of the members of each side. People process information differently: some are predominantly fact-oriented; some are more receptive to abstract argument; others tend to focus on the relationships involved in a situation; and others are primarily interested in creatively finding a break-through idea. A group of people, formed into a negotiating team, will operate in a dominant style that is characteristic of the majority of its members or of its leader. This factor—how groups process information as they work—operates implicitly, but its power in affecting the course and outcome of negotiation talks cannot be overestimated.

Positions and strategies: the substance of negotiation dynamics

Undefined vital interests, molded by the structural considerations described in the previous section, emerge as each party's primary negotiating position or "official bottom line." We identify this as Position I, and in boundary negotiations it is typically expressed as a line on a map that is kept secret throughout negotiations—even from the mediators, who may be sent out of the room when it is brought out and used as a point of reference for the talks. Position I defines the line from which there will be no retreat. It is usually not seen as defining "what we want" as much as indicating "the least we will accept." The definition of Position I plays at least two important functions in setting up the dynamics of the negotiations. First, by defining its bottom line, the team establishes its identity and is drawn together into a unit. Second, the clear definition of the bottom line serves to protect the team from itself. It can go into the rough-and-tumble of negotiations knowing that it knows where to stop. The line is insurance that the team will not inadvertently give away too much. Like any insurance, this affords a measure of security that can promote flexibility or openness in the negotiations themselves.

A party will not, of course, enter a negotiation by bidding its bottom-line position at the outset. Rather, it will utilize its skills and its assessment of the situation to formulate a strategy for approaching the negotiation in a way that will maximize its outcomes. This will lead to the formulation of a second position, Position II, which typically will be far different from Position I. Indeed, for strategic reasons, Position II may be deliberately overdrawn (though it will be rational to the initiating party) and hence may communicate little or nothing about the party's true position. Position II, in deliberately overstating the case, is looked upon as a device for disorienting the other side so as to open opportunities for perhaps serendipitous gains.

We cannot say, however, that even Position II, as defined by the proposing party, is communicated to the other side. That is, inside the chambers of the party that formulates it, it is one thing, but when embodied and presented to the other side in the negotiation setting, it necessarily becomes something else. Making and responding to proposals are critical points in negotiations—one reason why mediators seek to set norms structuring these events. A variety of communication formats and techniques are available to a team presenting a position, ranging from the heuristic, informal probe delivered outside the meeting room to the formal speech presented at a joint session of the governing boards. The medium, if it does not in fact *become* the message, at least comes to bear heavily in the definition of it. Illustrations of this effect will be provided later; the transformations of meaning that take place are sometimes marvelous to witness. The most frequent one is that a proposal intended to invite and initiate a series of bids back and forth becomes in the hands of the presenter a rigid or dogmatic demand that insults the receiving party and brings the talks to the edge of collapse.

Hence, Position II *as and when presented*, becomes still something else: Position III. It is Position III to which the receiving party responds. At this point the stage is set for a rich and complex pattern of intergroup and interpersonal dynamics to begin. Since the presenting party most likely does not see the distinction between Position II and Position III (they are unaware that a redefinition of it occurred in the presentation), they are likely to be puzzled by the response of the receiving side. Hence, the presenter's subsequent response will be partly confused, leading possibly to suspicions on the part of the other side, then mutual suspicion, and so on. As these dynamics proceed, two further effects occur: First, yet another position, Position IV, emerges from the negotiational dynamics. Second, actual experiences in the negotiations feed back to the two parties' perceptions of each other. This can lead to a redefinition of the situation, a revision of strategy and of Position II, and so on, in a continuing loop or cycle, all of which will go on beneath the surface, creating important but unacknowledged influences on the talks.

It should be clear from the model that negotiation in intergovernmental boundary cases (and other cases) is by no means the rational, straightforward process depicted in our stereotypes about negotiation. Myriad nonrational factors come into play at every point. The purpose here is to use this model for discussing how mediators can understand, work with, and intervene in these dynamics so that the capricious effects they tend to create in negotiations can be reduced. A subsidiary purpose is to illustrate and document these dynamics from experience in a number of annexation-immunity cases.

The psycho-social dynamics of negotiations

We must recall that the mediator, in order to build and maintain credibility, is best advised to emphasize the "harder"—more technical or structure-oriented—aspects of the role. With most clients, to present oneself as some sort of "communications" or "interpersonal relations" specialist would undermine his or her effectiveness. Extending this point, we can note again that mediators are not therapists. This is ironic, because perhaps the most helpful thing mediators could do in annexation-immunity cases is conduct a kind of group therapy session with each side to distill as clearly as possible its vital interests. The limits of appropriateness, however, dictate that the most the mediator can legitimately do is work at the surface of the negotiations—at the level of intergroup dynamics and with individuals. The mediator must be circumspect, however, and where possible operate under cover of substantive discussion. At the same time, though, it must be noted that as a case proceeds, more actions can be taken at the deeper levels (definition of vital interests and perception of the situation). Hence, much of the time the mediator must pay heed to one definition of the role, while acting from a much broader definition of it.

From this broader role orientation, the mediator can work along parallel lines (1) to establish valid relationships with individuals on the two sides, so that the individuals feel that the mediator fully understands their point of view and appreciates them as people and (2) to develop membership, in the sense of a *role presence*, with each of the parties as a human group. The mediator must work past being a stranger in the midst of the two sides.

First level: vital interests   In examining the details of negotiation dynamics, let us begin again at the basic level, the area of vital interests and wants. Since each party will feel that it has a clear definition of these—as represented in its (secret) Position I—it will usually not be easy for a mediator to focus attention on clarifying these and developing a coherent, cohesive viewpoint on them. This matter can be approached at least obliquely in a number of ways, however. For example, one of the major contributions a mediator can make is in mediating the inevitable *intra*team disputes over position and strategy.

In many cases negotiations become stalled because one or both of the negotiating teams cannot "get their act together" well enough to deal effectively with the other party. By working through these intrateam disputes the mediator paves the way for better communication with the other party, often resulting in clarification of vital interests and increased openness. In caucus sessions, the mediator can sometimes help each side clarify and discuss its vital interests as a way of working toward intrateam cohesion and harmony.

A second way of working at this level is to ask each party to state what it sees to be the broad vital interests of the other side and to compare this statement with a similar statement of its own. By so doing, of course, the party will have to reflect on its own general and vital interests.

A third technique is for the mediator, at appropriate points, to feed back to a side what he or she sees to be their vital interests—

given what they have been saying in the negotiations. Response to this feedback might lead to further clarification of the party's interests.

Second level: perception of the situation   At the next level, how the party perceives and interprets the situation, the mediator can sometimes be much more directly active and potentially helpful. The setting for these interventions, of course, must be the caucus or single-side meeting. Perhaps the most powerful type of intervention here is when the mediator can draw on experience in past cases or point out nuances of law, administrative procedure, or policy that lead the party to redefine the situation in such a way that options are opened up and possibilities for movement appear where previously there were none. Of course, on technical points, the parties will defer to their own technical experts. Also, no two cases are exactly alike, and the parties will be quick to remind the mediator that experience does not transfer fully. Hence, the mediator does face some definite limits in working at this level. Relevant information from other cases is useful and appropriate when it is offered simply as something to consider, and in more technical areas, the mediator should restrict inputs to those that might inspire imaginative, creative thinking.

Another area for intervention by the mediator at this level is the matter of psychological projections toward the other team. Anyone who has worked much with groups knows that a great deal of the perception in intergroup relations is really *projection*—where negative traits of one's own are imputed to the other side. This process accounts for perhaps *most* of the negative emotionalism and communication tangles that can characterize difficult negotiations.

One outstanding example was an instance where a member of one negotiating team solemnly told the mediators, "We have decided that if they come in tonight with a proposal as ridiculous as *our* last one, we are going to walk out!"

In another instance, a party complained to the mediators that the other side was not negotiating in good faith, as evidenced by the fact that they had come to the negotiation session with a press release ready to pass out at the end of the evening. When the mediators pointed out that the speaker's own team had gone into the meeting with a prepared press release, he was somewhat taken back as he realized it was true. However, he quickly (and defensively) retorted, "Well, but ours was only handwritten; they had theirs typed out!"

In some cases, projections can be centered in interpersonal relations across teams and involve professional egos, making them particularly difficult to deal with. In one case, the planning staffs of the two sides saw each other in precisely the same terms—as mostly incompetent sellouts to development interests. In another, the staff attorneys for the two sides described each other to the mediators in almost verbatim (nearly scurrilous) language. It is important that the mediator have built something of a trust relation, with informal channels of communication, with the parties before attempting to intervene in psychological projections. A humorous retort from the other side's point of view can often gently jar the subject into self-reflection. Working through projections is particularly difficult, as the sides will want the mediator to buy into and share its projections. Hence, the mediator must be cautious, subtly using objective data from joint sessions—for example, statements from one side that are at odds with the other side's projections. It is sometimes remarkable to see the extent to which the two sides in a negotiation misperceive each other. Such problems can only be sorted out by helping each side, slowly, to stop projecting and come to a more accurate sense of the other side on their own.

Third level: communication format and technique   There are basically two types of strategy for the mediator to follow at the level of communication format and technique. At this level, the reader will recall, the parties are presenting their strategized position (Position II) and are altering it in the process. One strategy is simply to be aware of the miscommunication that typically occurs at this level and deal with it *in situ* as it occurs. This can be done by caucusing and providing feedback or by "process interventions" such as asking the receiving team to restate the position being presented.

In one case, a curious reverse example of miscommunication at this step occurred. One side presented a position openly, hoping to evoke a counterproposal. Instead, the receiving team retorted arrogantly that the proposal did not please them and a new proposal would have to be made before they would respond. An emotional blowup, complete with cursing, ensued. The mediators made a few process interventions, but the emotionalism of the incident itself led the team receiving the proposal to believe the authenticity of the other team's desire to negotiate in good faith. This was a good illustration of how "the medium is the message" in negotiations and how the manner of presentation is often the critical factor in communicating to the other side. By being sensitive to what is happening during a presentation, a mediator can help move the parties' understanding of each other closer to their intentions.

As mentioned earlier, however, the more typical problem at this level is that a party will formulate a position intended to lead to a counterproposal, to which they can respond in turn, and so on, but then they *present* the position in such a way that the receiving side reads it as an (unacceptable) final offer.

In order to ward off such misunderstandings, the mediator can

(1) ask the side after it has formulated its position to consider *how* they wish to communicate it so that they will get the intended response, or (2) actually take the presenting member aside and coach him or her on how to go about the presentation. Even then, the problem may arise. In one case the presenting side decided to run an idea up the flagpole to see the other party's response. The mediator coached the presenter, suggesting a low-key if not casual introduction and a tentative statement of the position. The presenter acknowledged that such an approach fitted his side's objective at that point and agreed to follow the suggestions. However, when he took the floor to present his team's position, he began with a long prefatory statement that he ardently hoped the proposal he was about to make would be accepted because "in the spirit of good faith and in hope of gaining agreement," his team members had pushed themselves as far as they could go in making concessions, and had reached the point where "their basic goals are in danger of being compromised." The mediator sat dismayed as the inevitable reaction unfolded.

Two other techniques mediators can use to cope with this problem are to take over a team's proposition and present it to the other side as his own or simply to carry one side's proposal to the other as a messenger. In either case, the mediator can exercise complete control over how a proposal is presented.

Fourth level: negotiation dynamics   Mediators can be most active at the surface level of negotiations—the interpersonal communication events that constitute the negotiation dynamics that lead to Position IV, the one that actually gets across to the other team as the talks proceed. A great deal happens at this level, and one of the major responsibilities of the effective mediator is to be conscious of and track the effects of as much of these dynamics as possible. In one case, for example, a member of a negotiating team—the mayor of the city involved in a dispute—failed through oversight to shake hands with a member of the county's team. This slight, though inadvertent, so angered and disturbed the offended member of the county team that he did not get over it through the entire course of the talks. The mediators made this matter an object of considerable discussion, however, and amends were made that were heard at least by other members of the county team.

In another instance, the mayor of a city had his team meet with the mediators prior to introducing them to the city council. A few members of the council arrived early and entered the meeting room, whereupon the mayor asked them to step outside and wait until the appointed time for the council to meet. Both the mediators present were immediately aware of the effects this move would have, but since this was their initial meeting in the case, they felt they had not yet laid a sufficient base of legitimacy for intervening. The results were nearly disastrous, for the negotiating team never gained the full trust and cooperation of the council.

A second area in which mediators can definitely help is the management of emotion through increasing the participants' awareness of how the language they use affects feelings on both sides. That is, in discussing the issues of a dispute, the parties will frequently employ language that they feel is innocuous but that will actually put off or even inflame the other team.

In one case, the two sides had attempted carrying on talks without mediation help for several weeks. They had even, wisely, agreed on a set of general ground rules for the talks. Yet, when the mediators were brought in, the sides had become so hostile that they were barely on speaking terms. After reestablishing talks and observing for a while, it became clear to the mediators that both sides were doing two things. First, they were using—innocently—a number of emotionally loaded phrases. Second, they were introducing irrelevant topics that were heating up the talks so much that neither side could continue to function in a rational manner. For example, the county team members would frequently refer, in the coolest, most objective tone, to their desire to "protect" a particular area of land from annexation. The city team would visibly rankle at the word "protect," for they read into it a variety of negative implications about city government. (The county, of course, believed some of these implications, but the point is that constantly stimulating such reactions on the city side impeded the talks.)

In addition, each side felt that it had been responsible for bringing about the commercial development that existed in the areas adjacent to the city that were under dispute. Hence, whenever one side would refer to "our development," argument would ensue.

In another instance one side brought up a case from the past history of the negotiations where it felt the other side had deceived it. This charge was matched with a counterexample, which was in turn matched, and so on. In all, eight such "button pushers" were identified by the mediators in this case. These were identified and discussed in separate meetings with each side. The teams agreed that bringing them up added nothing to the talks, and they acknowledged how heavily loaded they were and how they had affected their interactions with the other team. Not only were the teams successful in virtually eliminating these from their discussions; they also showed an increased awareness of how their language affected the other side, often putting in hedges and provisos in their statements that were designed to ward off misunderstandings and consequent needless emotionality.

Another area where the mediator can help is the *efficiency of listening* and its corollary, *semantic tangles*. Organizational research has amply documented that the efficiency even of work-related (hence "important") communication is astoundingly low—one estimate of 12 percent is probably representative. The same holds true in negotiation meetings. Sometimes parties simply do not hear each other, and other times they misunderstand; but they seldom are able to get their messages to connect, as intended. In one negotiation at a key point, the mediator stopped a participant who was just beginning to respond to a statement from the other side and asked him to tell the other team what he understood the other side to have just said. Perplexed, he blurted out, "I don't have the slightest idea what they just said!" Mediators must track the dialogue of talks very closely and quickly interject probes, interventions, or clarifications that will prevent misunderstanding or improve comprehension. A great help can be provided here with only a small effort. Those engaged in the fray can use the help of an outside observer in identifying what they are both saying and hearing.

One of the early moves for the mediator is to establish a set of norms, ground rules, or negotiating conventions as a framework for the talks. The enforcement of these norms is perhaps the single most important thing the mediator can do to improve the dynamics of negotiations. In representing these norms the mediator is establishing himself or herself as the symbolic authority figure who defines appropriate behavior. This role is important more at the symbolic level than in actual practice, because no mediator would get very far in actually issuing fiats about the behavior of the negotiators. That is, the presence of the mediator itself refers the talks *out* to the broader setting of society and government generally, where "reasoned discourse" and "fairness" are broadly accepted norms. Further, the mediator represents a norm of *positive strategizing*— that is, strategy that concerns how to achieve settlement. He or she is a counterweight to the tendency for parties in a dispute to move toward extreme positions. To the parties, the mediator must symbolize moderation and balance.

While it may be disappointing, it is nonetheless true that, lacking such an operative symbol, negotiation talks can quickly sink into the morass of interpersonal dynamics, where anything but reasoned discourse takes place. The negotiation setting is an unfamiliar, even normless place to the participants. As Harold Garfinkel's studies show, in such circumstances people will seek to find benchmarks indicating what behaviors are appropriate. The mediator embodies such benchmarks, and they are expressed to a large extent through the norms he or she proposes for the negotiations. This symbolic impact is the main way in which the dynamics of the talks are structured. To play this role effectively the mediator must take actions in the name of the norms only sparingly and carefully, but when this *is* done it should be done firmly, ranging from simply reminding the participants of a norm to calling a halt to the negotiations. A not unimportant side dimension is management of the physical arrangements for the joint sessions, for press announcements, and for any other meetings. The meeting ground is neutral territory and hence appropriately the province of the mediator, who can take an active role in arranging it.

The most difficult aspect of the mediator's role, perhaps, is that he or she becomes privy to information about one side's position that cannot be divulged to the other side. No precise rules or even guidelines can be defined for dealing with this dimension of the role. However, one thing can be noted: often, in joint meetings, one side will make hints or suggestions about its position that it does not wish to reveal explicitly for what it sees as strategic reasons. The mediator, by knowing what he or she does about that side's position, can recognize these hints as a coded form of proposal making and can initiate an exploration of them by, for example, asking the receiving side to "feed back" what it understands the signal to mean. This device can frequently open new lines of discussion without the slightest compromise of a team's position by the mediator.

In sum, while the level of negotiation dynamics is the surface level, and hence the least connected to the give-and-take that is the heart of the process, there is nonetheless a great deal that can be done here to both reduce negative factors and provide positive impetus to the proceedings. The payoffs make it well worth the effort required to track and work with these surface dynamics. In doing so, though, it is useful to try to avoid a number of actions. It bears repeating, in this context, that the mediator must make it a principle not to reveal information from one side to the other. Also, mediators must not fall into the trap of pressuring one side and not the other to compromise. This is simple advocacy and has nothing to do with mediation. The mediator is not an arbitrator or judge and should avoid this position even when the parties pressure him or her to assume it—as they will, frequently. Last, while expertise can be shared with the sides, mediators are not consultants and must avoid offering authoritative analyses or opinions on the technical aspects of proposals.

Conclusion

This article has attempted to show, conceptually, some of the complexities that beset the negotiation process in annexation-immunity cases. These complexities often cause the position taken by each side, as finally understood by the other, to be far removed from its own concept of its position or from its vital interests. A number of illustrations of these dynamics and effective mediator interventions were also described. Experience in negotiation shows that it is not the rational, objective process we so often think it to be. Rather, it must be regarded and dealt with as a complex, ever-changing, even volatile psycho-social process while at the same time paying homage to the image of it as rational.

By doing this, the mediator can manage the caprice of the process, improve communication, and increase the comfort each side feels in dealing with the other. As comfort with the negotiating relationship grows, so does trust. The bottom-line payoff of mediation is that it nurtures the trust required as a foundation for the parties' moving to dialogue at the level of vital interests and wants. It is at this fundamental level that the magic of negotiation produces a winning resolution for both sides, even where it seemed initially that one must win and one must lose.

References

Archibald, K. A. "Three Views of the Experts Role in Policy Making," *Policy Sciences* (1970), pp. 73-86.

Fisher, Roger, and William Ury. *Getting to Yes: Negotiating Agreement Without Giving In*. Boston: Houghton Mifflin, 1981.

Garfinkel, Harold. *Studies in Ethnomethodology*. Englewood Cliffs, N.J.: Prentice-Hall, 1967.

Johnston, Robert W. "Negotiation Strategies: Different Strokes for Different Folks," *Personnel* (1982), pp. 36-44.

Keirsey, David, and Marilyn Bates. *Please Understand Me*. Del Mar, Calif.: Prometheus Nemesis, 1978.

Laing, R. D., H. Phillipson, and A. R. Lee. *Interpersonal Perception*. London: Tavistock Publications, 1966.

Morely, Ian, and Geoffrey Stephenson. *The Social Psychology of Bargaining*. London: George Allen and Unwin.

Richman, Roger. "Mediation in a City-County Annexation Dispute: The Negotiations Process," *Environmental Impact Assessment Review* (1983), pp. 55-66.

Schein, Edgar. *Process Consultation*. Reading, Mass.: Addison-Wesley, 1969.

Walton, Richard E. *Interpersonal Peacemaking: Confrontations and Third Party Consultation*. Reading, Mass.: Addison-Wesley, 1969.

Zartman, I. Wilham, and Maureen Berman. *The Practical Negotiator*. New Haven: Yale University Press, 1982.

PART 4

Applications

Man
in the
Middle

Mark Woodhams

The time is now. The place is a small American city beset by some
large, but not atypical, problems: an out-of-date master plan, vacant
downtown storefronts, an aging housing stock, and a declining industrial base.

Amid much fanfare, the mayor convenes a commission of business and civic leaders to address these issues and develop a list of
goals for the year 2000. The mayor himself chairs the commission—
to make sure that the discussions don't deviate from his political
agenda. Eventually, the commission agrees on a multigoal wish list
that the mayor happily proclaims is "do-able." The local paper
praises the commission's foresight and concern for the community.

End of story? Perhaps. Those who have gone through such a
goal-setting exercise will recognize the pitfalls in this hypothetical
example. Because the commission wishes to please as many interest
groups as possible, some of the goals it sets are conflicting or unre-
alistic. Some are weighted in favor of one interest or another. Whatever the reason, the exercise fails to generate any long-term results
and ends up gathering dust in the city clerk's office.

But there is another way, one that its advocates say can separate politics from the goal-setting process and extract commitments
to make sure the goals are achieved. Known as a negotiated investment strategy (NIS), this technique was used successfully in the financially strapped Boston suburb of Malden, Massachusetts.

What made the effort unusual—those involved often use the
term "unique"—was the process of getting the city's major stakeholders to agree to be partners in planning for the city's future. No
backroom deals were cut, no developers taken out to lunch, and no
laundry lists of goals adopted. Instead, over a year's time, three

teams representing Malden's citizens, government, and businesses met on an equal footing to hammer out a 148-recommendation agenda for this primarily working-class community. "We've tried to evolve a new way of participatory planning," says city planning director Edmund P. Tarullo.

The process was brought to Malden by Lawrence E. Susskind, professor of urban studies and planning at the Massachusetts Institute of Technology and executive director of the interdisciplinary Program on Negotiation at Harvard Law School, at the invitation of Mayor Thomas Fallon, who had heard Susskind speak on NIS. Long an advocate of intergovernmental cooperation, Susskind had participated in a negotiation project in Columbus, Ohio, in the late 1970s. That project, backed by the Kettering Foundation, sought to coordinate local and federal policies and funding criteria in several areas. It was a success, in Susskind's view.

A team approach

Susskind saw in Malden an opportunity "to nurture the process" by adding citizen and business groups to the roster of negotiators. "What I was interested in," he says, "was the notion of building teams to represent the city's different interests. I don't believe in hand-picked blue-ribbon commissions."

Thus, says Susskind, the process developed for Malden engaged the entire community, not just developers and not just the mayor. The result, he feels, is a unique and effective partnership.

NIS is a variant of the better known types of environmental negotiation that have emerged in recent years as a means of settling environmental or public policy disputes. Most of these disputes involve specific sites. In contrast, Malden's NIS is aimed at long-term agreement about local goals.

What sets NIS apart from traditional goal setting is the use of an independent mediator—Susskind in Malden's case—to guide the negotiations. The mediator not only sharpens the focus of the discussion, but also helps eliminate political grandstanding and irrelevant detail. Moreover, because the NIS sets unanimous agreement on the issues as a goal, its participants become committed to seeing the process through.

"The thing the NIS does is get people on record with commitments, and, in a sense, the public enforces them," says James Kunde, program manager at the Kettering Foundation, which helped develop the NIS model. In Kunde's view, the Columbus NIS and two others conducted at the same time in St. Paul, Minnesota, and Gary, Indiana, have proved that the concept works. All three were initiated by the Federal Regional Council for Region V and aimed at developing highly targeted urban policies.

In Columbus, for example, two-thirds of the recommendations

were carried out within a year, Kunde says. And St. Paul got UDAG commitments to help with three major projects set as goals in the NIS process: development of an energy park, renovation of a large downtown warehouse district, and redevelopment along the Mississippi River.

The Gary project resulted in an improved working relationship between the city and U.S. Steel, according to Kunde. The state also delivered on several major bond issues, resulting in airport and freeway projects.

The NIS process in Malden began in the summer of 1983, a year after a University of Massachusetts study described the city as one of the state's most financially pressed. Like other Massachusetts cities, Malden (pop. 50,000) was coming to terms with Proposition 2½, a statewide referendum passed in 1980 that placed a 2.5 percent ceiling on growth of property taxes. Malden's property tax revenues had been declining since 1977. By 1982, income from the tax had dropped by 57 percent.

This loss of revenue, coupled with a generally acknowledged deterioration in the public school system and a 2,500 drop in population over 10 years, contributed to the community's negative self-image. "It turned out to be a very tough place to work because there is so little activism," says Susskind. "The business community is very sluggish and the neighborhoods not very well organized. Looking back on it, if you were to ask me if I'd choose a place like Malden again, I'd say, 'God, no.'"

The goals of the NIS were to identify problems and recommend solutions in six areas: city pride and beautification, public education, economic development, public safety, human services, and city finances. Each of the teams—city, business, and citizens—placed a representative on tripartite subcommittees responsible for fact finding in each area. Susskind says the use of issue-oriented subcommittees was a unique feature of the Malden NIS.

Even after the project was begun, there was still considerable skepticism, notes William Breslin, former executive editor of the Malden *Evening News* and now director of publications for Harvard's Program on Negotiation.

Malden, only a few miles from both Boston and Cambridge, had been used before as a laboratory for university studies, including an extensive survey of the public schools by the Harvard Graduate School of Education. "People were jaded," Breslin says. "'Here they go again,' they said. 'They'll come out and write their dissertations, and then everything will stay the same.'"

The NIS was able to overcome some of this cynicism, its participants say. In fact, although the NIS agreement was formally drafted only last June, private volunteer efforts have already completed a city beautification program.

Nuts and bolts

Susskind and his staff from the Program on Negotiation volunteered their time to mediate the proceedings. The only funding was a $10,000 grant from the Lincoln Land Institute in Cambridge to cover administrative costs.

Although the process was initiated by the city, the teams had equal say in the negotiations. No agreements were reached without approval from each team. The city team, headed by planning director Tarullo, included the mayor and representatives from the city council, the school committee, and various city departments. Local clergy brought together representatives from civic organizations and neighborhoods. The business team was led by Bernard Rotondo, manager of human resources for Data Printer Corporation, Malden's largest employer.

All told, the proceedings involved a diverse lot of 47 participants. "It took a while to get going," Rotondo says. "We were asking diverse groups to pull together and initially that was difficult."

Once under way, the process was successful both in identifying community problems and coming up with solutions, the NIS participants say. The final agreement, an inch and a half thick, is a far-reaching "action plan," targeting volunteer, private, and public resources.

Perhaps the most controversial recommendation of the 148 agreed upon by the three teams was a one-year override of Proposition 2½. "Present economic trends and conditions in Malden indicate a serious threat of financial failure," the group concluded. "All possible means of alleviating the city's financial problems should be explored."

The NIS teams also agreed that the city should update its 1970 master plan in a manner consistent with the NIS process. This means that input from citizen and business groups will be sought before a final plan is adopted.

Seeking consensus is at the heart of the NIS, as Susskind pointed out recently in an article called "Mediating Public Disputes," which appears in the January 1985 inaugural issue of *Negotiation Journal*, a quarterly edited by Jeffrey Z. Rubin of Tufts University.[1]

Some of the other Malden recommendations include:

1. Initiating a biannual citywide cleanup effort, with city equipment and volunteer labor.
2. Offering incentives for early payment of property taxes.
3. Creating a public-private coalition to monitor the delivery of human services.

4. Holding public meetings in each ward to address the issue of juvenile crime.
5. Encouraging the creation of community gardens on vacant land.
6. Expanding development in commercial areas through federal community development block grant and urban development action grant funds.

The hitch

The NIS process does not guarantee, however, that these recommendations will ever be implemented. For one thing, the city government is not legally bound by the negotiated agreement. For another, some recommendations—such as the Proposition 2½ override—appear to be politically infeasible. To help in the implementation, Susskind and his staff prepared an implementation appendix to the agreement describing how certain actions can be taken. For example, the appendix suggests that the recommendation on updating the master plan be presented as an official motion to the planning board. The staff also developed a monitoring plan that calls for the team leaders to meet every six months to review progress. The overall intent of the appendix is to commit city agencies and other groups to take action.

For Mayor Fallon, it is too early to tell how many of the recommendations will be enacted. "If you're looking for something immediate, you're not going to get it," he says. "It's 10 years down the line. I'm not going to be here [as mayor] to see it."

But Fallon insists that the process was worth going through. "Things that were merely minor irritants to people came out in the process, small things that only required an administrative decision to effect a solution," he says. "How do you place a value on that? I saw people get informed about things that they otherwise wouldn't be informed about. There are an awful lot of intangibles that go into this that no value can be placed on."

Concern about whether the NIS will produce results lingers in the community. "There's still some cynicism," business leader Rotondo acknowledges. Political considerations, which were mostly divorced from the process, "are unavoidable now," he says. "You have some very difficult decisions down the road that city government is going to be faced with."

One political problem is the potential for a high rate of turnover in city government. Both the mayor and members of the city council are elected every two years, a method Susskind calls "cuckoo." He believes the NIS can be more effective in cities with a "more professionalized" city manager-mayor-council form of government.

For his part, Fallon believes now that he tried too hard to keep politics out of the Malden NIS. "Don't be too wary of the politics involved," he advises mayors considering a similar effort. Including more local political leaders in the process would have "enhanced my ability to get our more information about what we're doing," he says.

Planner's view

Similar advice to planners comes from the local planning director, Tarullo. "You have to work within the political spectrum," he says. Tarullo is cautious in evaluating the NIS results, but he believes the process "cultivated some food for thought and created a greater understanding of the problems we face.

"I've been reluctant to answer when people ask, 'Does it work?' but now I'm ready to say, 'I think it has,'" he says.

A city planner's role in the NIS is still "up for grabs," says Susskind, who was encouraged by Mayor Fallon's decision to name Tarullo to head the city team. "In another city, the mayor would have been more likely to appoint his personal deputy," he says. "The fact that Ed [Tarullo] had the mayor's confidence suggests to me something out of the ordinary."

Susskind is optimistic about the results of the NIS process. "My view is that, if the city of Malden can really get its act together, it can sit down with state and federal governments and say, 'Look, we speak with one voice. We're going to leverage private and voluntary commitment. What are you going to do for us?'"

Heart of the strategy

The notion that a community can draw together its disparate interests to confront existing or potential problems is at the core of the negotiated investment strategy, says Susskind. "When you get people together face-to-face, you can deal with conflicts directly. You don't need to create new institutions for better policy administration."

Because the NIS is inherently confrontational, those who went through the Malden process believe strongly that an experienced, impartial mediator is required to keep the sessions on track. "Getting people together—that's a key role," says Mayor Fallon. "The negotiator has to be someone who conveys authority, someone with the appropriate training."

The 38-year-old Susskind likens his negotiating style to that of former Secretary of State Henry Kissinger because of its "activist" nature. The mediator in an NIS has to create relationships that never existed before, he says, and find ways for the participants to confront their differences.

How to do it

To cities interested in doing an NIS, Susskind offers this basic advice:

1. A commitment from city government is the "quintessential ingredient." Although an NIS doesn't have to be initiated by the city, it will require city involvement and cooperation to be successful.
2. Finding a capable facilitator or mediator to manage the process is the next important step. The mediator should be nonpartisan and, ideally, funded through a grant to avoid being beholden to any of the NIS participants. Susskind points out that there are several groups, such as the Kettering Foundation, that may have funds available for an NIS. A written agreement between the mediator and the NIS participants spelling out the ground rules is also necessary.

An NIS handbook will be published later this year by the National Institute for Dispute Resolution, 1901 L St., N.W., Washington, DC 20036; 202-466-4764; it will include how-to information for cities interested in the process. More information is also available from Susskind or Denise Madigan, the staff assistant, at the Program on Negotiation, Harvard Law School, 500 Pound Hall, Cambridge, MA 02138; 617-495-1684.

1. *Negotiation Journal* is available for $25 a year for individual subscribers ($50 for others) from Plenum Publishing Corporation, 233 Spring Street, New York, NY 10013.

Mediation in an Annexation Dispute

Roger Richman

Annexation is an often controversial process by which municipalities expand their boundaries to incorporate land from surrounding political jurisdictions. In states where urban annexation involves competition for land, annexation initiatives can generate important disputes between governing bodies of adjacent communities. Leaders of a community facing annexation may, that is, see the initiative as a challenge to their local sovereignty—a threat to their tax base, to local political alignments, and to their land. In Virginia, the setting of the negotiation described in this article, cities and counties do not overlap or share tax bases or population. Therefore, city-county separation creates a win/lose scenario in annexation and a particularly sharp polarization of interests between neighboring local governments. Virginia annexation disputes are the state's most controversial interjurisdictional issues; traditionally, they have been settled only after lengthy intergovernmental litigation.[1]

This paper describes a formal negotiation between a city and county over a city petition to annex some six square miles of county land, including commercial centers, the only regional shopping mall, an industrial park, and several thousand county residents. The negotiations, organized by an independent mediator, spanned three months and resulted in a comprehensive settlement ultimately approved by the courts.[2] Lengthy intergovernmental litigation was avoided and a settlement was reached that went far beyond the narrowly framed issues traditionally submitted to the state boundary

This paper is a revised version of an article, "Mediation in a City-County Annexation Dispute: The Negotiations Process," originally published in the *Environmental Impact Assessment Review*, volume 4, no. 1 (1983), pp. 55–56. Reprinted with permission of Plenum Publishing Corp.

commission for fact finding and to a special annexation court for adjudication.

The objective here is to describe various roles mediation can play in structuring intergovernmental negotiations. The mediation detailed in this article has many substantive and stylistic variations. However, a review of the overall process suggests that when viewed as a structured, neutral, and authorized procedure, mediation can enable public officials to resolve the political and technical issues in a dispute that has reached an impasse. Mediation can also complement more traditional dispute resolution models, such as *ad hoc* political negotiations and more formal proceedings before state adjudicatory agencies, and the courts.

Another aim of this article is to offer a view of a complex negotiation as a process that *evolves* in a sequence of separate developmental phases. In each phase in the case presented here, the parties engaged in different negotiating behaviors, conditioned in the main by their perception of their adversaries' orientation toward the negotiation. The phases thus are important to an understanding of the evolutionary nature of complex negotiations. In this case five phases were noted:

1. Exploring positions
2. Competitive bargaining; proposals and counterproposals
3. Breakthrough into a problem-solving mode
4. Competitive bargaining; secondary issues
5. Development of an agreement in the form of a detailed contract.

These phases are reviewed below.

The parties and the issues

In September 1981, Spotsylvania County in Virginia, located midway between Washington, D.C., and Richmond, Virginia, filed a petition with the Virginia Commission on Local Government for immunity from annexation from the city of Fredericksburg. Within a few days the city filed its formal annexation petition in which it proposed to annex approximately six square miles of the county. In the usual annexation proceeding the parties would eventually have their petitions adjudicated by a special three-judge court appointed by the Virginia Supreme Court. In this case, however, the Commission on Local Government met with the parties' elected officials and their attorneys and urged them to enter formal negotiations with a mediator to attempt to resolve the dispute.[3] Though the parties were not optimistic about the likelihood of a negotiated settlement, each feeling the other side would be intractable in negotiations, they agreed at least to attempt formal talks. Each side felt they would soon return to litigation to settle the dispute, yet each side strongly felt that as local officials they could fashion a better settlement than could the court.

Cast as a dispute over a proposed boundary shift, the issues reflected a conflict between each community's view of its right to benefit from recent economic development and growth surrounding the central city. The city's spokesman pointed to empty downtown stores that had relocated to suburban shopping areas in the county, noting that the city needed to recapture its lost commercial base. The city claimed that it was the employment generator for thousands of new residents who were using city services but, not living in town, were not paying taxes. The city claimed that while it was a good neighbor to the county, in order to remain a fiscally viable government it was forced to extend its boundaries to capture the spillover growth across its borders. The county, on the other hand, claimed that Fredericksburg was seeking to take an important part of the county. County spokesmen noted that the county government had attracted new residents and shopping areas because it had funded the public infrastructure to support them. County spokesmen pointed to the county's relatively new schools, to its decision to place utility lines to serve a major commercial investor, to its development of an industrial park with county funds, and, above all, to its competence to provide modern public services as efficiently as the city. The county argued, in the press and before the state commission, that the proposed annexation was proposed theft by the city of county territory and of county people (voters, school children, and taxpayers). The county vowed to fight the annexation to the Virginia Supreme Court if necessary.

Initiating negotiations

At an initial meeting with the mediator, representatives from the city and county agreed to nominate negotiating teams, to select a neutral site for the negotiations, and to schedule a first joint meeting of the teams. In the interim the mediator met separately with each team and other elected officials to gain an understanding of their positions toward the negotiations and their specific positions on the issues. In these separate meetings the mediator and the parties exchanged views on the probable course of the negotiations, and on what the parties might expect in the process of the formal talks. As the county had filed a formal proceeding with the Commission on Local Government, and as a date approximately six weeks from the initiation of negotiations had been set for a public hearing by the commission, the negotiations were seen by both sides as focused and time-bounded, and not as tentative or exploratory sessions.

Both sides nominated negotiating teams of senior elected officials and policy executives. The county's team included the chairman of the county board of supervisors and two other elected officials, the county administrator, the county attorney, and a special counsel retained to handle the county's immunity suit and defense of the annexation suit before the commission and the state court. The special counsel was designated by the county team as their primary spokesman during the negotiations. The city's negotiating team included the mayor and three other members of the city council plus an alternate council member who sat in during negotiations. The elected officials did not comprise a majority of the twelve-member council, but did represent some of its most prominent members. The city's team also included the city manager, the city attorney, and a special counsel retained to argue the city's annexation case before the courts.

Exploring positions

Prior to the initiation of negotiations the parties had established public positions on the central issues. The county had formally requested the state, through the Commission on Local Government and the courts, to grant it immunity from annexation from the city along most of their joint border. The county was silent on the fate of the relatively limited borderline for which it was now seeking immunity from annexation. The city's public position was that it had, in past years, studied and considered annexing a relatively large area from the county and that it was now proposing to annex only a modest six square miles of land.

In the first phase of negotiations, the teams explored how far each might be willing to compromise its public position. In the exploratory phase each party took readings of the other's sense of compromise. Based on that reading, each party decided whether to go forward with the negotiations. In this phase, the degree of flexibility demonstrated by each side was just as important as the specific proposals offered.

A second function of the exploratory phase of negotiations was to give each team its first opportunity to work together to develop individual points of view on issues in the process of reacting to the proposals of other team members. The creation of a focused team identity in relation to the issues was an inevitable and crucial step in developing the negotiations process. Differences between individual members of negotiating teams surfaced and were considered in the reformulation of proposals received from the other side. These internal negotiations, the internal group development, and position-forming behavior took place in caucus sessions throughout the negotiating process. They were most important elements of the agreement-seeking process.

Competitive bargaining

After the negotiators examined each other's initial proposals and found a certain amount of flexibility, they rather quickly moved toward more competitive bargaining. Initial positive exchanges between the negotiators were soon replaced by more cautious position taking. The parties indicated to each other that they had gone very far in their initial offers, and that it would be almost impossible to go further. Both sides, to a greater or lesser degree, had worked out in advance what they believed their bottom line positions were. These positions had been developed unilaterally and did not account for the variability that surfaced in interactions between the two sets of negotiators. However, the original positions did serve as frameworks within which parties reviewed progress in the negotiations.

 The competitive bargaining process surfaced naturally in the presentations made by each side on the primary issue, the determination of a new boundary line between the communities. Isolated from the wider context of interlocal concerns, the boundary line controversy itself could only be won or lost. This win/lose context was reinforced by each party's determination to not appear to be the loser in exchanges. The competitive bargaining around the narrow issue of the new boundary line was thus stimulated by the nature of the problem.

Competitive bargaining did enable the parties to sharpen their views of the significance of the boundary line for each. Conflict and confrontation in joint sessions carried over to caucus sessions as each team reviewed its positions in light of the sharp points made by the other side. The confrontational aspects of the negotiations provided important information for the reformulation of proposals in preparation for joint meetings.

The negotiating process was able to maintain itself even in the context of limited confrontational bargaining. During this phase there was constant tension between the parties' desire to work out an agreement and the option to leave the process for more explicit and formal adversarial procedures.

The structure of the negotiations helped to maintain the process despite open conflict between the two sides. Meetings were conducted in the evening, at a neutral site, with separate caucus facilities available. The negotiating teams would frequently request a caucus period when issues surfaced that could not be immediately resolved in direct exchanges. New proposals and reconfigurations of current issues or of past issues would generally emerge from these caucus sessions. At certain critical points the two special counsel, who knew each other well, would suggest that they meet apart from the formal negotiations to attempt to bridge particularly difficult gaps between the parties. These meetings complemented the joint negotiations and assisted the teams in moving toward settlement.

Throughout the process the mediator monitored the negotiations and intervened selectively in two contexts. First, in caucus sessions with the parties and in the periods between the negotiating sessions, the mediator met with the parties and reviewed positions and characterizations of the negotiations. In certain instances the mediator actively assisted one party in developing proposals by focusing on key interests of the other negotiating teams.

In another role the mediator functioned as a facilitator in the joint meetings—in setting the initial agendas, in monitoring the flow of exchanges and, on occasion, in intervening to help clarify understanding of positions and points of discussion, and to modify certain dysfunctional exchanges between the parties.

Joint problem-solving

The third phase of the negotiations emerged after the parties had apparently reached impasse over key issues in competitive bargaining. A complete shift in orientation of the parties toward each other was made possible by the initiative of one individual, a city councilman. He looked beyond the boundary issue and formulated a proposal on the major utilities issues that was both comprehensive and of significant benefit to both sides.

The county and city had disagreed over water and sewer service issues for years. The most significant recent problem had involved the county's desire to have the city support its initiative in purchasing a retired industrial plant and converting it to a major waste water treatment facility. For various reasons the city had adamantly refused to participate in the new plant. The future of the industrial plant had become a sore point in city-county relations.

After the mediator's intervention, the city team acknowledged that further progress in negotiations required resolution of the issue of this plant. The city councilman on his own initiative developed a new approach to treating the water and sewerage requirements of the city and of that portion of the county in the same watershed as the city. His plan was a technically feasible and cost-effective alternative to the existing city and county utilities programs. He tested his proposal in caucus with city negotiators and in selective private contacts with members of the county negotiating team. It was a significant breakthrough and impressed all the negotiators with its scope and good sense.

The parties then fell into a joint discussion of how to improve the plan and how to implement it. Some limited bargaining took place, but the plan was so well conceived that, in the main, each side recognized its advantages and worked together to improve and clarify it. A professional engineer, employed as a consultant by both the city and county, was called upon to join the discussions. Both sides dropped the adversarial approach adopted in earlier negotiations to concentrate on jointly settling on the common major utilities scheme.

Return to competitive bargaining

After both negotiating teams accepted the concepts of the joint utilities initiative, they were again eager to complete negotiations on the boundary issue. However, the discussion of the boundary line again became competitive as each party sought concessions from the other side. In caucus sessions the parties reinforced their adversarial view of the negotiations. Positions hardened for the moment and the discussions were on the verge of breaking up. The negotiations lasted till late one night and recessed at impasse.

However, the positive gains of the negotiations had not been lost on the parties. Most of the land issues had been worked out in the previous round of competitive bargaining. Those agreements, added to the major achievements on the utilities, left both sides with the sense that they were close to an overall agreement and that they would best serve their communities by compromising on the final bits of land remaining. Against this feeling that an agreement was achievable, lay the sense, in each negotiating team, that they had gone about as far as possible. There were two dimensions to this feeling. First, each party felt that the still contested land represented significant economic resources for the community that "won" the boundary line controversy. Lesser political factors were complicated by each side's feeling that its original position had already been significantly compromised. Each felt that further compromise, without reciprocity from the other side, would be tantamount to losing in a win/lose context. As the remaining contested land involved relatively marginal concerns, the parties felt that any concessions made would not be reciprocal, but rather unilateral. They resisted the idea of compromise without reciprocity.

The next morning the two special counsel, the mediator, and the professional managers of the city and county met for breakfast and developed a compromise. Negotiations throughout the morning proceeded with the parties separated from one another and with the attorneys and the mediator meeting face to face and by telephone. Through these processes a final agreement on the new boundary line and on the immunity of the county from further annexation was developed in principle.

The written agreement

Translation of the agreement in principle to a written form took four days of detailed negotiation, primarily between the attorneys for the parties, the community managers, and the mediator. As unresolved differences surfaced they were recorded and later reviewed in special negotiating sessions involving key members of the negotiating teams. Through give and take, the parties sought to avoid any fatal impasse which could "unstick" the agreement. Each party competed to maximize its advantage on the details, within the framework of the major agreements. The time pressure created by the county's formal proceedings before the State Commission on Local Government discouraged the tactic of waiting out the other side on points of disagreement. The time factor was most important in focusing the parties on the necessity of striking the final compromises when they could.

The written agreement was reviewed by each negotiating team and presented to each full board of elected officials. Within two days the two full boards met in an extraordinary joint session, and each unanimously adopted the written agreement. In its final form the agreement consisted of a detailed seventeen-page contract and attachments delineating an expanded boundary for Fredericksburg, immunity from annexation for the county for twenty-five years, and a major joint public services contract covering water and sewer services in the region for twenty-five years. The immunity from further annexation and the joint utilities agreements may be extended at the parties' option for five years or longer after expiration of the initial twenty-five-year period.

The decision to enter mediation

A review of some key features of this case reveals a distillation of the dynamics of the mediation process in such disputes. The reader who is familiar with local government politics may assume that local elected officials would be most wary of entering a dispute settlement process with which they were unfamiliar. In this instance, the city and county entered mediation only after they were convinced on five points:

1. The process was authorized and endorsed by the state agency to whom the parties were required to submit their adversarial briefs. (Acceptance of the process was not mandated and remained a voluntary decision for each party.)
2. The parties each had in place formal adversarial proceedings that were procedurally unfolding during the period of negotiations. Thus the parties would easily return to formal proceedings leading to a court decision should negotiations break down.
3. The procedures attendant to formal proceedings under the controlling statute established a bounded time frame for negotiations, which could be modified only by mutual agreement of the parties.
4. The mediation role was indeed a neutral and nondecision-making one, and the mediator unbiased and experienced.
5. Each party desired to negotiate a settlement if possible.

Before entering the process the county checked with another county, and the city with another city that had participated in a mediation of an annexation case. They reviewed the process, the potential problems to their vital interests, and the mediator's role. In addition, each party took an initial reading of the other through formal channels and decided that true negotiations might be possible. The parties agreed that a negotiated settlement in which they could make the essential compromises would be preferable to a court-ordered settlement imposed upon them.

The negotiating process

With the parties' agreement the mediator structured a formal negotiation process, using a university board room for joint sessions with assigned separate caucus rooms for private discussions among team members. The formality of the framework was reinforced early in the negotiations when the parties adopted a short list of ground rules addressing such issues as a requirement for confidentiality in negotiations, an agreement that the mediator would make all press statements, and an agreement on the status of proposals should negotiations break down. The individual negotiators signed this negotiating document that the mediator drafted as directed by the parties.

In consultation with the parties and their attorneys the mediator designed a negotiating process that emphasized the development of formal written proposals first from one side, then from the other—a series of counterproposals addressing a package of issues raised through joint discussions and reflecting both marginal compromises from preceding positions and the addition of new ideas. The emphasis on formality was deliberate. The negotiating teams (elected and appointed officials and special counsel) were able to use the formal structure of the negotiation as a vehicle within which they could engage in tactical adversarial maneuvers (as they were determined to) and still feel that the negotiating process would be sustained. That is, in most phases of the negotiation the parties insisted on approaching the issues as adversaries seeking to "win" on certain points and, just as important, to avoid "losing" on certain points. Given this natural tendency to demonstrate "toughness" as individuals and as teams in a risk-filled environment with significant issues under discussion, the formal structure of proposals and counterproposals provided a frame of reference for the review both of formal positions and of the negotiators' feelings about how their adversaries were responding to their good-faith initiatives.

Negotiations typically became most heated when officials from one community, one team, challenged the good faith of the other team in making or commenting on proposals. The mediator did not always intervene in such confrontations, sensing that the conflict exposed in certain instances was beneficial to the progress of the discussions—as individuals forced one another to move off calculated positions and engage in discussions of their real interests and requirements.

In other instances, however, the mediator did intervene in the dynamics between the parties when, in his judgment, the negotiation itself was threatened. These interventions were purposely infrequent, reserving the neutral process role for selected important moments. The mediator was more fully involved in the substance of the issues, particularly in assisting one party in organizing its positions (the other party's special counsel attended the talks and helped his client develop positions).

As described above, movement toward agreement was unsteady, with points of agreement separated by periods of impasse and confrontation. The merit of the formal negotiation was to provide a means for the containment of adversarial relations within a wider context of agreement seeking. At points of impasse the process teetered on the edge of failure as the parties considered their positions and options.

Conclusions

The mediation process afforded the city and county a formal means to pursue structured negotiations toward dispute settlement. In the usual history of annexation disputes in Virginia the parties each would have expended large sums of money in purely adversarial case making before a special court which would have rendered a binding decision based on the submitted briefs. In this instance, however, the parties were able to negotiate their own settlement of the issues. This possibility offered two important positive outcomes to the disputants.

First, the local elected officials and managers most aware of the competing values at stake and the facts of the case were able to maintain a primary decision-making role in the case. Thus, those most expert in the equities of the situation were able to resolve the issues. They did not relinquish the dispute to a court for an external judicially imposed settlement that undoubtedly would have been different and less satisfactory to the parties than their own mutually determined outcomes.

Second, by maintaining an open negotiating process instead of relying on formal positions recorded in briefs for litigation, the parties were able to look beyond the immediate causes of the dispute to fashion a settlement that encompassed much wider interjurisdictional concerns. More than a decade of interlocal fighting over water and sewer issues were resolved in the settlement in this dispute. This wider concern would not have been considered in more traditional court processes. The mediation process enabled the parties to pursue political and technical negotiations within an organized forum for as long as they cared to do so. It deepened the possibility of achieving settlement of complex issues by providing a structure for their consideration. While it is possible that traditional political negotiating styles might have resolved the issues, it is not likely. Recourse to the courts was, after all, the tested and accepted procedure for resolving these interlocal boundary disputes.

Where third party mediation has been employed in dispute negotiations in the intergovernmental setting, it has generally been favorably reviewed by participating public officials. It is likely that mediation will become accepted as a means for intergovernmental dispute management if it is endorsed as a formal process by senior executives in agencies, and is authorized in enabling statutes. The evidence suggests that the process of providing a structured forum for political and technical negotiations of complex intergovernmental issues can transform traditional means of dispute resolution, and can improve the quality of intergovernmental decision making.

1. Chester W. Bain, *Annexation in Virginia* (Charlottesville, Va.: University of Virginia Press, 1966).

2. In an interesting development in the case, a group of concerned citizens formed an organization and determined to enter the case as intervenor before the court. The Commission on Local Government, in a fact-finding report advisory to the court, sustained the major components of the negotiated settlement, and endorsed the localities' agreements with two changes. The commission saw these changes as representing the state's interest in maintaining viable communities in the long run. The localities, the county in particular, saw the commission's proposed changes as inimical to their interests, and strenuously objected to any changes made by a state agency to an interlocal agreement. The court specially convened to hear evidence in the annexation case took the intervenor's comments and the commission's report under consideration and rendered a decision that sustained the negotiated settlement with only a minor change in the negotiated boundary line. The city and county accepted the court's decision. The mediation process thus took place within an administrative and judicial context in which the interests of those not at the bargaining table were able to be represented before the court prior to the effective date of the negotiated settlement.

3. In 1980, under a new statute, negotiated settlements were endorsed as an alternative to litigation to settle intergovernmental boundary disputes in Virginia (Code of Virginia, Section 15.1 945.7). Between 1980 and January 1985, of twenty-one annexation-related petitions, eighteen have been settled through negotiations. Seven cases have been settled through direct bilateral negotiations; in ten cases independent mediators were appointed; and in four cases the state agency provided technical assistance/conciliation services. Negotiations led by mediators have led to seven agreements.

David vs. Goliath: Shuttle Diplomacy in a Water Rate Dispute

Thomas E. Taylor and Matalyn Harp

This paper is purposely written in a style that attempts to capture the perceptions and biases inherent in the dispute; to illustrate the polarization of the principals that was developing; and to outline the issues that had to be addressed before genuine agreement was possible. Because of the purpose and writing style, there is some sacrifice of historical and technical accuracy.

Dallas provides retail water and wastewater service to its 900,000 citizens—plus wholesale services to several cities in the region. For years, the wholesale water services program provoked disputes with many of the cities. The disputes over contracts, rates, and services continued on and off for 20 years. In recent years the disputes were decidedly on—rather than off.

All efforts to settle the disputes met with failure. The circumstance called for a sure and final solution. The participants selected an age-old method: The mayors and the city managers of Dallas' 16 customer cities, with hatchets in hand, confronted the mayor, city manager, and utilities director of Dallas. This historic meeting took place in a cottonpatch outside the Dallas city limits on August 23, 1979. But, this historic meeting should not be misinterpreted. These city officials met, not to fight, but to sign a peace treaty and to bury the hatchet. They agreed never to fight over water again.

Now for the rest of the story.

History—Dallas' viewpoint

All good stories about water should include a drought. In north Texas it began with the great drought of the 1950s—the worst ever

Reprinted from *1982 AWWA Annual Conference Proceedings* by permission. Copyright © 1982, the American Water Works Association.

recorded in the area. Dallas ran short of water. The suburban cities ran short also, but much sooner than Dallas. Dallas shared its limited water supplies and began regular service to its first customer city. Many of the growing suburban cities recognized the need for a more dependable water supply, and Dallas offered that opportunity.

The drought was severe, continuing unrelenting for more than six years. In the last stages of the drought, only poor quality water was available. These difficult times made a lasting impression on Dallas. The leaders committed that "never again" would Dallas experience a shortfall in its water supply. A blue ribbon citizens' committee developed a master plan to provide adequate surface water supplies for Dallas and nearby "county towns"—a supply that would be adequate for anticipated growth between 1958 (the date of the plan) and the year 2000.

Dallas continued to serve suburban cities. In the beginning, the contracts were surplus water contracts to supplement the various cities' groundwater supplies. But as the water table began to fall and as the wells became inadequate to provide for the growth of the suburban cities, most switched to permanent contracts with Dallas. Before service to other cities began, Dallas already had two major surface water supply reservoirs. An aggressive development program produced three additional reservoirs within a few years. The five reservoirs provided an abundant capacity, sufficient for growth of the entire service area until the year 2000. Yet, the rates Dallas charged customer cities were far less than the cost would have been had they developed their own supplies.

Dallas took all the responsibility to plan, finance, and build water supply reservoirs, transmission lines, and treatment plants. Customer cities took no responsibility. They seemed complacent about the immense financial and technical responsibilities. They just wanted cheap water and plenty of it.

History—customer cities' viewpoint

The cities went to Dallas to obtain permanent water supplies because they had no choice. Dallas—the big city—had tied up all the water rights in the region and effectively blocked customer cities from any direct access to their own supply. Additional water supplies from out of the region had to be developed and the customer cities supported Dallas in the acquisition of those water rights. In return for that support, Dallas promised to serve. Dallas was not doing the customer cities a favor.

Dallas offered contracts to the suburban cities; however, it was on a "take it or leave it" basis. There were no genuine negotiations. In fact, Dallas tended to use water as a tool for control of growth in the region. Suburban cities had encircled Dallas, so Dallas could not grow. But through its control of water supplies, Dallas was able to affect other cities. Two cities gave up the fight and decided to consolidate with Dallas. In spite of the efforts of Dallas, the suburban cities continued to grow faster than Dallas and became a force to be reckoned with.

Yes, customer cities had contracts; but Dallas would unilaterally change the contracts and the rates. Contracts specified that service would be provided "at cost." Dallas included a profit in its rates; customer cities believed that "cost" should mean just that: "at cost." Also, who was to pay for these reservoirs constructed for the future growth of Dallas and the various cities it was serving? Dallas claimed for its exclusive benefit the older reservoirs for which the water development cost was less than 5¢ per thousand gallons. The customer cities were to pick up the cost of the new reservoirs constructed at a cost several times that of the old reservoirs. Dallas may have considered this method a fair distribution of cost—but the customer cities certainly did not. The rates were already high and this policy would have led to astronomical rates for customer cities, and the subsidization of Dallas' growth by customer cities. The customer cities tried to talk to Dallas, tried to reason with it. The only recourse appeared to be litigation.

The dispute—Dallas' viewpoint

The drought of the 1950s was barely over before one city began grumbling about its water contract and the rates it was paying. Before long, two cities were involved. One of the cities even used its police department to create a confrontation with the city of Dallas. By 1973 these two cities had filed suit. At first the suit was not perceived to be a problem. Dallas defended its program and an outcome favorable to Dallas was expected. However, other cities eventually joined the suit. Ganging up on the big city seemed to be great sport for the suburban cities.

The dispute—customer cities' viewpoint

The dispute as Dallas saw it was oversimplified. There were some real issues involved.

Negotiation of contracts   There was no genuine negotiation. Dallas wrote the contracts and offered them to customer cities on a "take it or leave it" basis.

Fairness of rates   Dallas set the rates too high. Customer cities were not involved and did not participate in rate determination.

Rate methodology   There was no agreement on how the rates were to be determined. Dallas was somewhat mysterious about its financial results.

Utility versus cash method   Dallas did not always use the same method for determining rates. On occasion it would use the traditional cash method practiced by municipalities. On other occasions it would use the utility method practiced by investor-owned utilities.

Decision making   Dallas made decisions without participation by customer cities. Dallas decided when and what to build and how much water to make available to customer cities.

Assurance of a firm supply   There was no such assurance. From year to year Dallas would let customer cities know how much they might have available.

Moratorium

Customer cities were concerned about "assurance of supply." But, there was one *big assurance that Dallas didn't have*. It had *no assurance* that it would ever get its money back for the tremendous investment in water supply reservoirs, transmission lines, and treatment facilities. A large percentage of Dallas' investment was made on behalf of customer cities in anticipation of their future growth.

Two years after litigation started there was no end in sight. The suburban cities seemed to be gaining strength in the fight as more joined in. Dallas got its belly full; the city council in 1975 declared a moratorium. Until the disputes were settled, there were to be:

1.   No more investments on behalf of customer cities
2.   No more construction on behalf of customer cities
3.   No new contracts with other cities.

Dallas had 16 customer cities—16 cities fighting Dallas. That was enough.

If the customer cities were not willing to pay Dallas its legitimate cost, then Dallas could not, in good conscience, take any further risk in their behalf.

A strategy for settlement—Dallas' viewpoint

The litigation continued five years with no letup. All 16 cities were now involved. Dallas' long-range planning was beginning to be affected. The moratorium was beginning to have its impact on the region, creating uncertainty. Suburban cities wouldn't negotiate nor cooperate on other regional issues of interest to Dallas. The water dispute was blocking progress.

The civic leadership became concerned; they got involved. Beginning in 1978 there was a continuous 12-month period of negotiation when various individuals and some groups were trying to get the matter solved. However, certain critical factors caused a settlement to remain elusive. Much of the effort was perceived to be an attempt to "sell" Dallas' position. Attempts to compromise were unsuccessful because, in part, the individuals had not yet fully comprehended the problem. Discussions typically were in group meetings; a few vocal members of the group resisted genuine compromise; the true feelings of the majority did not surface. The high profile approach was not working.

Many people of good will had tried to bring the disputing parties together in agreement—but without success. Might as well forget a mutually satisfactory agreement and let the litigation run its course—right? Wrong! All that was needed was a new initiative.

In 1979, Dallas city manager George R. Schrader realized that all the veterans at city hall (and some outside city hall) had tried and failed. He offered a bold new strategy. The city manager took himself and the other responsible officials (city attorney and utilities director)—all of whose viewpoints were well known—out of the process. There were two new kids on the block: Dr. Camille Barnett, the new assistant city manager, and Tom Taylor, the new assistant director of water utilities. The city manager assigned Barnett and Taylor as a team with delegated authority to assess the situation and determine if a settlement were possible. If not, the alternative to continuing the litigation remained. If they determined that settlement was possible, the city manager authorized them to negotiate and bring about agreement. All discussions were to be confidential without participation by or influence from those who had been taken out of the process.

Barnett and Taylor adopted a strategy, an approach not previously used locally, but one that was responsive to the situation. Shuttle diplomacy it was to be, with emphasis on "one-on-one" informal discussion, a formidable task—recognizing that there were 16 cities involved. The steps:

1. Meet with each city manager or mayor.
2. Do little talking. Listen.
3. Offer no opinion. Listen.
4. Don't defend Dallas. Listen.
5. Determine what the problem is.
6. Identify the issues blocking agreement.
7. Identify the leaders whose support would be necessary for a settlement.

After several rounds of discussion, Camille Barnett and Tom Taylor developed a list of issues and alternative scenarios for addressing the issues. Each alternative was rated against rigid criteria that included such topics as saleability, financial soundness, regulatory compliance, etc.

The issues and response to the issues were discussed in another round of one-on-one meetings. Only after there was reasonable confidence that the effort was approaching a mutually satisfactory end result was the first group meeting called for a collective response. In the group meeting it was explained how the proposed settlement took into account all the views, all the problems, and all the concerns that had been expressed by each of the managers individually. In subsequent meetings the group reviewed, revised, and ratified the compromise solution.

Strategy—customer cities' viewpoint

Dallas likes to take credit for its brilliant strategy and how it brought about a settlement. The settlement was possible, really, because of what the customer cities were doing. The customer cities had formed a committee for fair water rates. That seemed a good name to call it. Money was put into the war chest. The committee hired an attorney. There was unanimity among the group as Camille Barnett and Tom Taylor were meeting with the managers one on one, discussing with each the issues and the problems. When Tom and Camille left one city manager's office, that manager would call ahead to let the rest know the nature of the discussion and the issues being discussed. There was coordination among the customer cities. Because they had done their homework and were coordinating and sticking together, a settlement was possible, and was achieved.

The winners!

The customer cities ratified the settlement because they won.

1. Customer cities got to share in the old, lower cost water from the regional reservoirs.
2. Rates were to be made on a utility basis at original cost—not the current or replacement cost that Dallas had been advocating.
3. The settlement allowed customer cities to have unlimited growth potential because Dallas had a plan for the year 2050 and was proceeding with reservoir development.

The methodology for making rates was fair and agreed upon in advance. Dallas would continue to finance the system. With its AAA rating, Dallas could finance facilities at lower cost than the customer cities.

Dallas ratified the settlement because it won. Dallas finally got a signed agreement covering most of the issues causing dispute over the 20-year period.

1. Customer cities expressly assumed their share of the responsibilities.
2. The litigation was dismissed.
3. The agreement did not require Dallas to give refunds for past charges.
4. The utility basis for setting rates, with its allowance for a fair rate of return on investment, gave assurance that Dallas would recover its cost. Customer cities would bear their share of the cost of new and future reservoirs.
5. In anticipation of suburban cities' growth being greater than that of Dallas, the agreement provided for customer cities to carry a proportionately larger share of reserve water supply costs.

The continuing process

Both sides thought that they won. But nobody would win if the process didn't continue. After the agreement Dallas began quarterly meetings at which the city managers, mayors, and utility directors communicate with their counterparts. These meetings provide for an exchange of information, an update on current projects, and committee reports. The committee system is used: on rates, on contracts, and on water resources. The customer city officials participate in all the key decisions.

A major participatory activity is rate making. Customer cities are involved through their committee during the cost of service study. Participation during the cost of service process provides the cities with an "ownership" in the outcome and reduces possible objections. There is open communication; there is input; and, there is cooperative decision making. The process is not highly structured and offers much flexibility. The process since the settlement has worked well and Dallas is now extending the concept to the cities provided with wastewater treatment services.

Results and benefits

The settlement provides that Dallas will continue a central unified management concept of regional utility services. This provides for maximum efficiency. It's a partnership arrangement, a peer relationship. History and the dispute were laid to rest. The parties look to the future without wasting energies on fighting each other.

The settlement and continuing agreement provide a solid basis for orderly planning. Planning is now underway for the period beyond the year 2000. Two additional reservoirs have been started since the settlement. Once these reservoirs are completed, all cities will have water supply adequate to the year 2035.

Each customer class is now carrying its fair share of cost. A cornerstone of the settlement is that it safeguards the regional concept which provides adequate water supply for all in the region at the lowest possible cost. Dallas is assured a return on its investment and can commit funds with confidence. And, finally, intergovernmental agreements on issues such as transportation and solid waste are now possible. Renewed vigor is being breathed into the economy of the region.

Postscript

It is working. The agreement signed in 1979 is standing up in the real world. In 1985 the regional system is meeting the needs of both the large central city and the many suburban cities. No one is losing. Everyone is winning.

Let Us Reason Together: New Tools for Resolving Local Disputes

Wendy Emrich

Imagine a landfill dispute (it's not hard) involving a town, city, county, local citizen groups, and two state agencies. The city, whose old landfill is nearly full, is engineering and licensing a new landfill to be located in the neighboring town. The state public intervenor (a statutory watchdog), supported by the citizen groups, goes to court challenging the adequacy of the state regulatory agency's environmental impact assessment. The town, concerned with such issues as hours of operation, noise, traffic, and recycling, files its suit against construction.

Each party feels a sense of urgency and realizes that it cannot win all it wants at a reasonable cost by going through litigation. The parties agree to seek settlement elsewhere.

Enter a new decision-making process—*environmental mediation*. A trained neutral mediator assists the parties in developing an agreement which is acceptable to all: the landfill can be built on the site but with limited hours of operation to reduce noise; the city must build a transfer station for compacting waste (which reduces truck traffic and creates the opportunity for recycling); and a plan is devised for cooperative siting of future landfills. The agreement is implemented through a consent order issued by the state agency and ordinance provisions enacted by the city and town.

Pipe dream. Sound too easy? In 1978, two mediators from the Wisconsin Center for Public Policy's Environmental Mediation

Wendy Emrich, "Let Us Reason Together: Environmental Mediation and Other New Tools for Resolving Local Disputes," *Environmental Currents*, newsletter of the Brandywine Conservancy's Environmental Management Center, Chadds Ford, Pennsylvania, Vol. 6, No. 2, Fall, 1981.

Project helped resolve just such a dispute over the Seven Mile Creek landfill in Eau Claire County.

"We were able to accomplish what we wanted and the other parties got what they wanted," explains George Kumferman, then acting city manager of Eau Claire. "We had to agree to some things that were hard to swallow, but without mediation, the other side would have held us up in court beyond the construction season. It was time to get the thing settled."

Use of mediation and similar techniques in environmental and land use disputes is on the rise, and it is easy to see why. Most people and groups handle public conflicts in one way: as adversaries. When you think about it, the processes we have been using in environmental disputes—public meetings, administrative hearings, court suits—tend to foster extremist and uncompromising positions which do little to solve the real problems. And look at the results:

1. Decisions dictated by others, not solutions developed cooperatively among the parties themselves.
2. Outcomes that often are rooted in procedural points, not in substantive issues.
3. "Winners" and "losers" who usually are more embittered and opposed to each other after the proceeding than before.

What is the alternative? There *are* some new techniques available which are meant to be "no lose" propositions. They all involve some type of joint problem solving or group negotiations which allow the participants themselves to invent solutions for their own problems. Better working relationships are formed so that future disputes can be handled more constructively.

This is not to say that adversarial methods are always "wrong." Environmental lawsuits in the last two decades have been crucial instruments for halting irresponsible and ill-conceived projects. In those cases where collaboration or compromise is conceivable and preferable, however, some innovative techniques—such as mediation, facilitation, and conflict assessment—are available and can be applied at the municipal level.

The same Wisconsin group, for example, recently conducted a mediation over provision of a new water system to a subdivision in the town of Fitchburg, near Madison. The 110-home subdivision was built 20 years ago in a semi-rural area and furnished with six community wells by the developer (who had a 10-year contract to own and operate the system). Following the contract's expiration, state testing revealed high bacteria counts during certain times of the year, forcing the state to order residents to boil their water. The controversy continued to build over the next 10 years when the developer, while feeling a moral obligation to maintain the system, finally had to disclaim responsibility or ability to make any further repairs. (This was due to the fact that the developer's sons had inherited the business and assets were not available.)

The property owners were at the end of their rope. The town refused to add the subdivision to its utility district. No one was budging.

The state Department of Natural Resources, preferring to avoid legal action or creation of a sanitary district which it might have to operate itself by default, called in the Wisconsin Environmental Mediation Project in 1979. Says Cynthia Sampson, associate director of the project, "Everyone told us, 'It will never work. Nothing short of litigation will solve this one.'"

But mediation did work. In one year—after extensive information-sharing, research, caucusing and negotiating sessions—the 10-year problem was resolved. The town agreed to construct a new water system to be operated by its utility district in return for a cash payment and various land donations (for new community well sites and an enlarged park) by the developer.

Tom Ruda, previously a supervisor on the Fitchburg Town Board, looks back on the dispute. "Without mediation," he says, "we'd still be there fighting."

Why does mediation work in these situations of stalemate? After all, parties to land use and environmental disputes are, in the main, always free to negotiate settlements. Howard Bellman, director of the Wisconsin Environmental Mediation Project, explains:

"Mediation simply adds the participation of a neutral person who applies the skills of a conflict resolution specialist. The mediator facilitates the negotiation process by conducting meetings, moderating antagonistic or unconstructive behavior, clarifying the issues, exploring the parties' priorities and areas of flexibility in private caucuses, and identifying areas of possible compromise not immediately apparent to the parties."

As useful and heartening as these mediation examples are, many municipalities are equally interested in resolving contentious issues *before* impasse occurs. What does the field of "environmental conflict management" offer in this regard? One approach, *negotiated development*, can be "mediation-like" in nature, but hopefully occurs before a stalemate and may or may not utilize the services of an outside third party. The best known case is that of White Flint Mall in Montgomery County, Maryland. Frustrated in its first attempt to construct a regional shopping center, Federated Department Stores hired a planning firm from Washington, D.C., to act as intermediary in negotiations among the company, the county, and the citizens.

After numerous sessions with neighborhood groups and government agencies, an agreement was reached which met the needs of all parties. The company got its rezoning and the go-ahead to build. The adjacent property owners won potential compensation for any future decline in the value of their homes, elimination of access to the shopping center through the neighborhood, and construction of a landscaped berm. To benefit the county, Federated agreed to reduce the net load on the county's sewage treatment plant by installing a water recycling system in the mall and treating some of the sewage from residential areas in its own nearby (and underused) treatment plant.

Malcolm Rivkin, principal of the Washington planning firm, likes to point out that while local governments and developers have been "negotiating development" for years, particularly over zoning modifications, the term as used here refers to a more open process which includes a wider range of parties and issues. Under this concept, citizen groups and individual property owners are able to join the process and help negotiate project components as varied as landscaping, lighting, storm drainage, impact mitigation, and compensation. "Third parties" which facilitate these negotiations need not be outside consultants. As conditions allow, that role can be filled by staff or local officials (e.g., a planning commissioner) who are viewed as sufficiently unbiased.

In a 1980 report titled *Negotiated Development: An Alternative Urban Strategy for the 80's*, issued by FORUM on Community and the Environment in California, municipalities showed increased awareness that, while broader community consultation at the beginning may take more time, it can, *if properly managed*, help avoid public opposition "in a stronger form at a later date, after a large investment of time and money."

"Properly managed" is the key. Given its track record, the prospect of *more* public participation in land use decisions may not be particularly alluring to local officials. Another rowdy neighborhood meeting is not what they need. Techniques which loosely fall under the heading of *joint problem solving*, however, are geared precisely to avoid a public free-for-all. A joint problem solving process is one that clarifies and resolves differences among groups, *before* positions become so entrenched that formal negotiations are required. Participants define and analyze problems, generate alternative solutions, and reach informal agreements. Instead of developing negotiating positions from which to bargain, they work collaboratively as a group to build consensus at each step.

To keep things in hand, (i.e., to assure "proper management"), such a process usually is conducted by a trained facilitator. A specialist in meeting dynamics, the facilitator makes sure that everyone's opinion is heard, assists the parties to define the key issues and rank them for orderly discussion, and ensures that agreements on process and substance are reached at each point along the way.

The *facilitation method* for running a meeting can provide a breath of fresh air when used in place of, or in addition to, a standard public hearing. After all, the agenda, meeting procedures, seating arrangements, and speaking format for most public hearings encourage competition, not cooperation. If government officials are really serious about seeking help in resolving environmental issues, then they may want to consider a forum that allows something besides rancorous testimonials made by opposing parties.

Case in point: developing controversial regulations. In Colorado, the State Air Quality Control Commission asked ROMCOE, Center for Environmental Problem Solving in Boulder, to develop a cooperative approach to designing air visibility protection regulations. (Such an approach would supplement, not replace, the formal public hearing process.) "The commission members were searching for a new direction," explains ROMCOE. "They were frustrated with the recurring syndrome of public hearings where angry interest groups all congregate to oppose regulations already drafted by the commission staff."

Toward the objective of involving the various interests early in the regulatory development process, the commission charged ROMCOE with bringing together some 40 different parties to come up with criteria and procedures for developing the regulations (but not to develop the regulations themselves). During four different sessions, ROMCOE, as facilitator, organized the parties (representing industry, state and federal government, and environmental organizations) into small working groups to tackle different sets of problems. Following the last session, designated members made a final report to the commission which detailed both the areas of consensus and the few remaining areas of disagreement.

While the entire air visibility protection program is now on hold (due to the uncertain future of the Clean Air Act), the commission was so encouraged by "the ROMCOE process" that, in a letter of appreciation to ROMCOE, it stated a desire to look for other opportunities where a similar cooperative approach could be used.

There is nothing particularly mystical about this type of approach. Stripped of its conflict management trappings, in many ways "early joint problem solving" simply represents "better planning." The assistance of a neutral third party and/or certain facilitation devices lend a new twist. But, these techniques aside, devising new ways of bringing together varied, if not opposing, interests earlier in the planning process to avoid later conflict is an expanding concern among managers and planners alike.

The "pre-application conference" is one such device. On the East coast, the Urban Waterfront Action Group, through a subcommittee on joint processing and permit coordination for the Delaware Estuary Coastal Zone, is using the conference technique. (The Zone includes all of the Delaware River frontage and Philadelphia and Delaware Counties and part of Bucks County.) The subcommittee offers the conference service to get waterfront developers and regulatory agencies together early in the process to resolve problems which—if left to fester—could result in worse delays and higher costs later on. *Coastal Tidings* (Pennsylvania Coastal Management newsletter) reported in its July 1981 issue, "Applicants who have participated in subcommittee conferences expressed strong support for the concept." A prime mover in establishing the pre-application conference has been the Delaware Valley Regional Planning Commission, which also manages the Delaware Estuary Coastal Zone program. Michael Wolf, program manager, DVRPC, observes, "The procedure has taken off. We are pleased by the response, and are working to make the system even more streamlined." Noting that the UWAG approach was inspired, in part, by the municipal sketch plan process for subdivision reviews, Wolf surmises, "Developers, while still rather overwhelmed by the number of permits needed, would rather get all their bad medicine at once than face continued hurdles later on." He notes that a major factor in the program's early success has been the willingness of the regulatory agency representatives to travel to one central location, thus relieving the applicant from coming to each of them.

Perhaps the simplest—but sometimes most important—function a neutral party can perform is a *conflict assessment.* This is exactly as it sounds: a hard look at a given conflict's dimensions, with suggestions for a way out of the dilemma. A written conflict assessment is meant to be a tool for the parties *themselves* to review the key issues in a new light, and then to devise a process for resolving them.

As an example, Grand Lake, Colorado, hired an engineering firm to develop optional plans for a new sewage treatment facility. EPA rejected five separate plans and then asked ROMCOE to do an assessment of the problem. After comprehensive interviews with a range of individuals and agencies, ROMCOE offered recommendations which then allowed the engineers themselves to design a system acceptable to the community and EPA.

When a municipality is not inclined to bring in the assistance of an outside third party, what can it do on its own? Local planning departments often are caught in the role of "conflict managers," whether or not they choose to be. And many planners, when jammed between a developer and a community group, find themselves wanting more than just survival skills.

At the request of the planning director in Boulder, Colorado, ROMCOE put on a one-day conflict management training session for the city's staff. Focusing on such communication skills as active listening, ROMCOE showed the staff how better to handle irate citizens, how to be more constructive in saying no to developers, how to work together as a support team in conflict situations, and how to mediate among various interest groups. The staff also learned about the nature of conflict, how it escalates, and the importance of doing an informal conflict analysis in problem situations.

Frank Gray, Boulder planning director, is enthusiastic about the results. "My staff continues to tell me that the training really helped," he reports. Budget permitting, he also hopes to provide facilitation/mediation training. "I feel very strongly that planners these days need to be professional facilitators," Gray adds.

While intriguing, these new approaches are not a panacea. They will only be appropriate in certain circumstances and must be used selectively. But they *should* be seen as additional tools for local governments so that public officials need not rely solely on existing procedures to anticipate, prevent, and solve disputes.

In Pennsylvania, the above-described landfill, subdivision water system, and regional shopping center cases may sound all too familiar. As in all states, however, Pennsylvania local governments must evaluate new mediation-type techniques in the light of state enabling laws for planning, administrative procedures, etc. The Municipalities Planning Code in Pennsylvania has certain rules concerning timing of applications and reviews, required public hearings, etc., which put some bounds on when and how new techniques could be used. But there remain ample opportunities, it would seem, for communities to experiment with additional approaches. It is up to the municipality to set the tenor for how such procedures might be tried.

There already are situations in Pennsylvania where localities are utilizing earlier cooperative measures with affected interest groups. The sketch plan mechanism, as one example, provides an opportunity for early consultation and collaboration. Pre-application or pre-proposal conferences (such as those held with the township engineer, as provided for in the EMC's model Storm Water Management Ordinance) are another instance. Informal arbitration of runoff-created property disputes also is part of the model ordinance; while philosophically somewhat distinct from the mediation techniques discussed here, such an arbitration process does represent a method available to local governments for resolving environmental conflicts outside "normal channels."

Who and How? Participation in Environmental Negotiation

A. Bruce Dotson

How negotiations are structured has significant consequences for the eventual outcome of the dispute resolution effort. Who participates and in what ways are among the key elements of this structure. The three negotiations over local land use described here illustrate how the element of participation was critical in each instance to the results achieved. In two of the cases, written agreements were reached successfully. Only partial success was achieved in the other case. The cases will be analyzed in terms of what they may suggest about participation generally.

Four aspects of participation deserve special attention. First, different modes of interaction (direct face-to-face negotiation, shuttle diplomacy, and indirect bargaining through the public hearing process) are illustrated in the described cases. Second, where direct interaction between the parties was involved, the cases also illustrate that different actors can fulfill a broker function by taking the initiative and suggesting mediation to the parties. A trusted outsider, a part-time counselor, and a full-time staff member each played this role in the cases here. Third, the motivation to participate in direct negotiations is often the result of pressure imposed by a less desirable but viable alternative, and shortage of time before that alternative becomes locked in. The cases here illustrate how both the presence and absence of such pressures condition the likelihood that participants will be able to reach a negotiated outcome. Fourth, negotiations are possible only if the larger political and legal system legitimates and empowers the negotiative process. The

From *Environmental Impact Assessment Review*, Vol. 4, No. 2, 1983. Reprinted with permission of Plenum Publishing Corp.

cases here illustrate different ways that local government officials legitimated the process, in one instance by personal participation and position taking in direct negotiations and in the other instances by more passive endorsement of the process generally.

All of the cases illustrate that the mediator must maintain an adaptive posture and adjust the structure of each dispute. The structuring process itself is a sort of negotiation between the mediator, with his ideas of what ought to be and what might work, and the other participants, with their attitudes toward each other and the kind of process they would be willing to participate in.

Warrenton townhouse dispute

In the Warrenton case, the results of face-to-face bargaining involving all parties can be contrasted favorably with the outcome of earlier positional bargaining that took place implicitly through formal public hearings. Face-to-face negotiations made it possible to open new options by uncovering underlying interests. The public hearing process led to compromises in initial positions but failed to resolve basic problems. (This element, interacting with other factors, illustrates the value of face-to-face negotiations compared to more traditional public participation mechanisms.)

Warrenton is a small town situated 45 minutes south of Washington, D.C. It is a quietly attractive place centered on an historic downtown. The town's many neighborhoods of older single-family homes appeal to long-term residents as well as an increasing number of new arrivals commuting to D.C. firms and offices.

The six-acre parcel of land that was the subject of this dispute lies along a tree-lined street in one of the town's designated historic neighborhoods. The parcel was vacant and had acted as a neutral zone between the neighborhood and a railroad, a light industrial area, and a low-income neighborhood. The residents felt that the disposition of this parcel would set the direction that the whole neighborhood would take in the future.

The parcel was long, narrow, and steeply sloping and, as a result, difficult to develop conventionally. It was zoned to allow up to 10 dwelling units per acre but would require a special use permit if the design flexibility allowed under a clustering provision was to be utilized. There had been periods of controversy about development of this parcel for several years. Neighborhood opposition plus a soft market had stalled the owner/developer's intentions. In the summer of 1982 he resolved to take whatever steps were necessary to develop the property and took out an application for a cluster development. Neighborhood residents and town-wide improvement league members organized a petition drive, wrote letters, and presented testimony at a series of public hearings. Considerable lobbying also took place outside the hearings.

The developer recognized that the considerable strength of the opposition might cause town officials to refuse the necessary permits. To head off such a denial, he was willing to modify his proposal to meet the multiple specific objections voiced at each hearing by the project's neighbors. This kind of indirect and unfocused exchange between the developer, town officials, and the neighbors resulted in the developer substantially modifying his proposal to the point that he felt it was fruitless to compromise further. He had reduced density. He had created a huge open space buffer between the townhouses and the street and proposed to fill this area with an evergreen screen that would shield his project from view. He had eliminated all driveways to the neighborhood street. He had made other concessions as well. However, the neighbors continued to object.

The town council finally denied the use permit. The developer's substantial concessions failed to gain assent from either the neighbors or town officials. He was convinced that his detractors just didn't want the land developed at all. In a dramatic exit from the council chambers, the developer vowed to forget the cluster approach and force a conventional development onto the property, as he legally could while meeting the letter of the law. If the town denied that proposal, he felt he would have a clear shot at winning a suit in the state courts. Many observers recognized that the situation had gotten out of control and had resulted in a lose-lose outcome. The parties' inability to agree on a better approach was leading to a development less desirable to all.

The second phase of the Warrenton process began when an official in an adjoining jurisdiction suggested privately to each of the parties that they consider mediation. The official was acquainted with both the developer and some of the neighbors and was familiar with the mediation process. At this point, the Institute for Environmental Negotiation was contacted. After several exchanges of phone calls and subsequent meetings between the mediator and each of the parties, they agreed to try face-to-face negotiations. At the same time, the developer indicated his intent to draw up and submit a conventional plan that would meet the letter of the zoning law. This was to be his insurance policy. A neighborhood meeting was subsequently held. A team of three negotiators was selected and priority issues were identified.

Town officials declined to participate directly in the negotiations or to formally endorse the process. They felt that there would be a role conflict if they took part in the discussions designing an alternative and then approved that proposal in their official capacity. They preferred simply to be kept informed. The town manager resisted efforts by the mediator to involve one or more people as town representatives. One person remarked that the absence of town participation wouldn't be crucial because the town council was simply reflecting the political pressures applied by others. Since the developer and the neighbors were going to meet face-to-face, it didn't matter that the town wasn't there. The town would likely go along with almost anything on which the parties could agree.

With team representatives selected, a series of joint bargaining sessions were held. What occurred surprised both sides. The neighbors discovered that they had a substantial amount of misinformation about the developer's earlier proposal, even though it had been aired several times in public hearings. They were not even aware of some of the concessions that his drawings showed. The developer discovered that the premise he held about the neighbors' concerns was off in the wrong direction. The concessions he made were the wrong ones. Rather than wanting to screen and buffer and separate the townhouse project from the neighborhood, the residents actually wanted to blend the development into the neighborhood so that it would not stand apart as being different. Once this organic issue and the neighbors' and developer's underlying interests became understood, it was then possible in a half dozen meetings to fashion a twenty-one-point agreement.

Buildings were moved up closer to the street to approximate the setback of the existing homes. The evergreen screen was removed and replaced with deciduous trees that would form a seasonal canopy like that already found along the street. Along the frontage of the project, density was lowered but it was made up elsewhere on the site without objection. The grouping of eight townhouses into a single structure was broken up with no grouping along the street to contain more than four units. Driveways to the front units were reinstituted. The parties agreed to specific architecture for each building. These were among the provisions arrived at and put into specific written language.

The developer agreed to propose that these stipulations be made conditions of his use permit from the town. The neighborhood team convened a neighborhood meeting where the negotiated plan won general support. At the hearings before town officials, both sides requested approval of the negotiated plan. The neighborhood spokesman in particular took pains to explain why this plan met underlying concerns of the residents. Town officials approved the plan intact with many congratulatory remarks.

This case illustrates several important aspects of participation. There are multiple reasons why this dispute was brought to a successful resolution, but one was the shift in the mode of participation that in the second phase brought the adversaries together for face-to-face dialogue. Clearly too, the pressure to find a better outcome was increased when the developer, at the end of the first phase, threatened to pursue a conventional design and then made good by doing so. However, that pressure alone does not explain the nature of the final agreements. Face-to-face bargaining made it possible for the parties to discover their own underlying interests and those of the other side. Since the town unanimously approved the agreement, apparently it was not crucial that the town did not participate in or even formally recognize the negotiations.

Other experiences reveal that under certain conditions, agency participation is more important than it was in Warrenton. In the next case, the town formally endorsed mediation and arranged to pay for the mediator. However, town officials preferred not to participate in the negotiations themselves.

Timberville assisted housing dispute

The outcome of the Timberville dispute, unlike that in Warrenton, was at best a partial success. The Timberville case illustrates how settlement can be frustrated by failing to have effective participation from a crucial stakeholder. The reasons for this include unusual bitterness as a result of the dispute and what appears to have been misunderstandings between the property owner and his attorney/ representative. In addition, shifts in federal funding caused the anticipated project to become financially infeasible. Secondly, the case illustrates the frequent need for mediators to prepare the parties, especially *ad hoc* groups, to participate in negotiations before joint meetings of the opposing sides can occur.

Timberville is a small rural town of only slightly over 500 households situated in the Shenandoah Valley region of Virginia. The main industries in the region are agriculture and food packing. Several food packing firms, employing a substantial number of lower wage workers, are located near, but not in, Timberville. The subject of this dispute was a proposal by an outside developer to build an assisted rental housing project in Timberville for low and moderate income occupants with Section 8 and state housing finance authority funding. Ninety-six units were proposed for a 10-acre site adjoining existing single family neighborhoods on three sides, and served by a narrow secondary street shared with two of the neighborhoods.

The arguments made against this project were multiple: too many assisted units for a town of this size, excessive traffic in relation to road capacity, rapid exhaustion of capacity in the town's sewage treatment plant, alleged understandings at the time of the property's rezoning years earlier, adverse impact on property values, lack of jobs in town, and what was seen by some as an effort to sneak this project into town without the neighbors knowing about it or being able to participate in the decision.

The legal basis of the controversy was a provision in the state housing finance authority's enabling statute. The statute provides that localities may disapprove VHDA financing within 60 days.

Even though the site was properly zoned, the town exercised its option to turn down the financing for this development. This occurred at the conclusion of a loud and somewhat ugly town council meeting.

The developer, a black man representing a firm from the much more urban northern part of the state, did not own the property but had planned to purchase it once financing was approved for the project. His firm had not prepared site plans or drawings that would show how the ninety-six units would be handled. The neighbors imagined the worst. The owners of the land were two brothers, respected in the community, who in earlier years had themselves built many of the single-family homes now occupied by the opponents of this project. One of the brothers currently was a member of the town council.

After the town rejected the financing in the heated atmosphere of the hearing and its aftermath, the property owners were incensed and felt genuinely injured. They vowed to drag the town into a messy court case and directed their attorney to file suit.

This is where the dispute stood when the attorney retained by the town suggested that the council hire a mediator to intervene between the neighbors and the property owners. One council member privately offered assurances that the town council would go along with any settlement that the parties could agree to. The council, however, did not want to participate in the negotiations because it didn't want to be caught in any more crossfire, especially with an election approaching. After being contacted by the town's attorney, the mediator made the customary round of phone calls to set up appointments with the property owners, the mayor who was speaking for the council, and one neighbor who had led a petition drive but who was characterized by others as being exceptionally level headed.

These interviews revealed major obstacles to negotiations and began to suggest an alternate structure for the negotiation process. In the interviews, the property owners characterized their numerous opponents as an irresponsible mob. There were in fact a large number of opponents with no organization representing them. The property owners said they were not willing to sit down face-to-face with their opponents because any such meeting would turn into a shouting match. Because they were preparing to file suit, the owners also said that their attorney was acting as their agent in this matter and that they would follow his advice. In a subsequent meeting with the mediator, the property owners' attorney indicated that he was personally comfortable with property development negotiation. However, he was not willing at that point to meet face-to-face with a room full of neighbors nor would he advise his clients to do so. He did feel that a solution was possible if the neighbors would stick to legitimate land planning concerns.

Before negotiation could begin, the mediator held several meetings with the neighbors to help them organize and to prepare for negotiations. They appointed a leader/spokesman and a steering committee. Soul-searching discussions among the neighbors enabled them to identify and agree on priority issues and to develop a familiarity with the notion of trade-offs and complex settlements. This prenegotiation stage required a half dozen caucuses by the neighbors.

The neighbors and the attorney representing the property owners then agreed to a second stage. This was essentially a "single-text" procedure in which the mediator shuttled between the parties to collect the preferences of each side independently. He then rendered a composite development scheme that reflected areas that the two sides might agree on. When there wasn't agreement, some points were given each side considering their stated priorities. Where both sides assigned high priority to the same issue, the scheme reflected a fifty-fifty compromise. Both sides agreed to give such a scheme open-minded consideration. Most importantly, both sides also agreed that if they did not approve of all of the features of the scheme—which wasn't expected—they would meet together and jointly criticize the scheme and work toward an agreement acceptable to each.

Without a development scheme to focus on, both sides felt that participation in face-to-face meetings would result in a useless exchange of interpersonal bitterness. Since the developer had been turned down by the town and since federal funds for new Section 8 housing had dried up, the developer had dropped this project. Thus with no developer to put forth a site-specific proposal, the single-text device was needed to get the opposing sides together to focus on a joint planning activity for the site in question.

The single-text scheme was prepared and provided to each side. The scheme had the following major features. The development would average 8 units per acre. The units were to be a mixture of single-family ownership units adjacent to the existing neighborhood and multiple-family rental units on the rest of the site. Ample open space and landscape buffers would be incorporated. Temporary access to the neighborhood street was granted with the promise of future access through adjacent property to a primary road when the adjoining property was developed. The other significant part of the scheme was an affirmative fair share housing policy. "Fair share" was to be a percentage of the region's assisted housing units equal to the percentage of the regional population represented by the town. At that time, the town had 0.7% of the region's population and under the policy would support 0.7% of the region's assisted housing, or, in this case, 20 assisted units.

The neighbors indicated that they saw the scheme very positively and accepted the scheme in principle. They were ready to meet face-to-face to negotiate its details and to make necessary adjustments. The property owners' attorney said the scheme looked pretty good to him but suggested several modifications before he presented it to his client. The mediator took these back to the neighbors who found them acceptable. The attorney then took the scheme to the property owners. The expected next step was a joint meeting.

However, the owners did not find the scheme or the process it embodied at all acceptable. They felt it gave the neighbors "meddling rights" which they should not have. Furthermore, the owners declared that they were not willing to participate further in the single-text procedure.

The neighbors and the property owners' attorney had agreed to give a status report to the town council in June regardless of the status at that time. By that time the election had passed and a new mayor had been elected. A neighborhood candidate failed to attract votes townwide. The new mayor vowed to get this matter settled. He scheduled a meeting where he would use his influence to get both sides to meet face-to-face to discuss their differences. Before that meeting occurred, however, the property owners dismissed their attorney from the case. A new attorney was hired and instructed to pursue litigation.

One year has now passed with no further action by any party. The actual project and developer precipitating the original dispute are no longer on the scene. However, the underlying problems of community relations remain. The case reveals the difficulty of achieving conciliation in the absence of a focus. Conciliation also requires face-to-face interaction at some points and various efforts to achieve this failed in Timberville. Without face-to-face participation and self-representation the likelihood of misunderstanding and difficult communication increases. Surprise reactions late in the process frustrated progress made by the neighborhood group. Having initiated the idea of negotiation, the town could have played a more active role in brokering face-to-face meetings. The Timberville case leaves the observer with the impression that if the sides would come together, a settlement and conciliation could be reached.

The next case describes a fully successful mediation effort that involved town officials as active negotiation participants throughout the bargaining process.

Blacksburg shopping center dispute

In Blacksburg, Virginia, the developer of a shopping center, abutting neighbors, a neighborhood foundation, and the town reached a negotiated agreement that was adopted and made a condition of development. This ended a long-standing dispute. The town planning director suggested mediation. He and the planning commission chairman acted as a negotiating team and interested party. The town's participation had the effect of legitimating the negotiation process in the eyes of the other participants and made it possible to expedite the subsequent formal review and approval process. The possibility of a quick decision was critical to the developer's willingness to participate in the negotiations at all.

Blacksburg is a medium-sized university community. The site of the dispute is a community shopping center in a planned unit development (PUD) containing a mixture of owner and renter occupied units. Students outnumber other residents by a considerable margin. The developer had a series of run-ins with owners of townhouses abutting the center in the company's effort to relax restrictions on the operating hours of the partially completed center. Late-night activity is what concerned the neighbors. The developer was seriously considering litigation. Several tenants of the center had not renewed leases and one explanation was the hours restriction. In addition, the center was unable to attract customers from the heavy volume of traffic that passed the site but did not patronize the existing supermarket, drug store, and assorted small retail shops.

The developer was now seeking approval to develop one of three remaining vacant parcels along the highway frontage of the center with a gas station, car wash, and convenience store. These he would operate well into the night and on holidays. The developer needed a quick decision in order to stimulate business at the badly faltering center. Unless that need could be met, he would not participate.

Town officials had reacted negatively to the developer's proposed scheme during an unofficial preliminary plan review. They feared that the proposed curb cuts and intense use of the site would aggravate congested traffic on the highway. Officials saw the highway situation as a critical concern for the town. They felt a need to participate to protect this interest. Some town officials were disturbed that the site plan dealt only with the one parcel the developer desired to develop at that time. It was not clear how the piecemeal development of the center would come together. It was clear, though, that the residents nearest the shopping center would object violently to the type of hours typically associated with uses like gas stations, car washes, and convenience stores.

Many of the neighbors were becoming battle-fatigued after earlier struggles over the shopping center. However, they were not about to ignore a threat to livability and property values in their carefully planned neighborhood. They saw participation in negotiations as a way of dealing with the shopping center once and for all.

The fourth party involved in this shopping center was an overall PUD association board, representing approximately 6,000 residents and the over-all PUD developer who owned the major share of the apartments in the complex. Deed provisions for the shopping center parcels granted certain final approval authority to this board. The board voted to deny approval to the preliminary sketches produced by the developer. Knowing that he faced opposition, the developer saw his only option as moving ahead as fast as possible so that he could proceed with a law suit he felt would go his way in the Virginia courts.

Town officials were aware that PUD zoning and regulating hours of operation were not clear cut areas of the law. The neighbors knew their greatest strength was local. The overall PUD board and the developer took the view that if the shopping center did not succeed, it would be a major problem to all in the area.

It was at this point that the town planning director suggested mediation and contacted the Institute for Environmental Negotiation after gaining approval from the town manager and planning commission. Institute personnel met with representatives of the developer and each of the other parties to discuss the advantages and disadvantages of trying mediation.

To deal with the apprehensions of each party, the mediators proposed that all parties agree to certain conditions before negotiations began. The town agreed not to require the developer to begin anew with permit processing even if the negotiations yielded a significantly revised plan. The town also expressed the desire to have the planning commission chair and two members of the planning staff actively participate in the negotiations. The developer agreed in exchange to negotiate about the whole shopping center and not just one of the three vacant parcels. The townhouse neighbors agreed to publicly support any plan that could be arrived at through negotiation. The PUD board agreed to participate actively in the negotiations and not hold out for a final veto of the agreements of the other parties. With these conditions set, all four parties agreed to participate.

Five negotiating sessions were held during the following five weeks. In April 1983 the town council gave final unanimous approval to the consequent agreement. The developer proceeded to obtain building permits so that the project could be completed the following summer.

The agreement hinged around trade-offs among three major issues. These trade-offs were hammered out in the face-to-face negotiations. There were, of course, a large number of facets to each issue plus an array of minor issues. While agreeing to a moratorium on further changes in hours of operation for five years, the developer succeeded in gaining expanded hours throughout the center but especially for the portion of property furthest from the residences and closest to the highway. The proposed uses were allowed after some redesign. Access was granted to the major highway but only after left turn movements and further requests for curb cuts were prohibited.

This case shows what can be accomplished through face-to-face negotiations involving direct participation by all stakeholders. Particularly interesting is the successful participation of town officials in the negotiation processes. In this case, it was important that the traffic and overall development plan concerns of officials had a strong spokesman. The town's ongoing participation also enabled the developer to continue to process his application while working toward a better alternative through negotiation. The town's willingness to pursue both "tracks" and to allow substitution down to the wire made this negotiation possible.

Discussion

The structuring of negotiations is a vital precondition for success. Even the most skillful meeting management tactics may not save an inappropriately structured negotiation. Who participates and how are crucial elements of structure.

Lawrence Susskind has identified nine steps that are frequent requisites to successful negotiations.[1] The first two steps, identifying the parties having a stake in the outcome and assuring adequate representation of these stake-holding interests, are both aspects of who participates and how. However, even after these tasks are accomplished participation questions can arise in many ways and can influence the success of conflict resolution efforts.

Success not only involved what Kai Lee has referred to as " . . . an obvious marker of success: achieving an agreement among disputing parties,"[2] but also includes the goals stated in the agreement, necessary procedural changes for implementation, successful renegotiation or modification if the need arises, and long-term satisfaction by the parties that the agreement advanced their objectives. Participation by all parties increases the chance for a successful outcome in each of these senses.

The three mediation cases described here illustrate some of the variations on the theme of participation. The cases suggest some recurrent issues related to participation. Compared to implicit negotiations that may take place through the traditional public hearing process or compared to shuttle diplomacy between disputing parties, face-to-face negotiations more effectively reveal underlying interests. As Roger Fisher and William Ury point out, underlying interests, rather than prior positions, provide a basis for seeking new options and possible settlements without "giving in."[3] Where parties are represented by others, it is especially important to have good communication and understanding between each representative and his constituent. When one party is reluctant to participate actively, the mediator might suggest an observer role. This would allow stakeholders to assure themselves of the adequacy of their representation and increase their awareness of the underlying point of view and potential for flexibility of the other side. Observers may gradually become comfortable with the process and begin to participate more actively. Where conciliation and repair of relationships are important, face-to-face participation, as opposed to the more buffered forms of indirect or intermediary bargaining, is especially valuable.

The participant role of the broker appears to have been especially important in these three cases. The broker is the person who raises the negotiation/mediation possibility and tests the idea with the other parties prior to mediator involvement. The broker can give initial credibility and legitimacy to the negotiated approach and make it easier for adversaries to decide to become participants. The cases here show that the broker can be an uninvolved outsider or a person who is a part of a stake-holding organization. A good argument can be made that the long-term success of mediation as a widely used process will depend in large part on the extent to which others are willing to trust a broker and refer cases for mediation.

Even after referral, participation itself is frequently the subject of negotiation and is often conditioned by the parties. The mediator can help to clarify these conditions and to combine them in a participation agreement giving all sides a basis to expect that the negotiative approach can advance their interests.

The time frame of the negotiations and the freedom to pursue alternatives to negotiation are frequently important conditions to project proponents. These conditions can motivate participants toward solutions. As part of the prenegotiation process, the mediator may need to help participants prepare for negotiations. This may involve developing an organization or clarifying values through internal negotiation within a group. The caucus is a related on-going activity that continues after the prenegotiation work. Neighborhood groups such as those involved in the cases discussed here may need prenegotiation and caucus assistance more than others. Groups coming together because of a new problem may especially need this help. The time and energy required to participate in negotiations may be a drain on neighborhood groups unless the process is structured to be efficient. Representatives must frequently check back with neighborhood constituencies to ensure that loyalties do not come seriously into question.

The participation of public officials in face-to-face negotiations poses a dilemma for some. They argue that elected officials should not participate in negotiations as well as pass subsequent judgment on the results of that negotiation. Though there is widespread agreement among mediators about the general value of having all interests represented and participating, many mediators also agree with Robert Stein[4] that there are circumstances where it is not appropriate for officials to participate. He observes that "No agency is obliged to produce a win-win situation. Why should the government give away power by being willing to negotiate through mediation?" Officials themselves, however, do not always share this view and can participate by designating a representative and/or by detailing staff to the task. As far as negotiated outcomes go, it seems most important that governmental concerns be represented if agency interests are significantly different either in substance or scale from those of the other parties. When an agency has agreed in advance to endorse the parties' solution, agency participation may not be critical. However, official participation can play a vital role in legitimating the negotiation process for other participants.

The element of participation, while having many forms and implications, is, of course, still only one variable in determining whether there are to be negotiations, how they are conducted, and what results are achieved. Other factors interact with participation in determining the eventual outcome. To the extent that we can focus on one element, however, we can come to understand it better. The three cases discussed here provide an initial step in that direction. Other cases will reveal other important dimensions to participation in environmental negotiations.

1. L. Susskind, "Environmental Mediation and the Accountability Problem," *Vermont Law Review* 6 (1981): 1-4.
2. K. Lee, "Defining Success in Environmental Dispute Resolution," *Resolve*, spring 1982, pp. 1-6.
3. R. Fisher and W. Ury, *Getting to Yes: Negotiating Agreement Without Giving In* (Boston: Houghton Mifflin, 1981).
4. R. Stein quoted in: "EPA, Looking for Better Ways to Settle Rules Disputes, Tries Mediation," *National Journal*, March 5, 1983, p. 505.

Bibliography

Adams, William H., III. "Would We Rather Fight Than Settle?" 51 *Fla. B. J.* 8, 1977.

Agranoff, Robert, and Lindsay, Valerie. "Intergovernmental Management: Perspectives from Human Services Problem Solving at the Local Level." *Public Administration Review* 43, 3 (1983): 227-237.

Bacharach, Samuel B., and Lawler, Edward J. *Bargaining: Power, Tactics and Outcomes.* San Francisco: Jossey-Bass, 1981.

Bacow, Lawrence S., and Wheeler, Michael. *Environmental Dispute Resolution.* New York: Plenum Press, 1985.

Ball, Milner S. "The Play's the Thing: An Unscientific Reflection on Courts under the Rubric of Theater." 28 *Stan. L. Rev.* 81, 1975.

Bartos, Otomar. *Process and Outcome of Negotiations.* New York: Columbia University Press, 1974.

Baum, Howell. "Politics, Power and Profession." *Planning,* December 1983, 18-21.

Bellman, Howard S. "Siting for a Sanitary Landfill for Eau Claire, Wisconsin." *Environmental Professional 2,* 1 (1980): 56-57.

Bellman, Howard S., Sampson, Cynthia, and Cormick, Gerald W. *Using Mediation when Siting Hazardous Waste Management Facilities, A Handbook (SW944).* Washington, D.C.: Government Printing Office, 1982.

Bleiker, Annemarie, and Bleiker, Hans. *Citizen Participation Handbook for Public Officials and Other Professionals Serving the Public.* 3rd ed. Laramie, Wyoming: Institute for Participatory Planning, 1978.

Boulding, Kenneth E. "Conflict Management as a Learning Process." In *Conflict in Society.* Boston: Little, Brown, 1966.

Boyer, Barry B. "Alternatives to Administrative Trial-Type Hearings for Resolving Complex Scientific, Economic or Social Issues." 71 *Mich. L. Rev.* 111, 1972.

Brown, Cherie R. *The Art of Coalition Building: A Guide for Community Leaders.* New York: American Jewish Committee, 1984.

Brown, L. Neville, and Lavirotte, Pierre. "The Mediator: A French Ombudsman?" 90 *L. Q. Rev.* 211, 1974.

Burger, Warren. "Let's Stop Building Major Cases out of Minor Disputes." *Bar Leader,* No. 2, 1977.

Busterud, J. "Environmental Conflict Resolution: The Promise of Cooperative Decision Making." *Environmental Science and Technology,* Vol. 15, No. 2 (February, 1981): 150-155.

Cappelletti, Maurice. "Fundamental

Guarantees of the Parties in Civil Litigation: Comparative Constitutional, International and Social Trends." 25 *Stan. L. Rev.* 651, 1973.

Cappelletti, Maurice, and Koch, K. F., eds. *Access to Justice: The Anthropological Perspective.* Sijthoff and Noordhoff, 1979.

Carpenter, Susan L., and Kennedy, W. J. D. "Information Sharing and Conciliation: Tools for Environmental Conflict Management." *Environmental Comment,* May 1977, 21–23.

Carpenter, Susan L., and Kennedy, W. J. D. *Consensus Building: A Tool for Managing Energy-Environment Conflicts.* Wye Plantation, Maryland: The Management of Energy-Environment Conflicts, May 20–23, 1980.

Chalmers, W. Ellison, and Cormick, Gerald W., eds. *Racial Conflict and Negotiation.* Institute of Labor and Industrial Relations, 1971.

Clark, Peter B. "Consensus Building: Mediating Energy, Environmental and Economic Conflict." *Environmental Comment,* May 1977, 9–12.

Cohen, Herb. *You Can Negotiate Anything.* New Jersey: Lyle Stuart, Inc., 1980.

Colson, Elizabeth. *Tradition and Contract: The Problem of Order.* Aldine, 1974.

Conn, Stephen, and Hippler, Arthur E. "Conciliation and Arbitration in the Native Village and the Urban Ghetto." 58 *Judicature* 228, 1974.

Coser, Lewis A. "The Termination of Conflict." *Social Change: Sources, Patterns and Consequences.* New York: Basic Books, 1964.

Cuomo, Mario M. *Forest Hills Diary: The Crisis of Low-Income Housing.* Vintage, 1975.

Danzig, Richard, and Lowy, Michael. "Everyday Disputes and Mediation in the U.S.—A Reply to Professor Felsteiner." 9 *Law and Soc'y Rev.* 675, 1975.

Davis, Kenneth C. "Ombudsmen in America: Officers to Criticize Administrative Action." 109 *U. Pa. L. Rev.* 1057, 1961.

Deutsch, Morton. *The Resolution of Conflict: Constructive and Destructive Processes.* New Haven: Yale University Press, 1973.

Doyle, Michael, and Straus, David. *How to Make Meetings Work.* New York: Playboy Press, 1976.

Drachman, Allan W. "Municipal Negotiations: From Differences to Agreement." *Labor Management Relations Service,* 1970.

Druckman, D. *Negotiations: Social-Psychological Perspectives.* California: Sage, 1977.

Eisenberg, Melvin A. "Private Ordering through Negotiation: Dispute-Settlement and Rulemaking." 89 *Harv. L. Rev.* 637, 1976.

Ehrlich, Paul. "Legal Pollution." *New York Times Magazine,* February 8, 1976.

Ehrlich, Thomas, and Frank, Jane Lakes. *Planning for Justice.* Aspen Institute, 1977.

Emond, P. D. "Resolving Development Decision-Making. Ontario Style." *Plan Canada* 20/1, March 1980.

Felsteiner, William L. "Influences of Social Organization on Dispute Processing." 9 *Law and Soc'y Rev.* 63, 1974.

Fisher, Roger, and Ury, William. *Getting to Yes: Negotiating Agreement without Giving in.* New York: Houghton Mifflin Co., 1981.

Florestano, Pat, and Gordon, Stephan. "Public vs. Private: Small Government Contracting with the Private Sector." *PAR,* Jan.–Feb. 1980, 29–34.

Ford Foundation. *New Approaches to Conflict Resolution.* 1978.

Fried, Bernard. "Resolution of Disputes under Government Contracts." 7 *Fernando Valley L. Rev.* 191, 1979.

Friedman, Lawrence. "Courts and Social Policy." 29 *Missouri B. J.* 460, 1973.

Fuller, Lon L. "Collective Bargaining and the Arbitrator." *Wisc. L. Rev.* 3, 1963.

Fuller, Lon L. "Mediation: Its Forms and Functions." 44 *So. Cal. L. Rev.* 305, 1971.

Getman, Julius. "Labor Arbitration and Dispute Resolution." 88 *Yale L. J.* 916, 1979.

Goldbeck, Willis. "Mediation: An Instrument of Citizen Involvement." *Arbitration Journal* 30, 4 (1975): 241-252.

Gordon, Thomas. *Leadership Effectiveness Training.* New York: Wyden Books, 1978.

Greenwald, "C. R. S.: Dispute Resolution through Mediation." 64 *A. B. A. J.* 1250, 1978.

Gulliver, P. H. *Disputes and Negotiations: A Cross-cultural Perspective.* New York: Academic Press, 1979.

Gulliver, P. H. "Negotiation as a Mode of Dispute Settlement: Towards a General Model." 7 *Law & Soc'y Rev.* 667.

Gulliver, P. H. "On Mediators." *Social Anthropology and the Law.* I. Hamnett. Academic Press, 1977.

Hofrichter, Richard. "Justice Centers Raise Basic Questions." *New Directions in Legal Services* 11, No. 6, 1977.

Horowitz, Donald L. *The Courts and Social Policy.* Brookings Institution, 1977.

Housing Courts. *Symposium Issue of Urban Law Annual.* 1979.

Isaacson, William J., and Zifchak, William C. "Agency Deferral to Private Arbitration of Employment Disputes." 73 *Colum. L. Rev.* 1383, 1973.

Karrass, Chester L. *The Negotiating Game.* New York: Thomas Y. Crowell Publishers, 1970.

Kennedy, W. J. D., and Lansford, Henry. "The Metropolitan Water Roundtable: Resource Allocation through Conflict Management." *Environmental Impact Assessment Review* 4:1, 1983.

Kettering Foundation. "Negotiating the City's Future." *Nation's Cities Weekly*, November 26, 1979.

Kidder, Robert L. "Afterword: Change and Structure in Dispute Processing." 9 *Law & Soc'y Rev.* 384, 1975.

Kriesberg, Louis. *The Sociology of Social Conflict.* Englewood Cliffs, N.J.: Prentice-Hall, 1973.

Laue, James. "Urban Conflict—What Role for Negotiations and Mediation?" Prepared for seminar at Institute for Mediation and Conflict Resolution, New York City, June 16, 1971.

Laue, James, and Cormick, Gerald. "The Ethics of Social Intervention in Community Disputes." In *The Ethics of Social Intervention.* Gordon Bermant, Herbert Kelman, and Donald Warwick, eds. Washington, D.C.: Hemisphere Publishing, 1974.

Li, Victor H. *Law Without Lawyers.* Stanford Alumni Association, 1977.

Lincoln, William F. "Mediation: A Transferable Process for the Prevention and Resolution of Racial Conflict in Public Secondary Schools." American Arbitration Association, Community Dispute Services, 1976.

McCarthy, Jane. "Learning from the Labor-Management Model." *Environmental Consensus*, Summer 1980.

McCarthy, Jane, and Shorett, Alice. *Negotiating Settlements: A Guide to Environmental Mediation.* New York: American Arbitration Association, 1984.

McGillis, Daniel. *Neighborhood Justice Centers: Recommendations for Legislators and Government Executives.* Washington, D.C.: Government Printing Office, 1979.

McGillis, Daniel. "Neighborhood Justice Centers and the Mediation of Housing-Related Disputes." 17 *Urb. L. J.*, 1979.

McGillis, Daniel. "Neighborhood Justice Centers as Mechanisms for Dispute Resolution." In *New Directions in Psychological Research.* Lipsitt and Sales, eds. 1979.

Milner, Alan. "Settling Disputes: The Changing Face of English Law." 20 *McGill L. J.* 521, 1974.

Moore, Sally Falk. *Law as Process: An Anthropological Approach.* Routledge and Kegan Paul, 1978.

Mumphrey, Anthony J., Jr., Seley, John E., and Wolpert, Julian. "A Decision Model for Locating Controversial Facilities." *AIP Journal* 37, 6 (1981): 397-402.

Nader, Laura. "Forums for Justice: A Cross-cultural Perspective." 31 *J. of Social Sciences* 151, 1975.

Nader, Laura, and Singer, Linda R. "Dispute Resolution and Law in the Future: What Are the Choices?" 51 *Cal. St. B. J.* 281, 1976.

Negotiation Journal: On the Process of Dispute Settlement. New York: Plenum Press.

Nicolau, George. *Training in Community Conflict Resolution Skills*. New York: Institute for Mediation and Conflict Resolution, 1973.

Nicolau, George, and Cormick, Gerald. "Community Disputes and the Resolution of Conflict: Another View." *Arbitration Journal* 27, 2 (1972): 98–112.

Nierenberg, Gerald I. *Fundamentals of Negotiating*. New York: Hawthorne Books, 1977.

Peck, Cornelius J. *Cases and Materials on Negotiation*. BNA, 1972.

Peck, Cornelius J. "Remedies for Racial Discrimination in Employment: A Comparative Evaluation of Forums." 46 *Wash. L. Rev.* 455, 1971.

Perin, Constance. *Everything in Its Place: Social Order and Land Use in America*. Princeton University Press, 1977.

Pruitt, D. G. *Negotiation Behavior*. New York: Academic, 1981.

Pruitt, D. G. "Strategic Choice in Negotiation." *American Behavioral Scientist*, Nov.–Dec. 1983, 167–194.

Raiffa, Howard. *The Art and Science of Negotiation*, Cambridge, Mass.: Harvard University Press, 1982.

Resolve. Washington, D.C.: Conservation Foundation.

Richman, Roger. "Intergovernmental Dispute Mediation." Unpublished.

Richman, Roger. "Employment Agreements between Managers and Governing Bodies." *Management Information Service Report*, Vol. 13, No. 7, July 1981.

Rivkin, Malcolm D. *An Issue Report: Negotiated Development: A Breakthrough in Environmental Controversies*. Washington, D.C.: Conservation Foundation, 1977.

Rubin, Jeffrey A. "A Causerie on Lawyers' Ethics in Negotiation." 35 *La. L. Rev.* 577, 1975.

Rubin, Jeffrey A., and Brown, Bert R. *The Social Psychology of Bargaining and Negotiation*. New York: Academic Press, 1975.

Sander, Frank A. E. "Varieties of Dispute Processing." 70 *F.R.D.* 111, 1976.

Satter, Robert. "Changing Roles of Courts and Legislatures." 11 *Conn. L. Rev.* 230, 1979.

Schelling, Thomas C. *The Strategy of Conflict*. Oxford University Press, 1963.

Schelling, Thomas C. "An Essay on Bargaining" in *The Strategy of Conflict*. Cambridge: Harvard University Press, 1969.

Simkin, William E. *Mediation and the Dynamics of Collective Bargaining*. Washington, D.C.: Bureau of National Affairs, 1971.

Smith, David. "A Warmer Way of Disputing: Mediation and Conciliation." 26 *Am. J. Comp. L. (Supp.)* 205, 1978.

Susskind, Lawrence E. *Citizen Involvement in the Local Planning Process: A Handbook for Municipal Officials and Citizen Involvement Groups*. Cambridge: Massachusetts Institute of Technology, Laboratory of Architecture and Planning, 1976.

Susskind, Lawrence E. *The Importance of Citizen Participation and Consensus-Building in the Land Use Planning Process*. Cambridge: Massachusetts Institute of Technology, Laboratory of Architecture and Planning, 1978.

Susskind, Lawrence, and Ozawa, Connie. "Mediated Negotiation in the Public Sector." *American Behavioral Scientist*, Vol. 27, No. 2, Nov.–Dec. 1983.

Susskind, Lawrence, and Persico, Sebastian. *Guide to Consensus and Development and Dispute Resolution Techniques*. Cambridge: Harvard Negotiation Project, 1983.

Talbot, Allan. *Environmental Mediation, Three Case Studies: The Island, the Highway, the Ferry Terminal*. Seattle, Washington: Institute for Environmental Mediation, 1981.

Thomas, Kenneth W. "Conflict and Conflict Management." In the *Handbook of Industrial and Organizational Psychology*. Marvin D. Dunnette, ed. Chicago: Rand McNally, 1976.

Traynor, Michael. "Lawsuits: First Re-

sort or Last?" *Utah L. Rev.* 635, 1978.
"The Value of Arbitration and Mediation in Resolving Community and Racial Disputes Affecting Business: A Symposium." 29 *Bus. L.* 1005, 1974.

Walton, Richard E., and McKersie, Robert B. *A Behavioral Theory of Labor Negotiations.* New York: McGraw-Hill, 1965.

Warren, Charles R. *National Implica-* tions of a Negotiated Approach to Federalism. Kettering Foundation, 1981.

Warschau, Tessa A. *Winning by Negotiation.* New York: McGraw-Hill, 1980.

Wehr, Paul. *Conflict Resolution.* Boulder, Co.: Westview Press, 1979.

Zartman, I. William, and Berman, Maureen R. *The Practical Negotiator.* New Haven: Yale University Press, 1982.

Practical Management Series

**Successful Negotiating
in Local Government**

Text type
Century Expanded

Composition
Unicorn Graphics
Washington, D.C.

Printing and binding
R. R. Donnelley & Sons Company
Harrisonburg, Virginia

Cover design
Rebecca Geanaros